Economic Policy and Manufacturing Performance in Developing Countries

Economic Policy and Manufacturing Performance in Developing Countries

Edited by

Oliver Morrissey

School of Economics, University of Nottingham, UK

Michael Tribe

Bradford Centre for International Development, University of Bradford, UK

Edward Elgar
Cheltenham, UK • Northampton, MA, USA

Published by
Edward Elgar Publishing Limited
Glensanda House
Montpellier Parade
Cheltenham
Glos GL50 1UA
UK

Edward Elgar Publishing, Inc.
136 West Street
Suite 202
Northampton
Massachusetts 01060
USA

A catalogue record for this book
is available from the British Library

Library of Congress Cataloging-in-Publication Data
Economic policy and manufacturing performance in developing countries / Oliver Morrissey and Michael Tribe : [editors].
    p. cm.
  Papers presented at workshops.
  Includes bibliographical references and index.
    1. Industrial productivity—Developing countries—Congresses. 2. Developing countries—Economic policy—Congresses. 3. Manufacturing industries—Developing countries—Congresses. I. Morrissey, Oliver. II. Tribe, Michael A., 1943–

HC59.72.I52 E36 2001
338.4'767'091724—dc21

                                                                    2001031365

ISBN 1 84064 518 0

Typeset by Manton Typesetters, Louth, Lincolnshire, UK.
Printed and bound in Great Britain by MPG Books Ltd, Bodmin, Cornwall.

Contents

Figures and tables

FIGURES

TABLES

vi

Notes on contributors

Isaac Acheampong is a Senior Lecturer in the Department of Economics, University of Cape Coast, Ghana.

T.G. Arun is a Lecturer in Economics, School of Public Policy, Economics and Law, University of Ulster.

Hossein Jalilian is a Senior Lecturer in the Bradford Centre for International Development, University of Bradford.

Ian Livingstone is Emeritus Professor in the School of Development Studies, University of East Anglia.

Wise Mainga is a Senior Lecturer in the School of Business, Copperbelt University, Kitwe, Zambia.

Alan Middleton is Professor and Associate Dean, Faculty of the Built Environment, University of Central England.

Muhammed Migdad is Lecturer in the Department of Economics, Islamic University of Gaza.

Oliver Morrissey is Reader in Development Economics and Director of the Centre for Research in Economic Development and International Trade (CREDIT), School of Economics, University of Nottingham.

Fred I. Nixson is Professor of Development Economics, School of Economic Studies, University of Manchester.

Nichodemus Rudaheranwa is a Lecturer at the Institute of Economics, Makerere University, Kampala, Uganda.

Kishor Sharma is Lecturer in Economics, School of Management, Charles Sturt University, Australia.

John T. Thoburn is Reader in Economics, School of Development Studies, University of East Anglia.

Michael Tribe is a Senior Lecturer in the Bradford Centre for International Development, University of Bradford.

John Weiss is Professor of Development Economics, Bradford Centre for International Development, University of Bradford.

As this book went to press the editors were saddened to learn of the death of Ian Livingstone. Ian had been a leading light amongst development economists for over three decades, and we hope that the chapter on Cambodian small enterprises in this book will represent a small and fitting tribute to his memory.

O.M. and M.T.

Preface

This book is essentially a product of the Trade and Industry Study Group (TISG) of the Development Studies Association (DSA). Oliver Morrissey and Michael Tribe have been co-convenors of the TISG since 1994, and while papers from TISG conferences and workshops during that time have often been published, this is the first collaborative effort on the part of the group. Most of the chapters in this book have, at an embryonic stage, been presented at TISG workshops or at TISG sessions in the annual DSA conferences, and plans for the book were initiated as long ago as 1998. Edited books are a slow process, and we wish to thank all of the contributors and the publishers for their patience and co-operation. We are also grateful for the financial support of the DSA for TISG workshops.

This volume does not reflect the proceedings of a specific conference. Rather, it represents an attempt to bring together a collection of case studies to address, from varying perspectives, an issue of general interest – how has government policy towards the manufacturing sector, and economic liberalisation in particular, impacted on subsector performance? Almost all developing countries have implemented major economic reforms over the past two decades, and these have often amounted to significant liberalisation of trade and industrial policy. However, there is no consensus either on how this impacts on manufacturing or on how policy could be adapted to support manufacturing. On the one hand, there is a widely held view that 'protection is dead' and trade liberalisation is the only direction; not least because multilateral liberalisation under the World Trade Organisation (WTO) may preclude many of the industrial policies that have been implemented in the past. On the other hand, there is an increasing perception that government has a role in fostering manufacturing subsector development. The contributions collected here explore the various impacts of policy on manufacturing performance, spanning, in the process, the major continents and both large scale and small-to-medium scale enterprises.

Oliver Morrissey and Michael Tribe
January 2001

1. Introduction: evaluating the relationship between economic policy and manufacturing sector performance

Oliver Morrissey and Michael Tribe

1 INTRODUCTION

One of the principal issues associated with the analysis of the relationship between economic policy and manufacturing sector performance lies in the definition of 'economic policy'. The term 'economic policy reform' has, in recent years, been linked in the literature principally with macroeconomic stabilisation, trade and exchange rate liberalisation, financial market liberalisation, and the removal of a wide range of controls and distortions that had become entrenched in many developing and transitional economies. However, 'economic policy' is a broader concept than this. Many countries have attempted to introduce policy instruments which extend beyond the conventional view of macroeconomic policy, especially, from our perspective, into areas of industrial policy (one could also include labour policy).

The essays in this volume do not attempt to employ a uniform definition of economic policy. Rather, they take as their focus an aspect of the performance of the manufacturing sector, and attempt to assess how and which economic policies have affected performance. From this perspective, some lessons for economic policy towards manufacturing can be drawn. The geographical range of the studies is intentionally wide. Although the majority of chapters relate to countries in sub-Saharan Africa (SSA), we include cases in South and East Asia, South America and the Middle East (thereby extending the study of Jalilian *et al.*, 2000). Furthermore, the chapters focus on various aspects of manufacturing – small enterprises, technology, the exporting sector and manufacturing in general. In this introduction we attempt to highlight some of the common themes and lessons that emerge.

Trade policy reform has been one of the most prevalent areas of economic policy reform in developing countries over the past decade or so, with direct implications for manufacturing. While Jalilian *et al.* (2000) addressed this primarily from the perspective of the impact on import-competing sectors, here the focus is more often on exporting. One of the aims of trade liberalisation is to stimulate export performance and encourage diversification. There is now considerable evidence to support the view that trade liberalisation contributes to export growth and diversification primarily through the removal of a bias against exports (see Section 2 below). Most of the evidence of successful liberalisation relates to high- and middle-income developing countries. The experience of low-income developing countries, which lack efficient physical infrastructure and rely extensively on the production of primary products, is less encouraging. This is particularly true in respect of manufacturing. A study of experiences in sub-Saharan Africa (SSA) suggests that while export diversification is slow to materialise, trade liberalisation is generally beneficial for the economy because it stimulates exports and efficiency gains due to reduced protection (Morrissey, 1999). However, low-income developing countries share characteristics that constrain export growth and limit the effectiveness of trade policy reforms. The analysis of the experience of a large number of developing countries from different backgrounds would provide a better insight into the response of liberalisation in different economic environments and enable the formulation of more appropriate policy measures, tailored to the specific needs of those countries. The aim of this volume is to provide such an analysis.

2   ECONOMIC POLICY REFORM AND TRADE LIBERALISATION

Motivated primarily by the World Bank under its policy of structural adjustment since the early 1980s, virtually all developing countries have engaged in economic policy reform, liberalisation in virtually all cases, over the past two decades. Trade liberalisation, the removal of restrictions on imports and reduction of discrimination against exports, has been the single most important area of policy reform in almost all cases (Greenaway and Morrissey, 1994). Liberalisation of exchange rate regimes, of agricultural policy (especially removal of price controls and state monopolies in marketing) and improved investment incentives have also been prevalent (Greenaway and Morrissey, 1993). All of these reforms have potential implications for manufacturing and these are discussed in this section. Policy reforms with a direct effect on manufacturing, such as privatisation and investment promotion, are of more recent vintage and are discussed in the next section.

The outcomes of the many liberalisation episodes have been mixed (see McGillivray and Morrissey, 1999; Papageorgiou *et al.*, 1991). There is evidence that liberalisation is associated with economic growth, though not necessarily in manufacturing. Onafowora and Owoye (1998) find evidence that growth is higher in more outward-oriented African economies as compared with more protective economies, and infer that trade liberalisation (which increases outward orientation) offers potential for low-income countries to increase growth rates. They recognise that the commodity composition of exports, especially dependence on a narrow range of primary products, can constrain the contribution of exports to growth. While the balance of the evidence suggests that outward orientation is associated with better growth, the link between trade liberalisation *per se* and better growth performance is rather weak (Greenaway *et al.*, 1997, 1998). Often this is because the anticipated export supply response fails to materialise following liberalisation. The econometric evidence should be interpreted very carefully as cross-country studies are limited to using simple measures of liberalisation (such as a dummy variable for when a reform episode occurred, or changes in average nominal tariffs). These simple measures are likely to be both inaccurate and misleading (Milner and Morrissey, 1999).

It is helpful to distinguish separate elements of trade liberalisation. Import liberalisation – the removal of quantitative restrictions (QRs) and the reduction of tariffs – reduces the price of imports and importables (domestically produced goods that compete with imports). This reduction of protection is expected to benefit the economy by reducing the inefficiencies in resource allocation typically associated with protectionist, import substituting (IS) policies. An important effect of reducing protection is that it reduces the bias against exports, although this alone may be insufficient to encourage investors to reallocate resources from the production of importables to production of exportables. Export promotion measures can directly facilitate and increase the return to exporting. Allowing exporters to retain export earnings is a simple (and potentially effective) export promotion measure. Devaluation of the exchange rate can also increase returns to exporters (as they receive more domestic currency for a given world price) and generally has the effect of increasing the price of exportables relative to importables (i.e. reducing the anti-export bias). There is evidence that the real exchange rate is the most important determinant of export growth (Noorbakhsh and Paloni, 1998).

Doubts that trade liberalisation may benefit developing countries remain strong (Rodrik, 1999). The removal of tariff subsidies and QRs exposes domestic firms (that may have become inefficient because of protection) to increased competition from imports. Consequently, trade liberalisation can have undesirable side effects in the short run. Greenaway (1998) argues that these will depend on initial conditions and the sequencing of reforms. The short to medium term responses to trade reforms are on the allocation of factors (especially labour but also investment) and the composition of output, as resources switch from inefficient import substitution to exporting. The medium to long term impact of trade reforms should be reflected in capital formation and growth of real output and trade. Often the adverse adjustment costs, as some firms close for example, are observed more immediately than the positive benefits. For example, for a variety of reasons, it can take some time before exports can actually be increased. As the impact of any policy reform takes time, and as typically a variety of reforms with often conflicting effects are implemented during a period, it is exceedingly difficult to identify the effects of specific reforms – see McGillivray and Morrissey (1999) for elaboration on this.

3   POLICY REFORM AND MANUFACTURING PERFORMANCE

Most studies of the impact of policy reform on manufacturing have studied performance during a period of trade liberalisation. Bennell (1998) finds that liberalisation does not appear to have had an adverse effect on the manufacturing sector in SSA countries in general, although some countries experienced a decline in output. Grenier *et al.* (1999) note that the manufacturing sector in Tanzania increased output during the period of trade liberalisation. Evidence from Nepalese manufacturing indicates some growth in manufacturing output following trade liberalisation; however, there was no significant productivity growth, although the rate of decline in productivity growth was reduced (Sharma *et al.* 2000). Acheampong and Tribe (this volume, Chapter 2) find similar results for Nepal and Ghana. Put simply, the evidence is mixed albeit generally favourable to some degree of liberalisation.

Mulaga and Weiss (1996) analyse the Malawian manufacturing sector over the period 1970 to 1991, using firm-level data. This was a period of substantial changes in trade policy. When the entire period is separated into relatively 'open' and 'closed' sub-periods, it is clear that productivity and value added tended to grow more when the economy was open. Of course, trade policy is only one factor affecting productivity, so that without careful analysis of other policy areas (and of other influences on manufacturing performance) it would not be possible to come to a strong conclusion (Rodrik, 1992b: 102). This caveat applies to all countries.

Helleiner (1994: 8–32) notes that when industrial output is decomposed using the Chenery methodology (Chenery *et al.*, 1986) into its demand-side constituents, most industrial growth during adjustment follows from growth in domestic demand. By comparison, studies of Ghana (this volume, Chapter 2) and Malawi (Mulaga and Weiss, 1996) suggest that much of the industrial recovery should be attributed to improved capacity utilisation, due to easier availability of inputs, and place the emphasis on the supply side rather than the demand side. For SSA countries, it should also be noted that the manufacturing industries that recovered were principally developed in an earlier import substitution period, suggesting that import substitution industrialisation has had a sustainable impact on the economy. This should be set against the rather negative view of import substitution that tends to appear in the literature. The recovery would not have been possible if the industries had not already been in place, so that long-term industrialisation can be based at least in part on an initial phase of import substitution.

The dichotomy between import substitution and export promotion is often overemphasised (Lall and Wangwe, 1998: 75 and 79). The experiences of Japan, South Korea and the other successful East Asian countries show that import substitution played a major role in the early stages of development (Rodrik, 1992a: 310). Chhibber and Leechor (1995) consider the extent to which the lessons from the East Asian experience can be applied to SSA countries. They emphasise the 'usual suspects' – human capital, financial institutions, public sector and economic management, institutional development, and the nature of political and economic risk – but suggest caution in interpreting the relationship between policy and manufacturing growth and efficiency. A number of factors other than the trade policy environment emerge in many studies as important determinants of the performance of manufactured exports:

a. Scale – Firms considered too large during the import substitution phase seem to be too small to be competitive (in foreign markets) in an export-oriented phase. In general, certainly for SSA countries, exporting firms are far more likely to be large firms and large firms are more likely to export (Grenier *et al.*, 2000; Söderbom and Teal, 2000). Middleton (this volume, Chapter 9) and Thoburn (this volume, Chapter 5) both emphasise the suitability of microenterprises for providing the goods demanded domestically by low-income consumers.

b. Finance – Access to long-term finance, rationed credit and high interest rates are all identified as major constraints. There is some evidence for this in Ghana (Acheampong and Tribe, this volume, Chapter 2) and Gaza (Migdad *et al.*, this volume, Chapter 10). Grenier *et al.* (2000) report similar evidence for Tanzanian firms. Livingstone (this volume, Chapter 8) discusses the problems facing small enterprises in Cambodia in gaining access to adequate credit; they also face rationing and high interest rates. Access to finance is a major determinant of investment, itself a principal determinant of manufacturing performance (Arun and Nixson, this volume, Chapter 7).

c. Raw material costs and availability create problems for exporting firms as well as for those supplying the domestic market (Migdad *et al.*, this volume, Chapter 10). This is especially a problem when tariffs increase the costs of imported inputs; Thoburn (this volume, Chapter 5) notes that delays and difficulties in getting refunds on tariffs and VAT paid on inputs places exporters at a competitive disadvantage.

d.   Technology – Technological obsolescence and poor equipment are major impediments to many firms, especially exporters, who blame these for low productivity and the difficulty in achieving product quality for export markets (Acheampong and Tribe, this volume, Chapter 2; Mainga, this volume, Chapter 3). This emphasis on the shortcomings of technical efficiency and technological progress as a major constraint on industrial development in sub-Saharan Africa is also emphasised by the African Development Bank (1998: 60).

e.   Infrastructure – many firms complain about the prices and unreliability of electricity and water supply. Livingstone (this volume, Chapter 8), in the case of microenterprises in Cambodia, and Milner *et al.* (2000) in respect of manufacturing in Uganda, note the major impediment to trade associated with high transport costs (largely due to a low quality of transport infrastructure). Livingstone (this volume, Chapter 8) also notes that microenterprises cite the high cost of power supply as a problem.

Lall and Wangwe (1998) provide an overview of the nature of and experience with industrial policy in SSA, distinguishing between trade policy on the one hand and specific policy relating to the industrial sector on the other. Although this distinction is important in clarifying the types of actions considered to be 'policy reform', it is not always drawn clearly. In considering broad macroeconomic policies relating to – for example – international trade and payments, it is very difficult in practice to identify which particular economic gains or losses are attributable to which particular aspects of policy change. For this reason, the contributions to this volume refer to 'policy' in a general sense, because economy-wide and industry-specific policy changes tend to be implemented together and their impacts are difficult to separate. Nevertheless, in some countries trade and macroeconomic reforms preceded, often by many years, specific measures aimed at industry. Where appropriate, the contributions try to isolate specific from general policy impacts. Another problem, of course, is that it is difficult to identify *when* policies have an impact – the significance of time lags is often underestimated (Acheampong and Tribe, 1998; Arun and Nixson, this volume, Chapter 7).

A particular concern of analysts of manufacturing in SSA is the potentially damaging effects of liberalisation:

Liberalisation has led large swathes of the manufacturing sector to be devastated by import competition. Industrial survivors and new entrants are basically in activities that have 'natural' protection from imports: very small-scale enterprises, making low-income or localised products, and larger enterprises protected by high transport costs or based on processing of local raw materials. (Lall and Wangwe, 1998: 81)

However, there appears to be no consensus about the precise definition of the phenomenon of 'de-industrialisation' let alone over the extent to which empirical verification should be undertaken. Several chapters in a recent book focused on sub-Saharan Africa address themselves to the 'de-industrialisation' issue (Jalilian *et al.* 2000). In addition to the above, others have also elucidated the *a priori* expectation that liberalisation (and structural adjustment in general) might lead to a decline in manufacturing production in African countries. This may be due to increased competition for formerly protected domestic industries from imports, and/or to the lack of global competitiveness provided by African industries in terms of manufactured export development – see in particular Bennell (1998). However, experience is mixed, with some countries (for example Ghana and Uganda) exhibiting strong recovery from economic decline (not least in manufacturing production) following structural adjustment and liberalisation programmes, and SSA generally experiencing sustained manufacturing growth during the 1980s and into the 1990s (Tribe, 2000).

This issue, and a number of other issues thrown up in the course of the Jalilian *et al.* (2000) volume were suggestive that a broader global view of the nature and impact of policy towards the development of the manufacturing sector in developing countries would be of interest. The chapters in this volume should therefore be viewed in this context. It is indisputable that the 1980s and 1990s have witnessed a sea change in attitudes to the role of government policy towards what has become predominantly private sector manufacturing sector development.

4   OVERVIEW OF THE VOLUME

Acheampong and Tribe (Chapter 2) note that generalisation about the level of, and changes in, manufacturing efficiency cannot easily be justified – some countries have performed worse than others, and some countries show signs of improvement while others have deteriorated. Subject to this caveat, calculations of total factor productivity growth (TFPG), a standard tool of analysis, is instructive; at the least, TFPG for countries in which manufacturing has performed poorly is not very encouraging. Many factors affect productivity growth at the enterprise level. Some relate to entrepreneurial or managerial actions of the firm – management restructuring, retraining of labour, reorganisation of labour to undertake new tasks. Others relate to investment and technology – increasing capital per employee, installation of new equipment or rehabilitation of machinery. These too are policies or actions of the firm. Government policies alter the environment – increasing availability of foreign exchange, increasing availability of inputs, growth in the level of demand and improved infrastructure. Improving the 'government policy environment' is a specific aim of adjustment or liberalisation.

Recent work on Ghanaian manufacturing has been based on a period which largely follows that covered in Acheampong and Tribe (Chapter 2), and is based on firm-level panel data rather than on sector-wide data from the Ghana Statistical Service. Teal (1998) finds that, over the period 1991–95, real value added for the sector grew by 17 per cent, or about 4 per cent per annum, but that over the five year period there was no evidence of a growth in underlying productivity. This conclusion is broadly consistent with the findings of Acheampong and Tribe (Chapter 2), whereby output growth has largely been achieved by increased capacity utilisation, with any changes in TFPG likely to have been negative – or at least very low – in the early 1990s. It appears to be the case, at least in Ghana, that 'substantial firm growth has occurred by increasing both labour and capital inputs with zero technical progress' (Teal, 1998: 9).

A common source of export growth is a widening of the market, which can be induced by a significant depreciation of the domestic currency relative to competitors. If accompanied by policy reform this can encourage firms both to increase exports and to increase production for the domestic market. Acheampong and Tribe (Chapter 2) suggest that this occurred in Ghana, and some firms reinforced this (i.e. responded to incentives) by improving product quality, adopting new production processes and diversifying product lines. Of course external events can cause the market to contract, and exports will decline for reasons outside the control of the country; Thoburn (Chapter 5) provides an illustration in the case of Indonesia. Nevertheless, appropriate domestic policies can strengthen the competitiveness of exporters, and may enable them to, at least partially, 'buck' global trends. Rudaheranwa (Chapter 4) shows that, for Uganda, domestic supply-side factors were more important in export growth than demand factors (growth in export markets).

Mainga (Chapter 3) emphasises the importance of developing firm-level capability building, particularly in the area of technological capabilities, as a basis for significant positive response to the opportunities presented by national-level economic adjustment programmes. Using Zambian firm-level survey data collected in the course of his doctoral research, Mainga assesses the extent to which specific capabilities have been demonstrated by firms, and the characteristics that have some explanatory power over responsive and adaptive behaviour. He emphasises that getting prices right is only part of the story; learning mechanisms determine the ability of firms to develop specific capabilities. This conclusion is consistent with the emphasis given by Chhibber and Leechor (1995) to the significance of managerial capability for responsive manufacturing development – a lesson from the Asian 'tiger' economies that had not been given prominence previously. Mainga's arguments are intuitively appealing, and his detailed discussion of forms and processes of 'technological learning', distinguishing between knowledge about i) productive technology, ii) work practices and the organisation of production, iii) customers, suppliers and complementary institutions, and iv) the evolution of target markets, is very illuminating. He also distinguishes between four different types of technology, relating to production, information, human capital and institutions. Essentially, the implication of Mainga's argument is that the capacity for manufacturing firms to respond effectively to policy shifts depends to a considerable extent on their technological and managerial capability. Liberalisation and adjustment would therefore be regarded as necessary, but not sufficient, conditions for the achievement of improvements in manufacturing sector competitiveness. The same line of argument would apply to the capacity for firm-level responsiveness to any other policy shift – for example in the area of environmental protection.

Rudaheranwa (Chapter 4) conducts a 'constant market share' analysis of the changing competitiveness of Ugandan exporters. It is clear that export performance is very sensitive to competitiveness; that is, just less than two-thirds of export growth is due to the competitive factor. It is also evident that supply conditions had the greater impact on Ugandan export growth (over 64 per cent) whereas demand conditions (in export markets) accounted for less than 20 per cent of growth. Most of the growth in Ugandan exports was in agricultural commodities, especially traditional exports such as coffee, which is to be expected given the structure of the economy. Nevertheless, there was significant growth in some manufacturing, mostly chemicals and textiles, to African and European countries. There is no evidence that manufacturing output overall declined during the 1990s (Rudaheranwa, 1999), and some evidence that manufacturing exports increased following liberalisation. More importantly, the results suggest that the limited improvement in Ugandan export performance, including manufactures, was largely attributable to Ugandan reforms (supply side conditions). This is evidence for a potentially beneficial effect of liberalisation, even if export response is slow. It is clear that Uganda will find it difficult to increase the volume and diversity (composition and destination) of exports without adopting a strategy that reduces costs arising from inefficient transport and associated infrastructure facilities.

Thoburn (Chapter 5) addresses the slow down in Indonesian export growth in the early 1990s. The main role of the government in support of exporters was in providing export companies with a more competitive domestic economic environment that is attractive to foreign investors. It is important that exporters have access to traded inputs at world prices, and face an undistorted choice between purchasing inputs locally or through imports. They also require a competitive exchange rate. Indonesia achieved much of this until the mid-1990s. Indonesia's export promoting trade regime was supported by export processing zones (EPZs) and institutions to refund taxes on inputs (tariffs and VAT), *Bapeksta* and the *EPTE* facility (which competed with each other in an institutional sense). The fact that *Bapeksta* became less effective in providing tax refunds, and devoted more attention to auditing against fraud, was one reason for the slowdown in exports, especially of textiles and garments, in the mid-1990s. What this study highlights is that effective export promoting measures are those that alleviate the adverse effects of policy barriers to trade – protection of imports tends to disprotect exports. An important question is whether the restoration of undistorted input and export prices (by providing tax refunds) is the optimal role for export promotion agencies. A liberal trade regime would achieve this, and the agencies could then devote their resources to providing market information and marketing assistance.

Sharma and Morrissey (Chapter 6) investigate the consequences of trade liberalisation on export diversification and growth in Nepal, a landlocked low-income country. There is some evidence for a rise in export intensity, especially for manufactured exports, and a fall in the export share of primary products following trade liberalisation. This provides some support for the notion that trade liberalisation contributes to export diversification and growth. However, the structure of the Nepalese economy is not conducive to export-led growth, primarily because manufactured exports are dominated by two items (carpets and garments) subject to quotas under the generalised system of preferences (GSP) scheme.

Arun and Nixson (Chapter 7) focus on the structural changes that have taken place in Indian policy towards manufacturing development since 1991. Before then the Indian government had maintained 'heavily protectionist' policies. Notably these policies included 'reserved' status for a large number of manufacturing subsectors, whereby only Indian public sector enterprises were permitted to develop capacity. However, despite the protectionist approach, the robustness and size of the Indian economy permitted sustained growth over the forty years from the 1950s to the 1980s. During this period manufacturing and mining increased from 15 to 30 per cent of GDP, and from the mid-1970s to the end of the 1980s manufacturing accounted for 80 to 85 per cent of the stock of direct foreign investment (DFI). However, the manufacturing sector tended towards technological obsolescence, high concentration ratios, and comparative lack of competition. After the 1991 liberalisation, deregulation, privatisation and more favourable policies towards DFI were pursued. DFI approvals increased substantially over the period 1991 to 1998, but over this period only about 30 per cent of the approvals by value were converted into actual investment. This slow conversion of 'approvals' into 'actuals' is a feature of 'liberalisation' which has also been noted in Ghana (Acheampong and Tribe, 1998) – emphasising *inter alia* the importance of time lags between policy change and response, and the build up of business confidence. Indian experience post-1991 has not demonstrated a clear 'watershed' in industrial development and performance. However, the indications are that increased market orientation and attention to the minutiae of competitiveness will reap dividends in the medium- to long-term. An important issue in this context is that of technological capability, reflecting the findings of Mainga in his study of Zambian manufacturing (Chapter 3).

Livingstone (Chapter 8) addresses the microenterprise sector in Cambodia, from the perspective of policies towards providing credit and generating employment. As has been noted above, manufacturing firms in general cite access to credit as a problem. This is more extreme in the case of microenterprises, which tended to be excluded from the 'formal' credit (banking) sector. Cambodia, like any low-income economy, exhibits a pattern of demand that is biased towards goods that are affordable by the poor. This implies that there is a market for 'informal sector' production, and microenterprise production can stimulate manufacturing development from the bottom up. Furthermore, the size of the domestic market limits the scope for any large scale production (with the possible exception of garment factories, directed towards export). The study shows, at least for Cambodia, that the successful NGO credit schemes have benefited primarily those in rural areas. While this is desirable in itself, it fails to address the problem of enterprise development. Microenterprises, especially in urban areas, are still denied access to credit.

Middleton (Chapter 9) finds no evidence that neo-liberal adjustment policies in Ecuador did anything but harm to petty manufacturers, a segment of the economy that is assumed to be dynamic. It appears to be small-scale manufacturers of subsistence goods that fared worst. In times of economic boom, they lost market share to larger-scale producers of basic consumption goods, whereas during economic decline their potential market shrank. On the other hand, small-scale producers of production goods, such as mechanics and printers, were able to grow by servicing the needs of larger firms. The rate at which firms were disappearing was high and reasonably constant across all activities. The big difference between the different types of activity was the rate at which replacements were taking place; the replacement was much higher for producers of 'production goods' (e.g. mechanics) than of subsistence goods. Overall, the numbers employed in 'informal sector' activities in Quito declined by over 20 per cent between 1975 and 1995; the numbers producing basic consumer goods declined by about half, whereas the numbers producing production goods rose, but only by six per cent. The two clear areas of growth were in bakers and beauty salons, where numbers employed almost doubled. However, on the evidence from Quito, most of the growth (and decline) was in numbers of microenterprises rather than in the size of enterprises. These patterns are not due to any active government policy. In fact, the government had no policy; the neo-liberal economic paradigm applied in Ecuador assumed that if markets were liberalised, dynamic entrepreneurs would benefit and grow. Although informal microenterprises were certainly dynamic in a practical sense, they tended not to grow (Teal, 1998 shows the absence of growth dynamics in small firms in Ghana). The evidence suggests that positive government policies are necessary to support a truly dynamic and growing microenterprise sector.

Migdad *et al.* (Chapter 10) conduct a detailed analysis of the industrial sector in Gaza. They find evidence of great diversity within the small firm sector, with high rates of start-up combined with high rates of closure, and some firms growing whilst others contract. However, within the small firm sector, performance does not appear to be related to size or to age (there is no evidence of learning by doing). Access to finance and scarcity of raw materials do appear to be constraints. The most significant finding is that clothing firms, especially those engaged in subcontracting for Israeli firms, are the most dynamic and perform best on most criteria. Such dependence on Israel for access to markets in low labour cost sectors is not, however, a viable development strategy for Gaza.

5   CONCLUSIONS

The explicit intention of economic policy reform is to alter the incentives facing different sectors in the economy so as to encourage the growth of the most efficient sectors. Specifically, the argument for liberalisation is that one is starting from a position of a distorted economy and it is desirable to remove these distortions. For example, a highly protectionist trade regime reduces the incentives to exporting but encourages inefficiency in IS industries. Domestic policies towards agriculture, industry or finance, for example, may exacerbate these distortions. Obviously, when these distortions are removed the previously sheltered or supported sectors will face increased competition. To the extent that they are unable to increase efficiency to respond to this competition, these sectors will decline. The issue in terms of the net impact on manufacturing is the speed and extent of decline in some sectors relative to the expansion in those sectors facing improved incentives.

All of the studies in this volume demonstrate that there remains a role for active government policy during periods of liberalisation. In particular, the government can facilitate the ability of firms to respond to the change in relative incentives. This is true whether firms are competing with imports or are exporting. In both cases, government policies towards or assistance in investment, adopting technology or finding new market opportunities can facilitate the speed of adjustment. The basic point is that macroeconomic or trade policy changes alter incentives, but microeconomic policies can affect the ability of firms to respond to these changes.

The principal microeconomic policies we have in mind are those relating to access to finance for investment, access to technology and capabilities more generally, and information about market opportunities. The government can also play a role in reducing the infrastructure and institutional constraints to manufacturing. There is nothing inherently new in these conclusions, but this does not make them any less deserving of emphasis. One of the problems faced in low-income countries is that the ability of the government to implement supporting policies is often limited. Infrastructure projects, for example, are expensive and have a long gestation period. Furthermore, the banking sector is often inefficient and credit-constrained (this is one major reason why foreign investment can play such an important role). The case studies in this volume do not offer solutions to these problems. Rather, they highlight the need for accommodating investment, industry and infrastructure policies in an environment of economic policy reform. It would be wrong to make the 'textbook assumption' that private agents can quickly respond to changes in relative incentives, even if these changes are desirable in themselves.

Nevertheless, the evidence from the case studies is not unduly pessimistic. Even in very poor countries such as Ghana, Uganda and Nepal, the manufacturing sector has responded reasonably well to liberalisation. In a large, albeit poor, country such as India the response is more encouraging. Liberalisation is not a panacea, but nor is it the evil it is sometimes portrayed as. Firms will respond to incentives, but governments should be aware of the types of assistance that are warranted. There is one note of caution: the studies in Ecuador, Cambodia and Gaza all highlight the particular vulnerability of small-scale enterprises. In an era of 'globalisation', this is an area of manufacturing policy that requires further study.

REFERENCES

Acheampong, I.K. (1996), *The Impact of the Economic Recovery Programme (1983–90) on Industrial Performance in Ghana*, unpublished PhD Thesis, University of Bradford.

Acheampong, I.K. and M.A. Tribe (1998), 'The Response of Ghana's Manufacturing Sector to Structural Adjustment', in Cook, P., Kirkpatrick, C. and Nixson, F.I.

(eds), *Privatisation, Entrepreneurship and Economic Reform*, Edward Elgar, Cheltenham.

African Development Bank (1998), *African Development Report 1998*, Oxford University Press, Oxford.

Bennell, P. (1998), 'Fighting for Survival: Manufacturing Industry and Adjustment in Sub-Saharan Africa', *Journal of International Development*, **10**, 621–637.

Chenery, H.B., S. Robinson and M. Syrquin (1986), *Industrialization and Growth: A Comparative Study*, Oxford University Press for the World Bank, New York.

Chhibber, A. and C. Leechor (1995), 'From Adjustment to Growth in Sub-Saharan Africa: the Lessons of East Asian Experience Applied to Ghana', *Journal of African Economies*, **4**, 83–114.

Greenaway, D. (1998), 'Does Trade Liberalisation Promote Economic Development', *Scottish Journal of Political Economy*, **45**, 491–511.

Greenaway, D., C.W. Morgan and P. Wright (1997), 'Trade Liberalisation and Growth in Developing Countries: Some New Evidence', *World Development*, **25**, 1885–92.

Greenaway, D., C.W. Morgan and P. Wright (1998), 'Trade Reform, Adjustment and Growth: What Does the Evidence Tell Us?', *Economic Journal*, **108**, 1547–61.

Greenaway, D. and O. Morrissey (1993), 'Structural Adjustment and Liberalisation in Developing Countries: What Lessons Have We Learned?', *Kyklos*, **46**, 241–61.

Greenaway, D. and O. Morrissey (1994), 'Trade Liberalisation and Economic Growth in Developing Countries', in Murshed, S.M. and Raffer, K. (eds), *Trade Transfers and Development*, Edward Elgar, Cheltenham, 210–32.

Grenier, L., A. McKay and O. Morrissey (1999), 'Exporting, Ownership and Confidence in Tanzanian Enterprises', *The World Economy*, **22**, 995–1012.

Grenier, L., A. McKay and O. Morrissey (2000), 'Ownership and Export Performance in Tanzanian Enterprises', in Jalilian, H. Tribe, M. and Weiss, J. (eds), *Industrial Development and Policy in Africa*, Edward Elgar, Cheltenham, 244–59.

Helleiner, G.K. (ed.) (1994), *Trade Policy and Industrialisation in Turbulent Times*, Routledge, London.

Jalilian, H., M.A. Tribe and J. Weiss (eds) (2000), *Industrial Development and Policy in Africa*, Edward Elgar, Cheltenham.

Lall, S. and F. Stewart (1996), 'Trade and Industrial Policies in Africa', in Ndulu, B. and de Walle, N. (eds), *Agenda for Africa's Economic Renewal*, US-Third World Policy Perspectives No 21, Overseas Development Council, Transaction Publishers, New Brunswick.

Lall, S. and S. Wangwe (1998), 'Industrial Policy and Industrialisation in Sub-Saharan Africa', *Journal of African Economies*, **7**, Supplement 1, 70–107.

McGillivray, M. and O. Morrissey (eds) (1999), *Evaluating Economic Liberalisation*, Macmillan, London.

Milner, C. and O. Morrissey (1999), 'Measuring Trade Liberalisation', chapter 3 in McGillivray and Morrissey (1999).

Milner, C., O. Morrissey and N. Rudaheranwa (2000), 'Policy and Non-Policy Barriers to Trade and the Implicit Taxation of Exports in Uganda', *Journal of Development Studies*, **37**(2), 67–90.

Morrissey, O. (1999), 'Trade Policy Reform in Sub-Saharan Africa: Achievements, Effects and Prospects', paper presented at the *4th SCUSA Inter-University Colloquium*, University of East Anglia, September.

Mulaga, G. and J. Weiss (1996), 'Trade Reform and Manufacturing Performance in Malawi 1970–1991', *World Development*, **24**, 1266–78.

Noorbakhsh, F. and A. Paloni (1998), 'Structural Adjustment Programmes and Export Supply Response', *Journal of International Development*, **10**, 555–73.

Onafowora, O. and O. Owoye (1998), 'Can Trade Liberalization Stimulate Economic Growth in Africa', *World Development*, **26**, 497–506.

Papageorgiou, D., M. Michaely and A. Choksi (1991), *Liberalizing Foreign Trade*, 7 volumes, Basil Blackwell, Oxford.

Rodrik, D. (1992a), 'Conceptual Issues in the Design of Trade Policy for Industrialisation', *World Development*, **20**, 309–20.

Rodrik, D. (1992b), 'The Limits of Trade Policy Reform in Developing Countries', *Journal of Economic Perspectives*, **6**, 87–105.

Rodrik, D. (1999), *The New Global Economy and Developing Countries: Making Openness Work*, ODC Policy Essay No. 24, Johns Hopkins University Press, Washington, DC.

Rudaheranwa, N. (1999), *Transport Costs and Export Trade of Landlocked Countries: Evidence from Uganda*, unpublished PhD Thesis, University of Nottingham.

Sharma, K., S. Jayasuriya and E. Oczkowski (2000), 'Liberalisation and Productivity Growth: The Case of Manufacturing Industries in Nepal', *Oxford Development Studies*, **28**, 205–22.

Söderbom, M. and F. Teal (2000), 'Skills, Investment and Exports from Manufacturing Firms in Africa', *Journal of Development Studies*, **37**(2), 14–43.

Teal, F. (1998), *The Ghanaian Manufacturing Sector 1991–1995: Firm Growth, Productivity and Convergence*, Working Paper Series – WPS/98-17, Centre for the Study of African Economies, University of Oxford.

Tribe, M. (2000), 'A Review of Recent Manufacturing Sector Development in Sub-Saharan Africa', in Jalilian *et al.* (2000), pp. 75–106.

2. Sources of industrial growth: the impact of policy on large and medium scale manufacturing performance in Ghana

Isaac Acheampong and Michael Tribe

1 INTRODUCTION

The principal objective of this chapter is to assess the extent to which the Ghanaian Government economic policies have affected the overall performance of the manufacturing sector over the period from the 1970s to the 1990s. In particular, the aim is to assess the impact of the Economic Recovery Programme and the Structural Adjustment Programmes which were introduced in the mid-1980s, and to form some judgement on the degree to which they have been responsible for a recovery of the large and medium scale manufacturing sector. The discussion will concentrate on large and medium scale industries, and will follow a 'before and after' approach based on analysis of data over the period 1970 to 1993. The analysis will attempt to identify the contributions of capital, labour and total factor productivity growth to output growth and to explore policy implications. Data for the estimation of the sources of industrial growth were obtained from published industrial statistics produced by the Ghana Statistical Service.

Industrial growth may arise from increases in factor inputs (that is physical and human capital and material inputs) and from productivity growth (due to increased efficiency in using factor inputs). Economic policies pursued in a particular period and relating to the economy as a whole, and to the industrial sector in particular, influence productivity growth. For example, the shift from a regulated to a liberalised economic regime in Ghana should have improved

Acknowledgements: This chapter is a revised and updated part of the PhD thesis of the first named author (Acheampong, 1996), which was supervised by Professor Colin Kirkpatrick and Dr Michael Tribe. The contributions of Colin Kirkpatrick to the evolution of the research are gratefully acknowledged by both authors. Acknowledgement should also be gratefully made for the Ghana Government scholarship which enabled the first author to undertake the research, and for the African Economic Research Consortium funding support for the data collection.

the incentive structure and ensured a stable macroeconomic environment influencing productivity growth positively. Better economic management, the economic recovery and the higher inflows of foreign exchange (linked to increased export earnings and positive capital flows) should have led to higher manufacturing capacity utilisation in the short run, and in the longer run to significant rehabilitation of existing capacity and capacity expansion. There were also specific policy measures relating to the industrial sector which should have had the effect of enhancing its performance.

Ghana embarked upon an Economic Recovery Programme (ERP) in April 1983 in order to reverse the declining trend in the economy.[1] The main thrust of the ERP was to provide a basis for economic growth and efficiency in the utilisation of scarce resources. The manufacturing sector was one of the sectors targeted under the ERP and changes were effected in industrial policy. The broad strategy of Ghana's industrial development policy since April 1983 has been to enhance the international and domestic competitiveness of manufacturing activity (through efficient import replacement and export development) and by removing supply constraints (through selective rehabilitation) that impede output and productivity performance (Republic of Ghana, 1992). The economic policy reforms involved the deregulation of economic activity, allowing market forces to work more effectively.

The policy changes that were effected during the ERP included:

- Changes in credit and interest rate policy;
- Overhauling the financial sector;
- Introduction of a market-determined foreign exchange rate;
- Removal of price and distribution controls;
- Promulgation of a new investment code (PNDC Law 116) and the reform of the Ghana Investment Centre into the renamed Ghana Investment Promotion Centre.

These policy changes were summarised in the Institute of Statistical, Social and Economic Research's annual economic survey for 1992 (ISSER, 1993: 156–70), and a broader review of policies which impacted on the manufacturing sector has recently been provided by Takeuchi (1999). A recent overview of the development of the manufacturing sector is provided by Asante, Nixson and Tsikata (2000).

In the pre-ERP era, industries were sheltered by a tariff wall, were protected by the rationing of foreign exchange (through import licensing with its associated rent seeking activities), and were dependent on large scale public sector investment (ISSER 1992: 122). In sum the ERP sought to promote the competitive performance of industry and to ensure higher growth of industrial production. A strand of economic theory holds the view that economic liberalisation leads to efficiency gains and productivity growth.[2] Theoretically, this is due to the fact that economic liberalisation:

- Exposes firms to international competition;
- Reduces static inefficiencies arising from resource misallocation and waste;
- Reduces rent seeking activities; and
- Enhances learning, technological change and economic growth.

Exposure to international competition forces domestic firms to raise their productivity performance to international levels. The expansion of market size through export development and import substitution allows more effective capacity utilisation in the short run and scale economies to be derived in the longer run. Improved availability of foreign exchange made possible by the effects of economic reforms also helps to improve productivity.

In the remainder of this chapter, Section 2 reviews the analytical framework which has been adopted, while Section 3 presents an overview of the performance of manufacturing industry in Ghana over the period 1970 to 1993. Section 4 focuses on the growth and structure of employment in the large- and medium-scale manufacturing subsector, and Section 5 reviews the nature and sources of growth in the subsector. Section 6 compares the results of some related studies, and Section 7 presents an overview of the results and conclusions of the analysis, including a discussion of the policy implications.

2   ANALYTICAL FRAMEWORK

The growth accounting framework that is used in the analysis estimates the growth rate of manufacturing output less the weighted average growth rate of identified inputs (where the weights are the shares of each factor in the value of total output). This is the approach which was used in path-breaking studies by the World Bank in the late 1970s (Krueger and Tuncer, 1980) and gives an insight into the sources of industrial growth. The growth accounting framework uses the production function as an accounting and not as an estimation framework as explained by the steps below. Given a production relation between inputs and output that is homogeneous of degree one and is subject to disembodied technical progress, the following formulation of a production function can be specified:

$$Q_t = A(t)F(K_t, L_t) \qquad\qquad [1]$$

where:

Q_t = Output over time

(t) = Hicksian efficiency parameter or cumulative effects of the shift of the production function over time (TFPG – total factor productivity growth)

F = Functional relationship

K_t = Capital employment over time

L_t = Labour employment over time

t = Time

Totally differentiating equation [1] with respect to time gives:

$$\dot{Q} = \dot{A}F + A\left[F_K K \cdot \frac{\dot{K}}{K} + F_L L \cdot \frac{\dot{L}}{L}\right] \qquad [2]$$

where

$$\frac{\partial Q}{\partial t} = \dot{Q}, \quad F_k = \frac{\partial F}{\partial K}, \quad F_L = \frac{\partial F}{\partial L}, \quad \dot{K} = \frac{\partial K}{\partial t}, \quad \dot{L} = \frac{\partial L}{\partial t}$$

Dividing through by $Q = AF$,

$$\frac{\dot{Q}}{Q} = \frac{\dot{A}}{A} + \left[\frac{AF_K \cdot K}{Q}\right]\frac{\dot{K}}{K} + \left[\frac{AF_L \cdot L}{Q}\right]\frac{\dot{L}}{L} \qquad [3]$$

where AF_K and AF_L represent the marginal products of capital and labour respectively and the terms in the square brackets are the elasticities of value added with respect to the two factor inputs. Under competitive equilibrium, factors of production are paid the value of their marginal products and so the output elasticities become equal to the income shares of the respective factors of production. Let the share of labour be $\alpha = [\partial Q/\partial L].[L/Q]$ and the share of capital be $\beta = [\partial Q/\partial K].[K/Q]$.

Substituting in equation [3], the following results are obtained:

$$\frac{\dot{Q}}{Q} = \frac{\dot{A}}{A} + \left[\beta\frac{\dot{K}}{K} + \alpha\frac{\dot{L}}{L}\right] \qquad [4]$$

The expression in parenthesis in equation [4] takes the form of the Divisia index number giving the rate of growth of total factor inputs as a weighted sum of the growth rates of individual factor inputs.

Rearranging equation [4] gives:

$$\frac{\dot{A}}{A} = \frac{\dot{Q}}{Q} - \left[\beta \frac{\dot{K}}{K} + \alpha \frac{\dot{L}}{L} \right] \qquad [5]$$

The right hand side (RHS) of equation [5] shows the difference between the percentage change in output and the percentage change in inputs weighted by α and β, which gives the equation for TFPG. The empirical application of equation [5] requires that continuous time derivatives are replaced by discrete changes. A Tornqvist index can be utilised whereby the resultant shares also become averages of current and previous shares.

3   OUTPUT GROWTH PERFORMANCE OF MANUFACTURING INDUSTRY

In this section we shall analyse manufacturing output growth performance concentrating on the growth of manufacturing real value added. The analysis will consider trends in the annual averages and average annual growth rates in manufacturing value added in relation to the other sectors of the economy in a 'before and after' ERP scenario. It is acknowledged that, in the context of ex-post evaluation of the impact of changes in economic policy, the 'before' situation is not equivalent to the 'without policy change' situation since it is not a satisfactory 'counterfactual' (Mosley *et al.*, 1995: 190). However, in the circumstances, the 'before and after' approach is the simplest and most straight-forward which can meaningfully be used in the Ghanaian case.

Table 2.1 shows that industry as a whole (which includes mining and quarrying, electricity and water, and construction, as well as manufacturing)

Table 2.1   Trends in real value added for industry and manufacturing 1970–92 (constant 1975 prices – millions of cedis)

	Gross National Product	Industry	Manufacturing
1970	5 335	1 033.0	678.7
1975	5 241	1 108.6	735.9
1980	5 453	838.4	579.4
1985	5 345	704.8	460.1
1990	6 724	994.3	628.4
1991	7 079	1 031.6	635.0
1992	7 359	1 091.1	652.3

Sources: Industry and Manufacturing data provided by the Ghana Statistical Service, GNP data from *Quarterly Digest of Statistics* and derived from Huq (1989: 47).

achieved improved real value added performance after the ERP. It can be seen that industry declined significantly in the period before the ERP (1973–82), and positive average annual growth rates were achieved after the ERP (1983–92). The growth performance of the economy as a whole improved considerably after the introduction of the ERP, and this improved growth performance is statistically significant. The difference between 'before' and 'after' the ERP is clearly apparent. For the industrial sector and for manufacturing, the mean level of value added after the ERP was markedly lower than in the entire period before, although the differences were not statistically significant.

The principal concern in this chapter is with the growth of the large and medium scale manufacturing sector, and Table 2.2 shows that between 1973 and 1982 this declined at an annual average rate of 5 per cent and then grew at 7 per cent per annum on average after the start of the ERP (1983–92).[3] It is notable that the manufacturing sector declined more rapidly than GDP in the period before the ERP, and recovered more strongly than GDP in the period after the ERP. One of the most obvious features is the steady recovery of manufacturing value added after 1983 to a level which is comparable with the 1970s. This performance might be attributed to the special attention that was accorded to the manufacturing sector in the first phase of the reforms. The manufacturing sector in Ghana depends heavily on imported inputs, which accounted for 73.1 per cent of all input requirements in 1982 (Ninsin, 1991: 78). The stagnation of the economy in the latter part of the 1970s led to a decline in capacity utilisation as imported inputs became a binding constraint. The importation of inputs under phase 1 of the ERP contributed immensely in this growth (Republic of Ghana – ERP 1 Vol 2: 47–54). Other complementary factors enhancing growth during the ERP era were the liberalisation of the exchange rate and imports, and the better availability of foreign exchange. These developments made it possible for industrial enterprises that had hitherto been starved of inputs and spare parts to obtain them and in turn this led to improved capacity utilisation. Furthermore, the growth of the industrial sector can be partly ascribed to the rehabilitation of existing plant and the availability of imported raw materials made possible by the easing of the foreign exchange constraint, particularly in the mining sector. Further discussion of the role of capacity utilisation will be found in a later section of the chapter.

The growth rate of the manufacturing sector was as high as 14 per cent per annum between 1983 and 1987, but declined to 3 per cent between 1987 and 1992.[4] This may be due to the fact that while competitive industries recovered (principally through improved capacity utilisation – as will be seen later) and then continued to grow, uncompetitive industries began to decline or close. Output in 1983 was particularly low due to the drought, electricity

Table 2.2 *Average value added and growth rates for industry and manufacturing 1970–92 (constant 1975 prices – million cedis/percentages)*

Sectors	Before ERP mean annual value added 1973–82	After ERP mean annual value added 1983–92	T statistic	Before ERP mean growth rate 1973–82	After ERP mean growth rate 1983–92	T statistic
1. GDP	5405.6	6150.0	2.1*	–1	5	2.7**
2. Industry	963.0	841.1	1.1	–5	8	1.9*
of which Manufacturing	625.0	533.0	1.3	–5	7	2.06*

Notes:
All values were computed in real terms at constant 1975 prices.
** significant at less than 5 per cent.
* significant at less than 10 per cent level.

Source: Computed from *Quarterly Digest of Statistics* and ISSER (1993).

rationing, shortages of foreign exchange and other factors. Recovery was therefore comparatively easily achieved in the early period, and the slow down in the growth rate of manufacturing value added reflected the lower growth of the whole economy (real GDP growth fell from 6 per cent between 1983 and 1987 to 5 per cent between 1987 and 1992), which affected the manufacturing sector more than any other.

Table 2.3 presents the average shares of industry and manufacturing in GDP before and after the ERP. Industry contributed a higher proportion of GDP before the ERP as compared with after, but there is evidence of steady recovery if the period 1983–87 is compared with 1987–92. The manufacturing sector contributed about 11 to 12 per cent of GDP before the ERP and 8 to 9 per cent after the ERP. However, the 1983–92 average conceals significant variations since the annual figures rose from 6.9 per cent in 1983 to 9.4

Table 2.3   Mean shares of industry and manufacturing in value added

Period	Share in GDP: industry	Share in GDP: manufacturing	Share in industry: manufacturing
Entire Period			
1970–92	16.02	10.26	63.92
Before ERP			
1970–82	17.92	11.54	64.33
1970–75	19.09	12.05	63.03
1975–82	17.42	11.45	65.56
After ERP			
1983–92	13.54	8.59	63.38
1983–87	12.74	8.19	64.08
1987–92	14.31	9.06	63.31
Significance Testing of Differences in Mean Shares 1973–92			
Before ERP			
1973–82	17.9	11.7	64.8
After ERP			
1983–92	13.6	8.6	63.4
T Statistic	4.0*	5.4*	1.4

Notes:
All values are computed in real terms – constant 1975 prices.
* significant at less than 5 per cent.

Source: Computed from *Quarterly Digest of Statistics* (several years) and ISSER (1992).

Table 2.4   Index numbers of manufacturing production 1978–91
            (1977=100)

	1978	1980	1985	1990	1991
Food	84.8	70.0	41.8	57.5	59.3
Beverages	77.0	70.2	59.3	94.0	93.0
Tobacco	66.1	67.0	61.3	57.1	49.6
Textiles	81.5	41.4	19.2	37.7	39.1
Sawmills	92.1	52.0	19.2	74.2	133.6
Paper	103.5	80.8	65.1	53.5	49.3
Petroleum	96.0	87.9	80.6	70.5	92.2
Chemicals	40.5	34.7	31.8	57.6	44.7
Cement	87.2	52.1	63.6	117.3	125.6
Iron and steel	39.3	73.9	46.2	5.2	n.a.
Non-ferrous metals	90.3	111.8	28.0	103.8	104.6
Cutlery	67.0	33.1	34.6	55.2	63.2
Electricals	73.2	26.1	28.4	25.5	40.0
All manufacturing	81.0	69.0	49.3	63.5	71.3

Source: Data provided by Ghana Statistical Service.

per cent in 1987 before declining slightly to 8.7 per cent in 1992. The manufacturing share in industry was about the same both before and after the ERP.

The shares in production contributed by individual manufacturing subsectors are presented in summary form in Table 2.4. The subsectors with the sharpest decline in the period before the ERP were textiles and sawmills, with the 1985 index declining to less than one-quarter of the 1978 level. By comparison the 1985 indices for the food, non-ferrous metals and electricals subsectors were less than half of the 1978 levels. In the recovery after the ERP, the important food and textiles subsectors were sluggish, but growth in sawmills, cement and non-ferrous metals was strong, with the index in each case ending the period higher than that for 1977–78. The petroleum subsector is significant in that the index remained relatively the same throughout the entire period 1978 to 1991, reflecting its significance for the surface transport sector of the economy.

Local sourcing of domestic inputs for the manufacture of food and beverages, soap and detergents, tyres and tubes and textiles and clothing, partly helped these manufacturing subsectors to increase output and growth. Among the priority sectors that benefited from the foreign exchange and trade reforms were domestic resource-based industries including wood products and furniture, textiles, rubber, minerals and certain food products. The textile subsector reached 1991 with a production index more than double the 1983 level, but still less than half of the 1978 level. Particularly notable is the substantial drop in the index of non-ferrous metal manufacture in the mid-1980s, accounted for by the 1983–84 drought which led to severe restrictions in the availability of hydroelectric power.

4 GROWTH AND STRUCTURE OF EMPLOYMENT

This section analyses the annual growth rates and mean levels of manufacturing employment in a 'before and after ERP' scenario, recognising that employment issues are of paramount importance to policy makers and have serious social consequences for the well-being of society at large.

It is generally observed that under a regulated economic regime, governments tend to maintain employment in state-owned enterprises at higher levels than is desirable within a distorted protectionist import substitution industrialisation strategy (World Bank, 1994: 150; Stein, 1994: 287–305). Overmanning is also an issue in the public sector at large. Two separate issues then arise in the context of the ERP and SAPs. First, in order to ensure increased efficiency in the utilisation of resources, and sustainable growth in output and productive employment, it is considered essential to reduce the size of the public sector and make it more efficient. Second, in order to support the development of an efficient and expanding manufacturing sector it is considered essential to move away from a focus on a protected industrial sector largely depending upon import substitution.

It is recognised that the considerable economic changes included in the ERP and SAPs are likely to lead to short-run transitional costs in terms of unemployment of labour, idle capacity, bankruptcies and other forms of business failure when resources are shifting from inefficient sectors to more efficient sectors of the economy. For example, the changes to the incentive structure associated with trade and other forms of liberalisation imply a bias against industries which have been protected (producing only for the domestic market) and in favour of industries which can compete equally in the domestic and international markets. In the short run this is likely to lead to a fall in employment in the first category of industries, while increases in employment in the second category might only be expected in the longer run; thus the decrease in employment may not be offset immediately by the expansion in the export sector, due to the fact that there may be a time lag before new investments take place, new skills are acquired, and export market penetration is achieved (Thomas *et al.*, 1991: 72–3). However, it is hoped that as the adjustment process gathers momentum, the net effect of the ERP and SAPs on employment will be positive (World Bank, 1994: 149–58; Michaely *et al.*, 1991: 72–102 and 284–5).

Empirical evidence from studies in other countries suggests that the loss of employment in the early stages of adjustment is a short-run phenomenon and that after resources have been reallocated, employment picks up again (Michaely *et al.*, 1991; World Bank, 1994: 150). These studies conclude that trade liberalisation is not associated with increased unemployment either in the manufacturing sector or in the economy as a whole. Thomas *et al.* (1991) argue that liberalisation policies are applied amidst other developments (and other policies) in the domestic and international economy such as, for example, a deterioration in the terms of trade. It is therefore difficult to attribute changes in the level of employment to liberalisation alone. They conclude that where renewed economic growth is robust following adjustment, employment tends to increase with reforms. It is not clear that these findings would necessarily apply without modification in the particular circumstances of Ghana.

Table 2.5 shows that for the manufacturing sector as a whole, grouping years into broad 'before' and 'after' periods of 1974–82 and 1983–91, the decline in employment improved from –15 per cent per annum before the ERP to –10 per cent afterwards. However, these averages conceal important changes in employment, as is clearer from Table 2.6. For example, the decline in public sector employment as a whole was actually faster during the adjustment period 1983–91 (–10 per cent per annum) than in the period 1975–82 (–7 per cent) (Achcampong, 1996). The rapid decline before the ERP was due to the fact that total employment in industry as a whole fell from 148.2 thousand in 1979 to 87.9 thousand in 1980, and then to 58.2 thousand in 1981. By 1983 industrial employment had increased to 91.7 thousand, recovering further to 131.6 thousand in 1987, after which it fell dramatically to 47.2 thousand in 1991.

Turning to the manufacturing sector in particular, it is clear that this subsector accounts for the highest proportion of employment in the industrial sector – ranging from one-third to a little over one-half over the period discussed here. Movements of manufacturing employment are very close to the movements in industrial employment as a whole. It is notable that employment in large and medium scale manufacturing ended the period at a level substantially less than half of that at the beginning of the period 20 years earlier, and only one-quarter of the recorded level of employment at its peak. This decline in employment tends to confirm the view that for many developing countries the large scale manufacturing sector does not represent a significant source of productive employment growth (Seers, 1963: 461–5). Other factors accounting for the deteriorating trend in employment are linked to the running down

Table 2.5 Mean employment levels and annual growth rates in industry and manufacturing 1974–91 (thousands/percentages)

Sectors	Before ERP mean level 1974–82	After ERP mean level 1983–91	T statistic	Before ERP mean annual growth rate 1974–82	After ERP mean annual growth rate 1983–91	T statistic
Industry	127.9	88.4	5.69***	−12.4	−9.0	0.48
of which manufacturing	62.9	43.8	3.5***	−15.4	−9.7	0.8

Note: *** Significant at less than 1 per cent level.

Source: Computed from *Labour Statistics & Quarterly Digest of Statistics* (several issues), Statistical Service, Accra.

Table 2.6   Employment in industry and manufacturing 1970–91 (thousands)

	1970	1975	1980	1985	1990	1991
Total employment		431.6		464.3	229.6	186.3
Industry	142.8	158.5	87.9	108.1	56.2	47.2
of which manufacturing	52.8	77.0	35.1	51.7	28.7	20.6

Note: 1975–9 is employment in establishments employing 10 or more persons and 1981–91 is employment in establishments irrespective of size. No data is available for 1980 from this source.

Source: *Quarterly Digest of Statistics, GSS*, (several issues).

of assets and closure of a number of enterprises due to their inability to adjust, the restructuring of existing enterprises, and the general constraints that faced industry as a whole in adjusting to the policies under the ERP (Weissman, 1990).

The declining trend in recorded employment for all the industrial sectors, and for the manufacturing sector in particular, during the later part of the post-ERP period from 1987 to 1991 was the result of, inter alia:

- Retrenchment and redeployment of workers from the public sector and parastatal organisations;
- Removing ghost workers from parastatal organisations;
- The private sector restructuring its operations in order to become more efficient in the new competitive environment;
- Closure of some firms following the import liberalisation policy;
- A slow response of the private sector and new investments to the policy changes;
- Divestiture of state owned enterprises.

5   SOURCES OF GROWTH IN THE LARGE AND MEDIUM SCALE MANUFACTURING SUBSECTORS

The purpose of this section is to examine the sources of manufacturing growth in the large and medium scale subsectors using the growth accounting framework described in Section 2. As a prelude to the analysis, we shall undertake an assessment of efficiency within the framework of partial productivity measures. Table 2.7 shows the growth rates of partial productivity measures and their arithmetic means.[5] Labour productivity declined at an increasing rate during the 1970s and early 1980s in the period before the ERP

Table 2.7 Growth rates of partial productivity measures in large and medium scale manufacturing 1970–89 (percentages and constant 1975 prices – 000s of cedis)

Year	Labour productivity growth (per cent)	Capital productivity growth (per cent)	Mean labour productivity (per annum)	Mean capital productivity (per annum)	Mean capital output ratio	Mean capital recovery ratio	Mean emolument per employee (per annum)
1. BEFORE THE ERP							
1970–82	–5	–3	6455.91	0.62	1.70	0.52	1065.07
1970–76	–3	1	7387.96	0.76	1.50	0.51	1670.41
1976–82	–7	–8	5657.01	0.52	1.80	0.53	546.18
2. DURING THE ERP							
1983–89	14	–5	5767.41	0.19	6.90	0.18	571.49
3. THE WHOLE PERIOD 1970–1989							
1970–89	–2	–10	6215.93	0.50	3.50	0.40	892.31

Notes: 1. Labour productivity is calculated as gross value added divided by total employment. 2. Productivity of capital is gross value added divided by capital stock. 3. Capital-labour ratio is defined as capital stock divided by total labour employment. 4. Capital-output ratio is computed as capital stock divided by gross value added. 5. Capital recovery ratio is expressed as gross value added minus total emolument to labour divided by capital stock. 6. Total emolument per employee is defined as total compensation accruing to labour divided by total employment. 7. Capital stock has been estimated using the perpetual inventory accumulation method. The expression is formulated as follows: $K(t) = (1 - d) K(t - 1) + A(t)$ where $K(t)$ is the real value of capital stock for year 't', $A(t)$ is the real gross investment for year (t) and 'd' is the rate of depreciation. 8. All the variables are expressed in constant 1975 prices using deflators from the Ghana Statistical Service. 9. The analysis is limited to 1970–89 due to the unavailability of data for later years at the time that the study was undertaken.

Source: Computed from *Industrial Statistics*, Ghana Statistical Service (GSS).

and fell overall by –7 per cent over the period 1976–82. Capital productivity also declined at an increasing rate before the ERP, reaching –8 per cent over the period 1976–82. In the period 1983–89, after the ERP, labour productivity growth recovered strongly and improved to 14 per cent per annum.

Average labour productivity was significantly higher in the period 1970–76 than in the periods immediately before and after the ERP (when the means are about the same at ¢5 700–5 800 per annum). It is notable that the mean annual emolument per employee fell substantially in real terms between 1970–76 and 1976–82, from ¢1 670 to ¢546, then remained at this lower level, on average, over the period after the ERP (¢571), reflecting the similar levels of labour productivity immediately before and after the ERP. The evidence of Table 2.7 is that capital productivity declined considerably over the period 1970–89, from ¢760 to ¢190 for the first and third of the periods identified. The higher capital output ratio in the period after the ERP confirms the low level of capital productivity, and is largely due to the increased capital inputs which became possible after the beginning of the ERP.

Table 2.8 shows that there is evidence that the mean productivity of labour and the mean compensation of employees for 1976–82 and 1983–89 are similar because the statistical test cannot separate them. The table also shows that there are statistically significant differences between the mean productivity of capital, capital output ratio, and capital recovery rate for the two periods before and after the ERP.

Table 2.9 shows that the average annual growth rate for gross value added in the post-ERP period (1983–89) was an impressive 20 per cent, whilst in the period preceding the implementation of the ERP (1976–82) the growth rate was substantially negative (–13 per cent). The partial productivity analysis does not show the efficiency with which total inputs were utilised. The total factor productivity growth (TFPG) approach within the growth accounting framework, which was explained in Section 2, provides a view of overall, rather than partial, productivity. From Table 2.9 it is clear that TFPG over the period immediately preceding the ERP (1976–82) was substantially negative at –12 per cent. After the introduction of the ERP, the rate of TFPG change turns around, so that although it is still negative, it is higher than before the ERP (–3 per cent over 1983–89 and –1.95 per cent over 1983–93). The implication of the new estimate for 1983–93 which is reported in this chapter is that for the period 1989 to 1993 TFPG was positive at about 1.08 per cent.[6] One of the reasons for the comparatively disappointing TFPG results after the inception of the ERP must be the significant additional capital inputs which were enabled and required,[7] and it will be recalled that in the period immediately after 1983, labour inputs increased significantly. It was only after the economy 'settled down' after the 'shock' of the ERP/SAPs and associated liberalisation, and the 'shake-out' of labour had taken hold, that TFP per-

Table 2.8 Mean labour and capital productivity and technical coefficients in large and medium scale manufacturing 1976–82 and 1983–89 (constant 1975 prices – 000s cedis)

Year	Mean labour productivity (per annum)	Mean capital productivity (per annum)	Mean capital output ratio	Mean capital recovery rate	Mean emolument per employee (per annum)
1976–82	5657.01	0.52	1.80	0.53	546.18
	(1325.43)	(0.26)	(0.46)	(0.15)	(274.39)
1983–89	5767.41	0.19	6.90	0.18	571.49
	(1987.01)	(0.10)	(4.11)	(0.10)	(230.58)
T-Statistic	0.24	4.39***	3.30**	7.90***	0.14

Notes:
** statistically significant at less than 5 per cent level.
*** statistically significant at less than 1 per cent level.
Standard deviations are in parentheses.

Sources: As for Table 2.7.

Table 2.9 Sources of manufacturing growth 1970–93 (constant 1975 prices)

Year	(1) Gross value added growth in real terms (%)	(2) Labour growth (%)	(3) Average share of labour in value added (%)	(4) Weighted growth of labour (2×3) (%)	(5) Capital growth in real terms (%)	(6) Average share of capital in value added (%)	(7) Weighted growth of capital (5×6) (%)	(8) Weighted average growth of total inputs (%)	(9) Total factor productivity growth (TFPG) (%)
1. BEFORE THE ERP (1970–82)									
1970–82	−3.00	2.40	15.00	0.40	0.90	85.00	0.90	1.20	−4.20
1970–76	4.00	7.00	22.00	1.50	3.00	78.00	3.90	5.40	1.40
1976–82	−13.00	−4.00	9.00	−0.40	−1.00	91.00	−0.91	−1.30	−12.00
2. DURING THE ERP (1983–89)									
1983–89	20.00	6.40	10.00	0.60	25.00	90.00	22.20	22.90	−3.00
1983–93	−2.05	1.61	26.00	0.418	−0.675	74.00	−0.50	−0.08	−1.95
3. THE TWO PERIODS 1970–89 AND 1970–93									
1970–89	−2.00	−0.10	13.00	−0.02	8.10	87.00	7.05	7.03	−9.03
1970–93	−2.50	0.09	20.00	0.02	0.31	80.00	0.25	0.27	−2.77

Notes:
1. In estimating TFPG by the value added approach, data is required to estimate growth in manufacturing output, capital, labour and shares of labour and capital in value added. The growth of the weighted sum of total inputs less the growth of value added gives total factor productivity growth.
2. Capital stock has been estimated using the perpetual inventory accumulation method. The expression is formulated as follows: $K(t) = (1 − d) K(t − 1) + A(t)$ where $K(t)$ is the real value of capital stock for year 't', $A(t)$ is the real gross investment for year (t) and 'd' is the rate of depreciation. The capital stock series have been deflated with the deflator for gross capital formation, with 1975 as the base year. The computation of capital stock series assumes that 5 per cent of the preceding year's capital stock is written off every year as depreciation in real terms. The value of capital in 1970 has been used as the benchmark. Output and compensation to labour have been deflated with deflators for manufacturing output and consumer price index respectively. The source of all deflators is the Ghana Statistical Service.

Source: As for Table 2.7.

formance became seriously encouraging. In other words, there is now evidence of efficiency gains linked with the economic liberalisation and structural adjustment programmes which Ghana embarked upon in 1983. The regulated economic regime which was in place throughout most of the 1970s and into the early 1980s was associated with significantly deteriorating TFP, while the liberalised economic policy regime which took over from 1983 has been associated with improvements to TFP performance.

TFPG is defined as the increase in economic and technical efficiency with which inputs are employed in the production process over time (Krueger and Tuncer, 1980; Nishimizu and Robinson, 1984). Nishimizu and Page (1991) explain that short-term changes in TFPG may be a reflection of changes in capacity utilisation. Helleiner suggests that 'much of the association between productivity growth and output growth is attributable to the impact of variation in the level of capacity utilization' (1994: 29). In principle, changes in productivity growth due to variations in capacity utilisation should not be included in estimates of TFPG. The production function analysis on which TFPG is based assumes either full, or constant, capacity utilisation, so that 'pure' TFPG abstracts from capacity utilisation (Mulaga and Weiss, 1996: 1269–70). Variations in capacity utilisation are easier to take into account in TFPG calculations when the data is at firm level rather than subsector or sector level. Data on Ghanaian capacity utilisation suggest that the improvement in TFPG reported in this chapter in the period after the introduction of the ERP may be accounted for largely by the changes in manufacturing capacity utilisation.

Most of the findings discussed earlier in this section confirm the theoretical underpinnings of structural adjustment programmes: the liberalisation process pressurises firms to reduce their price cost margins and improve their efficiency, while the better availability of imported inputs and capital goods and improved infrastructure services enable firms to improve their capacity utilisation and production performance. Many hypotheses have been advanced and discussed concerning the relationship between development policies, growth and productivity change (see for example: Nishimizu and Robinson, 1986; Nishimizu and Page, 1991; Helleiner, 1994: 8–32), and some of these are summarised below:

- A positive relationship exists between productivity growth and the rate of growth of output: this relation is referred to as Verdoorn's law (Nishimizu and Page, 1991: 253; Helleiner, 1994: 29);
- International competition triggers increases in domestic efficiency. An implied challenge-response mechanism induced by competition compels domestic industries to adopt new technologies, increasing efficiency and reducing costs;

- Easing of the foreign exchange constraint makes imported inputs available and thereby enables better productivity performance;
- Better levels of capacity utilisation improve industrial efficiency and competitiveness;
- Improved infrastructure enhances industrial performance.

Table 2.10 shows summary data for Ghanaian manufacturing capacity utilisation, and the original source shows that utilisation increased from 18 per cent in 1984 to nearly 46 per cent in 1993 (Republic of Ghana, *Quarterly Digest of Statistics*, 1997: 12).[8] In footnote 8, a small correlation exercise shows that there is a fairly significant statistical relationship between aggregate manufacturing capacity utilisation and the index of manufacturing

Table 2.10   Ghana – manufacturing industries: estimated rate of capacity utilisation (large and medium scale factories: percentages)

Sub-Sector	1978	1980	1985	1990	1993
Textiles	40.0	20.1	19.7	35.0	41.3
Garments	38.1	29.9	25.5	22.0	53.3
Metals	28.2	28.4	16.2	49.0	80.0
Electricals	32.1	17.8	33.2	13.4	23.9
Plastics	10.6	19.1	28.0	40.0	45.0
Vehicle assembly (bicycle/motor cycle)	18.4	n.a.	19.9	25.0	16.4
Tobacco and beverages	50.0	30.0	39.6	65.0	76.3
Food processing	40.8	30.0	31.2	55.0	52.3
Leather	31.3	20.9	21.5	12.0	10.0
Pharmaceuticals	25.0	16.8	16.6	30.0	40.0
Cosmetics	33.4	8.0	n.a.	25.0	16.2
Paper and printing	31.0	28.4	14.5	30.0	45.0
Non-metallic mineral manufactures	47.0	29.7	35.0	48.0	72.8
Chemicals	42.0	28.0	20.2	30.2	40.0
Rubber	21.6	16.4	16.0	48.0	54.0
Wood processing	36.0	27.3	32.5	70.0	65.0
Miscellaneous	55.9	44.9	n.a.	n.a.	n.a.
All manufacturing industries	40.4	25.5	25.0	39.8	45.7

Note: Data for individual industries are obtained from Ministry of Industries. The estimate for all manufacturing industries is a weighted arithmetic average using weights proportional to the value of gross output in 1973.

Source: Republic of Ghana; *Quarterly Digest of Statistics*; various issues and June 1995 Table 10:12.

production. Individual manufacturing subsectors performed in a very diverse way over this period, and particularly high levels of capacity utilisation were achieved by metals, tobacco and beverages, non-metallic mineral manufactures and wood processing in 1993. Poor levels of capacity utilisation were experienced in 1993 for vehicle assembly, leather and cosmetics.

The statistics for manufacturing capacity utilisation are consistent with the main objectives of the rehabilitation programme embodied in ERP 1, which were to provide raw materials, spares, equipment and other inputs in a selected group of priority industries that:

- produced essential consumer goods for domestic use;
- generated government revenue;
- earned or saved foreign exchange; and
- employed labour intensive production methods and thus promoted employment.

The industries that were given priority attention were textiles, soap, cutlasses (agricultural hand implements), matches, sugar, beer, cigarettes, wood products, tyres and batteries (Republic of Ghana – ERP1 vol 2: 48). Most of the subsectors improved significantly, due essentially to the availability of imported raw materials and parts and to the rehabilitation of plant and machinery.[9] Following the adoption of the ERP in April 1983, changes in macroeconomic policies (including exchange rate policy) made the acquisition of foreign exchange easier through the open market, thus making it possible for industries to improve upon the levels of their capacity utilisation.[10] The liberalisation of imports and improved availability of foreign exchange helped industrial enterprises which had hitherto been starved of regular inputs and spare parts.

Prior to the ERP, most firms operated with obsolete machinery and equipment, but after its inception some firms were able to embark upon the rehabilitation of their plant and equipment in order to improve their efficiency. The efficiency gains came about through improved capacity utilisation and through improved production coefficients. The improved capacity utilisation was based on:

- higher levels of consumer demand based on the recovery of the economy;
- lower levels of downtime because of the breakdown and slow repair of equipment, caused partly by age and partly by poor maintenance (due in turn to poor cash flows and unavailability of parts);
- improved availability of inputs, both imported and locally sourced;
- lower levels of downtime due to improved infrastructure – for example less frequent breakdowns in electricity supply.[11]

Stein (1992: 87) draws attention to the capacity utilisation issue in his critical review of African industrial development under Adjustment.

It should be emphasised that the rehabilitation of plant and machinery, as well as the privatisation of state-owned enterprises (SOEs), can only be achieved over a period of time. The time lag between investment planning and the installation and operation of plant and machinery in the form of new investment means that any higher levels of TFPG arising from new technology following on from the adoption of trade and other forms of liberalisation will only be observed some considerable time after the policy change. This time lag relates to new investment plans as well as to rehabilitation, re-equipment or extension of existing plants (Acheampong and Tribe, 1998: 69–71); this would also apply to the advertisement, sale, purchase, and rehabilitation of SOEs under the divestiture programme, and is also related to uncertainty and business confidence on the part of private sector institutions responsible for investment decisions and their implementation (Pattillo, 1998).

6   COMPARISON WITH OTHER STUDIES ON GHANA

The introduction to this volume has surveyed some of the broader literature which has focused on manufacturing growth performance, and specifically on TFPG in other sub-Saharan African countries and in other continents. Here the focus will be on studies which have considered Ghanaian performance in particular.[12]

The implication of the conclusion that much of the Ghanaian industrial recovery must have been accounted for by improved capacity utilisation due to easier availability of inputs, is that the emphasis is on the supply side rather than the demand side. In fact it is necessary to take account of the effects of improvements on both the demand and supply sides of the economy. Helleiner (1994: 8–32) notes that when industrial output is decomposed using the Chenery methodology (Chenery *et al.*, 1986) into its demand-side constituents, most of the industrial growth during adjustment followed from growth in domestic demand. Thus it is important that the focus is maintained on both the supply and demand sides of the analysis. It should also be noted that the Ghanaian manufacturing industries which recovered were principally developed in an earlier import substitution period, suggesting that import substitution industrialisation has had a sustainable impact on the economy. This should be set against the rather negative view of import substitution which tends to appear in the literature. The recovery would not have been possible if the industries had not already been in place so that long-term industrialisation could be based at least in part on import substitution. The dichotomy between import substitution and export promotion is often overemphasised (Lall and Wangwe, 1998: 75 and 79). The experiences of Japan, South Korea and the other successful East Asian countries, for example, show that import substitution industrial activities played a major role in the early stages of development (Rodrik, 1992: 310).

Recent work on the Ghanaian manufacturing sector by Francis Teal has been based on a period which largely follows after that covered in this chapter, and is based on firm-level panel data rather than on sector-wide data from the Ghana Statistical Service (Teal, 1998). He finds that, over the period 1991–95, real value added for the sector grew by 17 per cent, or about 4 per cent per annum, but that over the five year period there was no evidence of a growth in underlying productivity. This conclusion is broadly consistent with the findings of this chapter for earlier periods, whereby output growth has largely been achieved by increased capacity utilisation, with any changes in TFPG likely to have been negative – or at least very low in the early 1990s. His final remark is that 'substantial firm growth has occurred by increasing both labour and capital inputs with zero technical progress' (Teal, 1998:9). This emphasis on the shortcomings of technical efficiency and technological progress as a major constraint on industrial development in sub-Saharan Africa is also emphasised in the *African Development Report 1998* (African Development Bank, 1998: 60).

A recent study undertaken on the development of Ghanaian manufactured exports has conclusions which are much more wide-ranging than applying simply to trade in manufactures (Baah-Nuakoh *et al.*, 1996: Chapter 6). The findings echo many of those in Acheampong (1996) and in Acheampong and Tribe (1998: 71–82). Some of the critical constraints identified in the study include:

a. Scale – 'Firm sizes which were considered too large during the import-substitution phase seem to be too small to make the transition to an export-oriented phase';
b. Finance – 'Most firms in the sample (87 per cent) were of the opinion that long-term finance was not easily available.' The survey responses included complaints about high interest rates;
c. Raw material costs and their availability created problems for exporting firms as well as for those supplying the domestic market;
d. Technology – technological obsolescence was considered a major impediment by about a quarter of the firms surveyed, and about one-third of exporting firms blamed the poor state of equipment for breakdowns, low productivity and difficulty in securing adequate product quality for export markets;
e. Infrastructure – a large number of firms complained about the unreliability of electricity and water supply, and about their prices.

Lall and Wangwe (1998: 80–82) provide a brief 'case study' discussion of industrial sector development in Ghana after the introduction of the ERP. In particular they draw attention to the slowing down of the growth of the manufacturing sector from 16 per cent per annum in 1984–86 to 2.7 per cent per annum in 1992–94, and make the following significant comment:

> Liberalisation has led large swathes of the manufacturing sector to be devastated by import competition. Industrial survivors and new entrants are basically in activities that have 'natural' protection from imports: very small-scale enterprises, making low-income or localised products, and larger enterprises protected by high transport costs or based on processing of local raw materials. (1998: 81)

Further discussion of Ghana's experience may be found in Lall and Stewart, (1996: 194–6).

Acheampong (1996) demonstrates that the factors accounting for productivity growth at the enterprise level ranged from the restructuring of firms, retraining of labour, reorganisation of labour to undertake new tasks, increasing capital per employee, installation of new equipment or rehabilitation of machinery, increasing availability of foreign exchange, increasing availability of inputs, growth in the level of demand, improved organisation, improved infrastructure and an improved government policy environment. Many of these factors were directly associated with the ERP/SAPs. The increased demand can be decomposed into domestic and export components. Increases in disposable incomes (for example through increased wages and salaries, higher cocoa prices and the payment of end-of-service benefits to retrenched workers) increased the purchasing power of some people and increased their effective demand. Improvements in exports were associated with a widening of the market, which can be explained by the significant depreciation of the cedi, which made some Ghanaian products cheaper and more competitive in international markets, and/or gave Ghanaian exporters more attractive prices for exported products. Thus the new incentive structure, together with policy reform, enabled firms both to increase exports and to increase production for the domestic market. Some firms embarked upon innovations such as improving upon product quality, retraining of workers to undertake new production processes and diversification of product lines.

In an interesting and wide-ranging article, Chhibber and Leechor (1995) review the extent to which 'lessons of East Asian experience' can be applied to Ghana. Many of their conclusions relate to broad areas of policy and development experience which transcend a narrow focus on trade policy and industrial policy *per se*. Human capital, financial institutions, public sector and economic management, institutional development, and the nature of political and economic risk all feature in their discussion. The article is suggestive of caution in interpreting the relationship between policy and manufacturing growth and efficiency, and provides some salutary lessons, not least on the long-term nature of economic growth and development.

7 CONCLUSIONS AND POLICY IMPLICATIONS

This chapter aimed to investigate the changes and sources of industrial growth with particular reference to large and medium scale industries in Ghana over the period 1970–93. The analysis reveals that much of the growth that occurred following the introduction of the ERP in 1983 was due to increased intermediate and capital inputs. Employment growth was not significant overall, and the level of employment in the manufacturing sector fluctuated considerably during the period under review. Due to retrenchment, redeployment of workers, the restructuring of firms and the recovery of manufacturing output during the adjustment period, labour productivity improved significantly – real wages also declined significantly over the entire period. It might be expected that in the future greater emphasis on investment in education, in retraining schemes for workers, and in research and development, might further enhance productivity growth performance (Lall, 1994: 16–19; Lall *et al.*, 1994: Chapter 7), and it is suggested that policy could focus on improving the technological and management capabilities of existing production units in order to provide a more secure basis for future productivity growth.

Much of the increased manufacturing output was attributable to improved capacity utilisation which reduced technical inefficiency. No attempt was made to separate productivity growth due to improved capacity utilisation from that due to changes in the intrinsic productivity of factors of production. The additional capital investment inputs due to rehabilitation and renewals gave rise to TFPG which appears to have been negative in the early part of the period under review, but which became positive in the latter part of the period. Manufacturing capacity utilisation is clearly a key issue in the policy arena, and it can be argued that greater attention should be given to it as a means of maintaining higher levels of industrial efficiency and competitiveness.

Increased availability of intermediate input imports contributed significantly towards industrial growth during the ERP because of the availability of foreign exchange that was made possible by the ERP. Intermediate imports constitute a binding constraint in production and are interlinked with the under-utilisation of installed capacity. The development of high quality and reliable sources for local raw materials would be one means of ensuring consistently higher capacity utilisation where foreign exchange shortages have been the major reason for under-utilisation.

Another factor which has clearly had a favourable impact on manufacturing growth is the improvement to the performance of infrastructure, including water, electricity, transport and communications. These services were given emphasis within the ERP/SAPs, and responses from surveys of manufacturers consistently refer to their importance in affecting firm performance. Improved manufacturing performance can also be accounted for partially by supportive macroeconomic management, supply-side policies and liberalisation of markets. However, the methodology adopted by the main statistical analysis within this chapter does not permit the association of specific policy measures with improved performance. It should be recalled that the results of the analysis give steadily improving TFPG, becoming positive in the period 1989–93, with much of the very substantial recovery of the Ghanaian manufacturing sector during the second half of the 1980s and early 1990s being associated with improved capacity utilisation rather than with structural efficiency gains. The discussion suggests that improvements in the fundamental productivity of the manufacturing sector are more likely to come later after a period of sustained investment, rather than as a short-term response to liberalisation. If a basis for sustained growth and fundamental productivity change is to be created there is a need for adequate supporting systems to be created for the development of technological and management capabilities.

ACRONYMS

ERP   – Economic Recovery Programme
ISSER – Institute of Statistical, Social and Economic Research, University of
           Ghana
SAPs – Structural Adjustment Programmes
TFPG – Total Factor Productivity Growth

NOTES

1. The three phases of the Economic Recovery Programme which was launched in April 1983 were implemented as follows. Phase 1 of the ERP was the stabilisation implemented from 1983 to 1986; Phase 2 was the structural adjustment implemented from 1986 to 1988; and Phase 3 was the sustainable phase implemented from 1988 to 1990 (see for example, Baffoe, 1992: 2).
2. Although there is a strong presumption that liberalisation of the trade regime, and of many other elements of economic management, is conducive to better economic performance (including growth), we are aware that there is considerable controversy surrounding the desirable extent of liberalisation and on the appropriate nature of government intervention in the economies of less developed countries (Helleiner, 1994: 26; Stiglitz, 1997; Wade, 1990; Williamson, 1996).
3. See for example, Ghana Industrial Census, (1987) *Phase 2 Report: Background and Results*, page 1.
4. The deterioration in the growth rate of manufacturing value added in the early 1990s has

been traced to import liberalisation and the rapid depreciation of the Ghanaian cedi (see Acheampong, 1996).

5. The rate of growth of all economic variables in period 't' is computed from a logarithmic regression of the variable on a time trend (Acheampong, 1996 and Acheampong and Tribe, 1999).

6. Given that the fall in TFP between 1983 and 1989 is 3 per cent, the 1989 value must be 97 per cent of the 1983 value. If the fall in TFP is 1.05 per cent between 1983 and 1993 then the 1993 value must be 98.05 per cent of the 1983 value. The increase in TFP between 1989 and 1993 must be $(98.05 \times 100/97) - 100 = 1.08$ per cent.

7. Elias (1993) also underscores the importance of capital growth to growth in TFPG in his study of seven Latin American countries. This evidence is supported by the study of four African countries by Shaaeldin (1989), and for Thailand and Indonesia by Urata and Yokota (1994) and by Osada (1994).

8. The Pearson Correlation Coefficient was calculated for the index of manufacturing production against manufacturing capacity utilisation for the period 1978 to 1993 (Republic of Ghana, *Quarterly Digest of Statistics*, various years). The correlation coefficient of 0.7255 suggests a fairly close association between the two variables, providing some evidence for the view that a high proportion of variations in manufacturing production was accounted for by variations in capacity utilisation. The data are as follows, with 1977=100 in the Index of Manufacturing Production:

	1978	1979	1980	1981	1982	1983	1984	1985
Cap Util %	40.4	33.1	25.5	24.9	21.0	30.0	18.0	25.0
Indx Man Prod	81.0	67.8	69.0	63.3	50.4	35.3	39.3	49.3

	1986	1987	1988	1989	1990	1991	1992	1993
Cap Util %	25.0	35.0	40.0	40.6	39.8	40.5	44.5	45.7
Indx Man Prod	54.2	56.8	62.1	63.0	63.5	71.3	76.9	87.3

9. The discussion in this section is informed by the findings of a questionnaire survey undertaken by the first-named author, reported in some detail in Acheampong (1996) and Acheampong and Tribe (1998).

10. It should be noted that the package of policy measures associated with the ERP/SAPs had implications for the manufacturing sector which were not simple. Greater availability of foreign exchange favoured manufacturing in general, while export retention schemes benefited exporters in particular (ISSER, 1993: 163–4). It is important to note that higher local cedi costs of imported materials and spare parts following devaluation and the 'controlled float' of the exchange rate were significantly lower than previous costs associated with purchases through the black market (Huq, 1989: 196).

11. It should be noted that in 1983–4, manufacturing industry, along with the rest of Ghanaian society, suffered from restricted availability of electricity from the principal Akosombo/ Kpong hydroelectric power source due to the prolonged drought. This partially explains the drop in capacity utilisation to 18 per cent in 1984 and the drop in production of non-ferrous metals (specifically at the aluminium smelter in Tema) (see Table 2.4).

12. A longer version of the paper on which this chapter is based is available from the authors on request (Acheampong and Tribe, 1999). It contains a somewhat larger comparative summary of the results of TFPG analysis for sub-Saharan African countries, as well as for some countries outside the African continent.

REFERENCES

Acheampong, I.K. (1996), *The Impact of the Economic Recovery Programme (1983–90) On Industrial Performance in Ghana*, PhD Thesis, University of Bradford.

Acheampong, I.K. and M.A. Tribe (1998), The Response of Ghana's Manufacturing Sector to Structural Adjustment, in Cook, P., Kirkpatrick, C. and Nixson, F.I. (eds*); Privatisation, Entrepreneurship and Economic Reform*, Edward Elgar, Cheltenham.

Acheampong, I.K. and M.A. Tribe (1999), *Sources of Industrial Growth: The Impact of Policy on Large and Medium Scale Manufacturing Performance in Ghana*, paper presented to the Annual Conference of the Development Studies Association, University of Bath, September (revised).

African Development Bank (1998), *African Development Report 1998*, Oxford University Press, Oxford.

Asante, Y., F. Nixson and G.K. Tsikata (2000), The Industrial Sector and Economic Development, in Aryeetey, E., Harrigan, J. and Nissanke, M. (eds); *Economic Reforms in Ghana: The Miracle and the Mirage*, James Currey, Oxford.

Baah-Nuakoh, A. *et al.* (1996), *Exporting Manufactures from Ghana: Is Adjustment Enough?*, Overseas Development Institute, London and University of Ghana, Legon.

Baffoe, J.K. (1992), Income Distribution and Poverty in Ghana 1987–1988, *African Development Review*, Volume 4, No. 1, pp. 1–29.

Chenery, H.B., S. Robinson and M. Syrquin (1986), *Industrialization and Growth: A Comparative Study*, Oxford University Press for the World Bank, New York.

Chhibber, A. and C. Leechor (1995), From Adjustment to Growth in Sub-Saharan Africa: the Lessons of East Asian Experience Applied to Ghana, *Journal of African Economies*, Vol. 4 No. 1, May, pp. 83–114.

Elias, V.J. (1993), The Role of Total Productivity in Economic Growth, *Estudios de Economia*, Universidad de Chile, Departamento de Economia, No. 20, Special Issue, pp. 19–47.

Helleiner, G.K. (ed.) (1994), *Trade Policy and Industrialisation in Turbulent Times*, Routledge, London.

Huq, M.M. (1989), *The Economy of Ghana: The First 25 Years Since Independence*, Macmillan, London.

ISSER (1992), *The State of the Ghanaian Economy in 1991*, ISSER, University of Ghana, Legon.

ISSER (1993), *The State of the Ghanaian Economy in 1992*, ISSER, University of Ghana, Legon.

Krueger, A.O. and B. Tuncer (1980), *Estimating Total Factor Productivity Growth in a Developing Country*, World Bank Staff Working Paper No. 422. World Bank, Washington, DC

Lall, S. (1994), *Industrial Policy: A Theoretical and Empirical Exposition*, Working Paper No. 70, Queen Elizabeth House, International Development Centre, University of Oxford.

Lall, S., G.B. Navaretti, S. Teitel and G. Wignaraja (1994), *Technology and Enterprise Development: Ghana Under Structural Adjustment*, Macmillan, Basingstoke.

Lall, S. and F. Stewart (1996), Trade and Industrial Policies in Africa, in Ndulu, B. *et al.*, *Agenda for Africa's Economic Renewal*, US-Third World Policy Perspectives No. 21, Overseas Development Council, Transaction Publishers, New Brunswick.

Lall, S. and S. Wangwe (1998), Industrial Policy and Industrialisation in Sub-Saharan

Africa, *Journal of African Economies* (African Economic Research Consortium Plenary Sessions May 1997), Vol. 7 Supplement 1, June.

Michaely, M., D. Papageorgiou and A.M. Mchoski (eds) (1991), *Liberalising Foreign Trade: Lessons of Experience in the Developing World*, Basil Blackwell, Cambridge, MA.

Mosley, P., J. Harrigan and J. Toye (1995), *Aid and Power: The World Bank and Policy Based Lending* Volume 1 (2nd ed.), Routledge, London.

Mulaga, G. and J. Weiss (1996), Trade Reform and Manufacturing Performance in Malawi 1970–91, *World Development*, Vol 24 No 7, pp. 1267–78.

Ninsin, K.A. (1991), *The Informal Sector in Ghana's Political Economy*, Freedom Publications, Accra.

Nishimizu, M. and J. Page (1991), Trade Policy, Market Orientation and Productivity Change in Industry, in De-Melo, J. and Sapir, A. (eds), *Trade Theory and Economic Reform, North, South and East – Essays in Honour of Bela Balassa*, Basil Blackwell, Oxford.

Nishimizu, M. and S. Robinson (1984), Trade Policies and Productivity Change in Semi-Industrialised Countries, *Journal of Development Economics*, Vol. 16, Nos. 1–2, pp. 177–206.

Nishimizu, M. and S. Robinson (1986), Productivity Growth in Manufacturing Industries, in Chenery, H. *et al.* (eds), *Industrialisation and Growth: A Comparative Study*, Oxford University Press for the World Bank, New York.

Osada, H. (1994), Trade Liberalization and FDI Incentives in Indonesia: The Impact on Industrial Productivity, *Developing Economies*, Vol XXXII No 4, December, pp. 479–91.

Pattillo, C. (1998), Investment, Uncertainty and Irreversibility in Ghana, *IMF Staff Papers*, Vol. 45 No. 3, September, pp. 522–53.

Republic of Ghana (various years), *Industrial Surveys*, Statistical Services, Accra.

Republic of Ghana (various years), *Quarterly Digest of Statistics*, Statistical Services, Accra.

Republic of Ghana (various years), *Quarterly Economic Review*, Ghana Commercial Bank, Accra.

Republic of Ghana (1987), *Ghana Industrial Census, Phase 2 Report: Background and Results*, Accra.

Republic of Ghana (1992), *Industrial Policy Statement*, Ministry of Industry and Science and Technology, Accra.

Republic of Ghana – ERP1 (1983), *Economic Recovery Programme 1984–1986*, Vols 1 & 2, Accra.

Rodrik, D. (1992), Conceptual Issues in the Design of Trade Policy for Industrialisation, *World Development*, Vol. 20 No. 3, pp. 309–20.

Seers, D. (1963), The Role of Industry in Development: Some Fallacies, *Journal of Modern African Studies*, December, pp. 461–5.

Shaaeldin, E. (1989), Sources of Industrial Growth in Kenya, Tanzania, Zambia, and Zimbabwe: Some Estimates, *African Development Review*, Vol. 1 No. 1, pp. 21–39.

Stein, H. (1992), Deindustrialization, Adjustment, the World Bank and the IMF in Africa, *World Development*, Vol. 20 No. 1, January, pp. 83–95.

Stein, H. (1994), The World Bank and the Application of Asian Industrial Policy to Africa: Theoretical Considerations, *Journal of International Development*, Vol. 6 No. 3, May–June, pp. 287–305.

Stiglitz, J. (1997), The Role of Government in Economic Development, *Annual*

World Bank Conference on Development Economics 1996, World Bank, Washington, DC, pp. 11–23.

Takeuchi, H. (1999), Some Suggested Measures for Industrial Development of the Republic of Ghana, *Journal of Development Assistance*, Vol. 4 No. 2, March, pp. 176–208.

Teal, F. (1998), *The Ghanaian Manufacturing Sector 1991–1995: Firm Growth, Productivity and Convergence*, Working Paper Series – WPS/98-17, Centre for the Study of African Economies, University of Oxford.

Thomas, V. *et al.* (1991), *Best Practices in Trade Policy Reform*, Oxford University Press, Oxford.

Urata, S. and K. Yokota (1994), Trade Liberalization and Productivity Growth in Thailand, *Developing Economies*, Vol. XXXII No. 4, December, pp. 444–59.

Wade, R. (1990), *Governing the Market: Economic Theory and the Role of Government in East Asian Industrialization*, Princeton University Press, Princeton.

Weissman, S.R. (1990), Structural Adjustment in Africa: Insights From The Experiences of Ghana and Senegal, *World Development*, Vol. 18 No. 12, pp. 1621–34.

Williamson, J. (1996), Lowest Common Denominator or Neoliberal Manifesto? The Polemics of the Washington Consensus, in Auty, R.M. and Toye, J.F.J., *Challenging the Orthodoxies*, Macmillan, London.

World Bank (1994), *Adjustment in Africa: Reforms, Results, and The Road Ahead*, The World Bank, Washington.

3. Firm-level capability building in less developed countries

Wise Mainga*

1 INTRODUCTION

Since the late 1980s, most African countries have undertaken efforts to re-structure their economies. Most reforms had to be undertaken after decades of economic decline. In some of the countries, the economic crises[1] had produced some degree of consensus that was needed to pursue wide-ranging restructuring reform packages. In countries like Zambia and South Africa,[2] relatively rapid and wide-ranging trade liberalisation policies were adopted as one means of revamping the manufacturing sector.

The effects of Structural Adjustment Programmes (SAPs) on the manufac-turing sector in countries of Sub-Saharan Africa (SSA) have proved to be very controversial, however. One view is that the across-the-board rapid liberalisation of foreign trade has not been conducive to industrial restructur-ing and upgrading. Not only has rapid exposure to foreign competition led to unavoidable destruction of inefficient high cost manufacturing, it has also resulted in wasteful deindustrialisation of accumulated capital stock that may have been viable in the medium term (Lall, 1995; Stein, 1992).[3] Some propo-nents of this view have urged that some of the liberalisation efforts have been too fast and have not provided enough time for firms to modernise and upgrade their competitive capabilities (Lall and Wangwe, 1998; Riddell, 1990). This view emphasises the need to address simultaneously the complex pro-cess of strengthening the technological competence of firms. The design, pace and implementation of SAPs must take account of such complexity.

The opposing view – which is often seen to be enshrined in most SAPs – assumes that manufacturing firms in most countries in SSA have been shel-

* I am grateful to Professor John Weiss for comments made on the earlier draft of this chapter, and the Commonwealth Scholarship Commission (UK) for financing the fieldwork survey which provided the data that is used in the empirical section. Neither Professor Weiss nor the Commonwealth Scholarship Commission are responsible for any errors or opinions contained in this chapter. An earlier draft of the chapter was presented at the Development Studies Association Annual Conference, University of Bath, September 1999.

tered from foreign competition for too long, and it is time for 'shock' type SAPs to be used to shake them out of their uncompetitive framework. The controversy over the effects of SAPs on the manufacturing sector is not based on whether reforms are necessary or not, but on the pace and content of these reforms.

The chapter is divided into seven sections. The introduction is followed by the background literature review in Section 2. Section 3 deals with definitions of some of the major concepts that are used in this chapter. Section 4 discusses the main components of the proposed framework model that links firm-level capability building efforts with other economy-wide variables. Section 5 examines the various subconstructs of firm-level technological capabilities and provides possible indicators that may be useful to measure the level of capabilities at the firm level. Section 6 presents an empirical example of how firm-level capabilities can be analysed, using survey data from Zambian manufacturing firms. Some conclusions from the study are outlined in Section 7.

2   BACKGROUND REVIEW

The Import Substitution Industrialisation (ISI) strategies that were undertaken by many African countries immediately after independence had a narrow definition of productive technology. Acquisition of productive technology was seen mostly as an acquisition of physical assets (plants, machinery and equipment). Where acquisition of knowledge and skills was acknowledged, it was often restricted, and understood to mean the acquisition of rudimentary operational skills, often complemented by a reliance on expatriate skilled labour. This dependence on expatriate skilled labour did not decrease over time as a result of technology absorption by local personnel, as the case was in most East Asian economies. As a result, the operationalisation of the ISI strategy culminated in a massive drive towards the acquisition of physical assets and a desire to increase industrial output through expansion of production capacity. The high protection that accompanied this industrialisation strategy, coupled with suppressed exchange rates, facilitated the acquisition of capital-intensive production techniques. Moreover, the acquisition of physical capital often outstripped the acquisition of capacity to operate such assets efficiently. The dismal performance of the ISI strategy has eventually led to an adoption of a much broader definition of technology, which has re-stated the centrality of capability building in any future industrialisation efforts in Africa (Lall and Stewart, 1996; Adei, 1990).

It is increasingly being accepted that the sluggish performance of the manufacturing sector following Structural Adjustment Programmes in less developed countries (LDCs) is partly due to the lack of firm-level capabilities (Biggs et al, 1995; Biggs and Srivastava, 1996). This chapter focuses on the various types of firm-level technological capabilities which need to be developed if manufacturing firms are to take advantage of the incentives thrown up by the liberalised environment. It is argued that firm-level capability building in the context of SAPs depends and is conditioned by a whole set of factors that go beyond the 'standard benefits' that are supposed to accrue from structural reforms.[4] Using the 'technological capabilities' approach, it is argued that the lack of managerial, organisational, technological and entrepreneurial capabilities, compounded by underdeveloped supportive physical and technological infrastructure, have all been very significant factors in the sluggish performance of the sector – factors that should receive serious consideration in parallel with the introduction of any comprehensive SAP. At the centre of the 'technological capabilities' approach is the realisation that knowledge is a factor of production alongside labour and capital.[5]

Indeed, it has been observed that most firms surviving the reform process in SSA are doing so on account of factors other than the achievement of international competitiveness. Apart from a few firms that have improved productivity (improvements often through increased work intensity due to lay-offs or 'one-time' improvement in capacity utilisation due to the availability of foreign exchange made possible by increased donor aid), many others that have survived are either: (i) dealing in products with low elasticity of demand (e.g., everyday groceries and traditional patterned clothes); (ii) manufactured products with natural protection (e.g., sheltered from external competition due to high transportation costs – for low value/high tonnage products like wood and cement products); or (iii) manufactured products like military and school uniforms (which have customers who are relatively immune from the overall performance of the domestic economy) (Proff, 1994: 231; Lall and Wangwe, 1998: 81). For many other firms, the risk of going bankrupt is ever present since their restructuring efforts do not represent any investment in upgrading long term competitiveness and dynamism. Long term survival is intrinsically linked to investment in building firm-level capabilities, as well as improving the overall social-economic, political and legal environment in which firms are operating.

3 DEFINITION OF CONCEPTS

3.1 Firm-Level Technological Capabilities (FTCs)

FTCs have been defined as consisting of a complex array of managerial, technical, organisational and entrepreneurial knowledge, skill and experience needed to acquire, comprehend, absorb, adapt and modify modern technology in ways which constantly improve its effective use (Lall, 1992; Ernst *et al.*, 1998; Weiss, 1988; Pietrobelli, 1994; Aw and Batra, 1998). The transferring of physical productive technology from developed to less developed countries needs to be accompanied by the transfer of 'capabilities'. Acquisition of firm-level technological capability takes place through a learning process – referred to as 'technological learning'.

3.2   Technological Learning

Technological learning has been defined as 'encompassing all those activities in a firm which assist the enhancement and expansion of knowledge and skill bases' (Dodgson, 1991: 133). Bell (1984: 188) defines it as the 'acquisition of additional technical skills and knowledge by individuals and, through them, by organisations'. Learning can therefore be seen as a process by which organisational activities are improved as more and better knowledge/understanding is acquired. The knowledge needed to be acquired by firms will normally fall into four categories:

i.   Knowledge about productive technology;
ii.   Knowledge about best work practices and organisation of production;
iii. Knowledge about customers, suppliers and complementary institutions;
iv.   Knowledge about evolution of target markets and necessary adjustments required.

   Learning involves complex interaction and information sharing within the firm, between firms and with the external complementary knowledge infrastructure. A firm learns from its operations (learning-by-doing, learning-by-using, trial and error experimentations), from external firms and institutions (learning-by-interaction, learning-by-imitation or watching, learning-to-learn), and from activated search (learning-by-searching, learning-by-environmental-scanning, learning from adaptive and generative research and development). Such efforts subsequently enable the effective utilisation and continual upgrading of a firm's productive assets (Romijn, 1997: 359; Wong, 1995: 790). Since raising firm-level capabilities involves learning, the 'learning capacity' of the firm is crucial to the acquisition of FTCs. For most learning processes to take place, however, explicit technological effort is required.

3.3   Technological Effort

Technological effort has been defined as a purposeful and costly expenditure of a firm's resources (human capital, financial, management time, etc.) aimed at acquisition, assimilation, adaptation and utilisation of technological knowledge (Romijn, 1997). Such expenditure might involve, for example, investment in workers' training (on/off-the-job training), sponsorships to relevant conferences, creation of knowledge networks with local complementary institutions and international knowledge sources, investment in computer information networks to provide access to on-line databases, forging strategic alliances with competitors to learn from them, environmental scanning efforts, etc. Firm-level capability building is therefore not an automatic by-product of involvement in production (Bell, 1984; Bell and Pavitt, 1993).

4 FRAMEWORK MODEL FOR CAPABILITY BUILDING PROCESSES AT THE FIRM LEVEL

In Figure 3.1 a prescriptive framework model links firm-level technological capabilities (FTCs) to various economy-wide variables. The main objective is to outline the main aspects of capability building processes that may require particular attention/strengthening as firms in less developed countries (LDCs) strive to improve their international competitiveness in the context of SAPs. Arguably, it is an abstraction from a complex interactive phenomenon and should be seen as a simplified policy guide for action. The prescriptive framework has been contextualised to environments that exist in LDCs, such as those in Sub-Saharan Africa (SSA).

In the proposed model, the firm is taken as the centre of all technological capability building and learning processes. A firm's technological building effort is a function of four components that comprise productive technology (Sharif, 1995: 129; Technology Atlas Team, 1987). The four components (as shown in Figure 3.1) are major 'building blocks' in capability building processes:

i.   Technoware – Object embodied technology. This comprises technology embodied in plant, machinery and equipment. Importation of capital goods for production activities is one of the main means of transferring this component of technology to LDCs.

ii.   Infoware – Record embodied technology. This comprises all documented knowledge, including operating and maintenance manuals, blueprints, equipment design parameters, input specifications, computer databases, technical theories and formulas relevant to production processes, etc. The productivity enhancing capacity of this form of knowledge to a firm's operations is dependent on the relevance, timeliness, reliability and easy retrieval of such stored knowledge. External information networks provide access to external knowledge, expertise and experience.

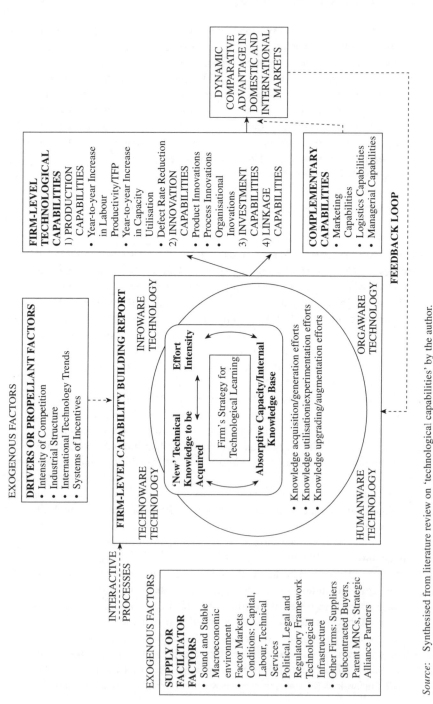

Source: Synthesised from literature review on 'technological capabilities' by the author.

Figure 3.1 Prescriptive framework model: various components of firm-level capability building efforts

iii. Humanware – Person embodied technology. This consists of skills, knowledge, cumulative experience and capabilities embodied in employees (individually and co-operatively). Such competence is a product of several factors: employees' skill levels, appropriateness of general and specific technical training offered to employees, creativity, relevant past experience, motivation, productivity orientation of employees, and entrepreneurial capacity. Some of these capabilities will be 'tacit' in nature and hence difficult to identify in an objective sense, e.g. imagination, adaptive knowledge, ability to react to challenge, ability to change, ability to try new things (Hall, 1993: 610; Lei, 1997). Such capabilities are essential if installed machinery and equipment are to be operated optimally.

iv. Orgaware – Institutional embodied technology. This consists of collective learning and experience that allow the efficient organisation of production. It represents the whole of the organisational framework within which work is undertaken. Such technology includes general managerial practices, corporate culture, norms and values, dynamic routines and communication channels, Human Resource Management policies, incentives structures, and organisational networks within the firm.

For a firm to be competitive in international markets, it must build up all the four components of productive technology. Moreover, continual upgrading of all these four components is essential if competitiveness is to be retained over time. Any underinvestment in any one of the components leads to sub-optimal use of the productive technology.

Figure 3.1 shows that technological capability building efforts are primarily driven by a firm's strategy to undertake technological learning. The company strategy dictates which types of learning can be done in-house or externally. The underlying assumption is that top management of firms has an awareness of the importance of investment in technological learning. This may not always be true in some LDCs, where firms may have to start with discovering better ways of improving their capacity to learn – what has come to be referred to as 'learning-to-learn' (Stiglitz, 1987). Where an explicit strategy for technological learning does not exist, any learning that takes place will be unstructured.

Technological learning implies the acquisition or assimilation of additional 'new' technological knowledge,[6] the source for which may be internal or external to the firm. The 'new' technical knowledge may, for example, be related to a more efficient way of executing production activities, modifications required when switching from imported to domestic inputs, or modifications needed to be made on products to suit specific market niches.

Figure 3.1 shows two other factors critical in facilitating technological learning in firms: the existence of a relevant internal knowledge base/absorptive capacity within the firm and of effort intensity. The 'internal knowledge base', in part, determines the content of the 'new' knowledge that a particular firm (at any one time) is able to absorb without incurring prohibitive learning costs. This underpins the fact that technological learning is cumulative and incremental – a function of past learning undertaken by firms. Effective learning requires more than exposure to new knowledge or information. It is necessary that there pre-exists 'the appropriate contextual knowledge necessary to make the new knowledge fully intelligible' (Cohen and Levinthal, 1990: 129). The 'new' technical knowledge that has to be acquired or learned in order to solve a particular complex operational bottleneck, should not be far removed from what the firm already knows (Pavitt, 1984: 353).

The third factor – effort intensity – has been defined as the amount of energy that organisational members expend on solving more complex operational problems or initiating creative solutions (Kim, 1997: 88). The capacity to solve more complex or higher-order problems is a function of experience by a firm in solving related but simpler problems in the past (Cohen and Levinthal, 1990: 131). Learning how to solve more complex operational problems is only enhanced incrementally. Effort intensity is often enhanced by intensive interaction and knowledge sharing, especially when a firm undertakes creative 'crises' – problem solving assignments within deadline dates (Kim, 1997).

Firm-level capability building efforts are conditioned by various exogenous factors. As shown in Figure 3.1, two sets of external factors are highlighted. One set of factors acts as 'drivers' in that they force firms to undertake productivity enhancing learning efforts. The second set of factors acts as enablers/facilitators, providing the appropriate environment supportive of firms in undertaking the necessary productivity-enhancing learning efforts.

4.1   Drivers/Propellant Factors

Four factors fall into this category: intensity of competition, industrial structure, international technology trends and the system of incentives. Intensity of competition refers to the competitive pressure firms experience from other players in their target product market. The competition may come from competing imports, other domestic firms, foreign subsidiaries operating in the local market, and foreign competitors in overseas markets. Such competition helps firms exert efforts in continuously re-tooling their competitive capabilities.

The industrial structure is also an important factor in forcing firms to invest in building their competitive capabilities. Structural Adjustment Programmes being undertaken in some less developed countries have led to higher levels of concentration in some manufacturing subsectors as a result of liberalisation efforts (Pack, 1993). The main cause is the differential rates at which firms enter and exit a particular subsector, so that a higher rate of exit than of entry in a subsector leads to higher concentration. This could lead to firms expending less effort in building up competitive capabilities where such firms enjoy a degree of natural protection, for example through high transport costs.

International technology trends also impinge on the amount of effort exerted by firms in building their competitive capabilities. In this case, the role of foreign subsidiaries is very important. Demonstration effects are likely to propel local firms into acquiring better technology through imitative efforts and a desire to offset the competition from foreign subsidiaries.[7]

The system of incentives has also played an important role in enhancing the supply response of the manufacturing sector in economies undertaking structural reforms. Getting the prices right is not the only type of incentive needed to influence firm behaviour (for example to make firms shift their production from non-tradables to tradables). However, the design of incentives, their focus and associated implementation capacity, is very important. A tax incentive linked to new physical capital would be a less efficient incentive for strengthening firm-level capabilities than a tax incentive based on meeting export targets or on training quotas of employees. The extent to which export targets are met can provide both the 'objective' international competitive benchmark of firms' performance as well as promoting efficiency in the utilisation of such tax incentives.

4.2 Supply/Supportive Factors

Supply factors act as an input to the capability building processes of firms. The relevant factors are varied and only a summarised outline is possible here. Moreover, it is the interactive process between these supply factors and domestic firms that is critical to the formation of competitive capabilities.

A sound and stable macroeconomic environment is crucial, if firms are to be induced to invest in technological development. For example, high inflation creates difficulties for the prediction of cost and revenue flows, which in turn makes it difficult for firms to make medium- to long-term investment plans. Equally important are the level of interest and exchange rates. High interest rates are likely to increase the cost of firms' investment and may create a disincentive for investment in the accumulation of technological capabilities. Flexible, market-determined exchange rates are important in reflecting a true and predictable cost of foreign exchange. In the past, massive repressed exchange rates in most African countries tended to lower the market cost of foreign exchange, which in turn, resulted in countries and enterprises investing in relatively capital-intensive technologies, which were unlikely to be in line with their comparative advantage.

In addition, exchange rates that are able to provide an impetus towards export expansion may help in expanding the size of the market for domestic firms. Sustained economic growth leading to a growing market size provides an incentive for firms to accept the risk associated with investment in technological development, and helps firms to focus strategies on long-term competitive potential. A sound regulatory and legal framework that enforces contracts fairly and effectively is equally important. The importance of maintaining a sound and consistent macroeconomic environment emphasises the importance of government capabilities. Sustained economic development can only take place in the context of an efficient, responsive and capable government (Ahrens, 1997).

Trade policies that expose domestic firms to foreign competition act as an impetus for firms to raise their technological competitiveness. Trade policies that shelter domestic firms from competition can be costly in terms of indirect subsidies to domestic firms.[8] In addition, protection may lead to technological efforts that do not necessarily enhance production efficiencies, for example through modifications which accommodate the use of poor quality local materials when 'prohibited' competing imported inputs are of better quality.

Equally important is the role of industrial policy. The appropriate definition of an 'industrial policy' is often controversial. Industrial policy may be defined narrowly as referring to state-led intervention in resource allocation that aims to favour specific sectors, firms or groups of firms. This intervention may be in terms of low interest rate loans or tax relief, direct subsidies, or protection from imports. The case for industrial policies has often been linked to the 'infant industry' argument. The fact that many 'infants' that were fostered by past industrial policies in many developing countries did not mature, emphasises the need to have an industrial policy that does not isolate firms from a framework (Tribe, 2000).

The high level information and administrative capacity required to get the intervention 'right' has been the main reason why government intervention is often not considered a recommended option for SSA. The case against any form of intervention is often set in the context of the high cost of intervention in the past. Taking a broader definition, however, a competitive industrial policy is still important for countries undertaking SAPs (Masuyama, 1997: 5). There is a growing realisation that the manufacturing sector may not necessarily thrive without an integrated industrial policy; 'SAPs should include a specific strategy for manufacturing. The expectations that manufacturing will blossom in the absence of a coherent strategy has not been borne out by African experience' (UNIDO, 1996: 15).

In general, any intervention will need to be light, and tailored to individual countries' institutional capabilities. In any case, the problem of firm-level inefficiency must never be reduced merely to the existence or non-existence of an industrial policy.

4.3 Factor Markets

The state of factor markets has an important impact on technological development of domestic firms. Markets for labour, capital and technical services are probably the three most important. The labour market should be able to provide the right mix of skilled labour needed by the productive sector. The curriculum of training institutions that offer pre-employment training, in-service training and off-the-job training all need to be synchronised with the evolving skill needs of industry.

The state of capital markets is crucial for the technological development of firms. The size, structure and availability of credit to the productive sector is important. Firms will only be able to invest in technological accumulation if they have access to financial resources at reasonable costs. The availability and access to long-term finance is a strong determinant in financing high risk investment with long gestation periods that typically characterises the capability building processes.

4.4 Technological Infrastructure (TI)

Technological infrastructure refers to all those external institutions and resources that directly contribute to the strengthening of capabilities of domestic firms (Roessner *et al.*, 1992: 103). Technological infrastructure[9] therefore complements firms' internal efforts to develop the capabilities or competencies needed to remain competitive in product markets. The increasing importance of technological capabilities for competitiveness has meant that the importance of TI has also increased. One of the main roles of TI is to assist firms absorb or assimilate new technology and improve its application in production (Goldman *et al.*, 1997). In order for TI to be partially or totally viable, its endowed capabilities must deliver services that are demanded by firms (demand-driven). The creation of technological infrastructure may be undertaken by the government, private sector or a collective of firms. The early introductory stage of any new technological services is likely to require some form of government support, since the absence of a ready market simply means that demand is not large enough to sustain the corresponding up-front investment.

5   THE MODEL'S DEPENDENT VARIABLE: FIRM-LEVEL TECHNOLOGICAL CAPABILITIES

The conceptual framework model outlined in Figure 3.1 depicts the broad hypothesis which is: higher firm-level technological capabilities (FTCs) require the conscious expenditure of resources in activities involving the accumulation of technological knowledge. As shown in Figure 3.1, FTCs, being a multidimensional construct, have been broken down into four subconstructs that are in line with the focus of this chapter: (i) production capabilities, (ii) innovation capabilities, (iii) investment capabilities and (iv) linkage capabilities. However, the discussion which follows mainly focuses on two capabilities: production capabilities and innovation capabilities.

Production capabilities are defined as 'skills and knowledge needed for efficient operation and subsequent improvement of production operations' (Lall *et al.*, 1994). Three indicators have been chosen to capture the dynamics related to the development of this type of capability: (a) year-on-year increases in labour productivity, (b) year-on-year increases in capacity utilisation, and (c) the rate at which efforts are exerted to reduce defective output (defect rate reduction). The overall aim is to determine the relationship between technical effort exerted by firms in terms of 'technical knowledge accumulation' and the rate of change in production efficiencies. It is reasonable to expect that efforts put into technical upgrading of the workforce should result in increased operational efficiency.

Innovation capabilities can be conceptualised as the capacity to undertake search activities that aim at continuously adapting and improving a firm's products, production processes and organisational structure in response to external and internal disequilibria (Wangwe, 1995; UNIDO, 1996; Ernst *et al.*, 1998). Innovation capabilities can be subdivided into three subgroups: (a) product-related innovations, (b) process-related innovations and (c) organisational innovations. Complementary capabilities, as shown in Figure 3.1, encompass all the knowledge and capabilities that are important for competitiveness, but do not fall into the four subconstructs of firm-level technological capabilities used in this chapter.

Finally, the framework model suggests that dynamic comparative advantage[10] is an interactive outcome of production capabilities, innovation capabilities, investment capabilities, linkage capabilities and the sum total of what has been referred to here as complementary capabilities. In the long run, the acquisition of dynamic efficiency by local firms in LDCs will require more than the achievement of 'allocative efficiency'. Efforts directed at 'knowledge accumulation' will play a critical role in ensuring long-term survival of firms. The feedback loop shown in the model indicates the importance of monitoring market performance, and the realignment of this performance with capability building efforts being undertaken by firms. Poor performance of manufactured products in the market place may suggest the need to strengthen the accumulation of specific capabilities in a firm's operations. In this way, capability building processes are partially responsive to signals from the market place.

6 ASSESSMENT OF EMPIRICAL EVIDENCE

When moving from the conceptual to the empirical level, there will always be a need to simplify most of the relationships. This is partly due to the fact that not all relationships are wholly reducible to measurable attributes. Our empirical analysis focuses on the relationship between capabilities and learning, but only one part of the relationships shown in Figure 3.1 is analysed. This discussion will concentrate on only one type of innovation capabilities – process innovation capabilities. It will examine which of the learning mechanisms have a significant explanatory power on this type of capability. We are interested in determining which of the modes of knowledge acquisition have a significant effect on enhancing the capacity to undertake productivity enhancing process modifications.

6.1 Data Sources

The data used in the analysis is from a fieldwork survey conducted on Zambian manufacturing firms between March and August 1997. Target firms were those classified as medium-to-large (≥ 30 employees). The definition of medium-to-large firms conforms to other studies done on a comparable country, Ghana (Baah-Nuakoh *et al.*, 1996; Steel and Webster, 1991). A structured questionnaire was delivered to 74 manufacturing firms across several subsectors. Forty-seven questionnaires were returned, but only 42 were usable. The response rate represents a 57 per cent return rate and 27 per cent of the sampling frame.

A firm may undertake incremental process modifications for various reasons. For example, the main aim may be to improve the quality of products being manufactured, to reduce the energy used during processing, or to adjust the production process to the use of domestic inputs. Whatever the reasons for undertaking process modifications, the whole process will normally require additional knowledge that goes beyond the basic capacity to undertake production. Technological effort to acquire the additional technical knowledge will be required. In this study, the capacity to undertake incremental process modifications (process innovation capabilities) is regarded as a multi-faceted concept, and is captured by a scoring system over a number of indicators.

Table 3.1   Measurement of process innovation capabilities: an example

Process Innovation types that were selected to capture this capability	Scores*	Scores≥4
Simplification of shop floor work activities	4	4
Improved efficiency by speeding production processes	2	
Production cost-reduction activities	5	5
Reduced manning levels (reduced number of employees assigned to specific jobs)	2	
Adjustments aimed at scaling down capacity to reduce operating fixed costs	1	
Reduced energy and materials used in manufacture of unit product	4	4
Integrated more local components into the manufacturing process	1	
Introduced use of automation/advanced productivity enhancing equipment	1	
Technical changes aimed at extending capacity of production processes beyond design limits	1	
Changed plant layout to reduce material flows	2	
Total sum score across the above outlined Process Innovations (PROCINVC1)	23	
Total sum of Process innovations with scores ≥ 4 (PROCINVC2)		13

Note: * firms were asked to rank implementation efforts along a Likert scale: 1 = none at all, 2 = very little, 3 = some, 4 = considerable, 5 = extensive implementation.

Source: Author's survey.

An example of how a firm's process innovation capability was calculated is shown in Table 3.1. Two related variables were selected to capture the process innovation capabilities of firms: (i) the total sum score across all the outlined process innovations types (PROCINVC1), and (ii) the total sum of process innovations types that scored ≥ 4 (PROCINVC2). The second indicator is meant to capture firms' capacity to implement process innovations fully, as opposed to being evaluated against a given list of process innovations. The sum total therefore consists of only those innovation types whose scores were ≥ 4 (representing considerable to extensive implementation on the Likert scale). A firm may introduce a specific innovation, but may fail to implement that innovation fully due to a host of factors such as uncertainty about how to proceed further, opposition from employees, or inability to complete the cost/benefit calculations of the innovation in the context of short-term unpredictability. PROCINVC2 therefore partly captures the capacity to overcome such impediments. The analysis in this section will be restricted to PROCINVC2 as the dependent variable.

6.2 Independent Variables

Independent variables were chosen to represent channels/means used to accumulate additional technical knowledge – referred to here as learning or knowledge acquisition mechanisms. The various independent variables, together with control variables, are summarised in Table 3.2. The number of technical staff among sample firms is captured by SKT2 (per cent of engineers/scientists in the labour force) and SKT1 (per cent of technicians/ technologists in the labour force). These two groups of employees are the ones primarily involved in absorption and mastery of productive technology. The level of skill among production workers (SKPW) is important if responsibility for quality output is to be devolved to such operatives. On-the-job training (ONJOBT1–5) and off-the-job training (OFFJOBT1–5) capture efforts exerted by firms to upgrade continuously the skill base and competence of various categories of employees in the organisation. The length of service of various categories of employees (EXPRNCE1–4), is meant to capture cumulative experience-based learning. In particular, it captures the firm-specific technical knowledge absorbed by employees. SCAN1 (Scanning efforts), SEARCH2 (important sources of technical expertise), RESEARCH (Adaptive R&D) and SUGGSCH (suggestion scheme) are all considered as technological search efforts directed at accumulating and/or generating new knowledge. These efforts may rely on internal activities or on tapping externally available knowledge. The RESEARCH and SUGGSCH variables are dummies, taking the value of 1 if a firm undertakes each of the activities and 0 if not.

6.3 Control Variables

Several variables were chosen to discriminate among firms according to specific characteristics. Capital intensity (CAPINT) and subsector dummies (INDSTRY1–8) are used to control for characteristics of production processes that are unique to specific industrial subsectors. Firm size (FMSIZE) was used to control for resources constraints. Firm size is based on the total number of full-time employees. The assumption is that larger firms are likely to have more resources, and hence be more likely to make technology-upgrading related investment. An export dummy (EXPTDMY) is used to

Table 3.2   Variables considered in the analysis

Control variables	Independent variables (learning mechanisms)	Dependent variable
	% of Engineers/Scientists in labour force (SKT2)	
	% of Technicians/Technologists in the labour force (SKT1)	
Capital Intensity (CAPINT)	Skill levels of shop floor operatives (SKPW)[1]	
Firm size (FMSIZE)	On-the-Job training (ONJOBT1–5)[2]	Process innovation capabilities –
Exporter or not (EXPTDMY)	Off-Job training (OFFJOBT1–5)[2]	PROCINVC2
Subsector Dummy (INDSTRY1–8)[5]	Length of Service (EXPRNCE1–4)[3]	
Ownership Dummy (OWNSHP1–6)[6]	Scanning Efforts (SCAN1)[4]	
	Sources of Technical Expertise to resolve operational problems (SEARCH2)[4]	
	Adaptive in-house R&D (RESEARCH)[7]	
	Suggestion Scheme (SUGGSCH)[7]	

Notes:

1. SKPW = (% of production workers in total labour force × % of production workers with secondary school education).
2. ONJOBT1–5 represent the average length of on-the-job training (in days per year) offered to various categories of employees: ONJOBT1 = On-the-job training offered to production workers; ONJOBT2 = On-the-job training offered to technologists/technicians who are also supervisors; ONJOBT3 = On-the-job training offered to technologists/technicians with no supervisory role; ONJOBT4 = On-the-job training offered to supervisors who have no technical qualification; ONJOBT5 = On-the-job training offered to engineers/scientists. The same categorisation was used for off-the-job training.
3. The average length of service of various categories of employees (in years) is captured by EXPRNCE1–4: EXPRNCE1 = Length of service of engineers/scientists; EXPRNCE2 = Length of service of technicians/technologists; EXPRNCE3 = Length of service of supervisors with no technical qualification; EXPRNCE4 = Length of service of production workers.
4. Indicators SCAN and SEARCH used a scoring system across several variables that make each construct (see Table 3.4 and 3.5 in Appendix 3.1).
5. Subsectoral dummies represent the following subsectors: Food and beverages; Textiles and clothing; Wood and wood products; Paper and pulp; Chemicals and chemical products; Rubber and plastics; Non-ferrous metal products; Fabricated metal products; Earth and stone-based products; 'Other' manufacturers.
6. Ownership dummies represent the following ownership categories: State owned; State-private (foreign) joint venture; Private (local); Private (foreign); Local-foreign (private) joint venture; Multinational subsidiary.
7. RESEARCH and SUGGSCH are dummy variables taking the value of 1 or 0.

60

capture the spillover benefits that accrue due to linkage with export markets. Other things being equal, exporters are expected to have higher capabilities than non-exporters. Six ownership dummies were used to control the effect of various ownership types. In particular, we were interested to see if multinational corporation (MNC) subsidiaries perform differently from other ownership types. MNC subsidiaries are likely to have access to more resources required to undertake technological efforts compared with other ownership types.

6.4   Regression Equation

Simple Ordinary Least Squares (OLS) regression analysis was used to determine which of the various technological learning mechanisms made a significant contribution to the variance of process innovation capability 2 (PROCINVC2). The regression equation used was of the form:

$$PROCINVC2 = a + b_i X_i + b_j CV_j$$

Where:
$PROCINVC2$ = Process innovation capability 2 (see Table 3.1)
A = constant
b_i, b_j = regression coefficients
X_I = is a vector of learning or knowledge accumulation mechanisms (see Table 3.2)
CV_j = is a vector of control variables; capital intensity, subsector dummies, firm size, exporting dummy, ownership dummies (see Table 3.2)

Because there were so many independent and control variables, a correlation analysis was initially run of all the variables shown in Table 3.2 against the dependent variable (PROCINVC2). This helped determine which of the independent variables had a significant correlation with the dependent variable and these were the only ones entered into the regression equations. The many other independent variables shown in Table 3.2 that did not have a significant correlation with PROCINVC2 (at 5 per cent significance level) were dropped from further analysis.

In all initial regressions, independent variables shown in Table 3.2 which were significantly correlated (at 5 per cent significance level) to PROCINVC2 were entered in the OLS regression equation. In subsequent regressions, the Backward Elimination Method[11] was used to remove variables with no significant explanatory power on the variance of PROCINVC2. The backward elimination procedure was chosen because it allows the entry and removal of variables in the regression equation based on the theoretical model underpinning the study. Independent variables with no significant explanatory power at 5 per cent significance level were deleted from subsequent regression equations, in successive steps. Only final regression results are shown in Table 3.3. Multi-collinearity among independent variables was examined using tolerance values generated by regression equations.

Table 3.3   Regression results

VARIABLES	EQUATION 1	EQUATION 2	EQUATION 3	EQUATION 4
Intercept	2.8375	3.2584	3.3267	2.7421
	(1.203)	(1.491)	(1.436)	(1.088)
SCAN1	–0.1435	–0.2339	–0.2234	–0.2353
	(–0.799)	(–1.379)	(1.231)	(1.370)
EXPRNCE2	0.3659*	0.3559*	0.3984*	0.3485*
	(2.293)	(2.413)	(2.543)	(2.317)
RESEARCH	7.8039***	6.0646***	6.8444***	5.9599***
	(4.943)	(3.774)	(4.165)	(3.620)
SEARCH2	1.2288**	1.2532**	1.1923**	1.1883**
	(3.168)	(3.496)	(3.150)	(3.020)
PRDINVC1		0.3760*		0.3812*
		(2.579)		(2.569)
PRDINVC2			0.2100	
			(1.661)	
ORGINVC1				0.0346
				(0.429)
Adjusted R^2	0.6197	0.6753	0.6390	0.6668
F	16.0749	16.3930	14.0976	13.3432
p	< 0.001	< 0.001	< 0.001	< 0.001
N	38	38	38	38

Notes:
1. Dependent variable: Process Innovations Capability (PROCINVC2) – see Table 3.1.
2. Significance levels: * = .05, ** = .01, *** = .001; t values are shown in brackets.
3. SCAN1 = Scanning efforts.
4. EXPRNCE2 = Length of service (in years) of technologists/technicians.
5. RESEARCH = Adaptive R&D.
6. SEARCH2 = Important sources of technical expertise used to solve operational bottlenecks.
7. PRDINVC1 = Product innovation capability 1 (number of improved versions of existing product lines introduced by a firm during the years 1995–7.
8. PRDINVC2 = Product innovation capability 2 (number of totally new product lines introduced by a firm during the years 1995–7.
9. ORGINVC2 = Organisational innovation capability 1 (see Appendix 3.1 for the calculation of this.

6.5   Regression results

The regression results are shown in Table 3.3. Equation 1 indicates that adaptive R&D (RESEARCH), length of service of technicians/technologists (EXPRNCE2) and the use of a few critically important sources of technological information and technical expertise needed to solve operational problems (SEARCH2) were the only significant explanatory variables of the capacity of firms to undertake extensive modifications of their production processes (PROCINVC2). Efforts at scanning the external environment for new improvement ideas (SCAN1) are not significant even at 5 per cent significance level. This outcome may mean either that the operating environment in which firms operate does not generate relevant information or that firms are not using this channel of knowledge acquisition to the level at which it would have a significant impact on strengthening their process modification capabilities. The overall predictive power of the regression equation is reasonably good, with an adjusted r^2 of nearly 0.62. The Beta coefficients are: -0.0914 for SCAN1, 0.2382 for EXPRNCE2, 0.5661 for RESEARCH and 0.3583 for SEARCH2. Examination of the Beta coefficients shows that adaptive R&D (RESEARCH) has a proportionally greater effect on the capacity of firms to undertake incremental process innovations.

Surprisingly, after backward elimination procedures, none of the on/off-the-job training and control variables appeared in the final equations. It was surprising that training variables have no impact on the capacity to implement extensive process innovations. The above outcome is likely to be caused by the nature of training offered by firms. It is more oriented towards imparting operational capabilities rather than capabilities to institute incremental modifications to production processes. All sectoral and factor intensity differences are not significant.

Equations 2 to 4 were run to examine whether the introduction of new product lines (PRDINVC1 and PRDINVC2) and the undertaking of changes in the way production is organised (ORGINVC1) precipitated any production process modifications.[12] Equation 2 shows that the introduction of improved versions of existing product lines (PRDINVC1) often precipitated some modifications of production processes that are needed to accommodate the manufacture of the new products. However, Equation 3 shows that the introduction of totally new product lines (PRDINVC2) – totally new to the firm – did not have the same effect on production processes of firms. An examination of the relationship between firms that made new capital investment in the years 1995–7 and those that had introduced totally new product lines reveals that there is a significant correlation between the two variables. It seems that for most firms, the introduction of totally new product lines into their operations was often facilitated by the purchase of new machinery rather than the modification of existing capital stock. This observation is further supported by the fact that the adjusted r^2 in Equation 3 changes only marginally from that of Equation 1 (from 0.6197 to 0.6390).

Equation 4 was run to test the interdependence between organisational innovations and process innovations. It has been observed that firms benefiting most from process innovations are those which simultaneously make changes to the organisational structure (Chandra, 1999). Equation 4 is basically Equation 2 with the extra variable ORGINVC1, which is used to capture the level of organisational innovation that has been undertaken in sample firms. The result in Equation 4 shows that ORGINVC1 has no significant association with process modifications undertaken by firms, indicating that firms undertaking extensive modifications of their production processes often did not change the way that work processes are organised. Two possible explanations may lie behind this outcome. First, the process modifications undertaken by firms may have been the type that did not require work reorganisations. Secondly, it may represent a failure among sample firms to take advantage of the synergetic benefits that flow from the complementarity that exists between organisational innovations and process innovations. From the survey data it was not possible to determine which of the two possible explanations was most likely to hold true for firms in our sample. Tolerance values of all variables in all the four equations in Table 3.3 were greater than 0.63, suggesting that multicollinearity is not a problem in the equations.[13]

7 CONCLUSIONS

The objective of this chapter was to present a framework model that links firm-level capability building processes to economy-wide variables. In addition, various indicators of production and innovation capabilities which could be used to examine firm-level technical competencies were outlined. The framework model basically argues that the process of strengthening the international competitiveness of manufacturing firms in LDCs undertaking SAPs is a complex interactive process involving multiple factors which the design and implementation of SAPs incorporate. The firm-level capability building which is an essential precondition of successful adjustment is the basis through which 'price-induced' incentives can take effect.

The empirical section of the chapter sought to give an example of how the effects of various learning mechanisms can be analysed to determine which had a significant effect on strengthening particular dimensions of firm-level capabilities. It is likely that different learning or knowledge accumulation mechanisms have different impacts on the various capabilities that are built up. Knowing which learning mechanisms are relevant to the building up of specific capabilities can assist focusing limited resources on technological efforts that maximise the use of such learning channels. In addition, such analysis identifies why certain learning mechanisms do not have a significant explanatory effect on specific dimensions of firm-level capabilities. Further research would be required to examine why on-the-job training and off-the-job training do not have a significant explanatory effect on the capacity of firms to undertake extensive implementation of process modifications.

The model suggests several avenues for further research. For example, the effects of various exogenous factors on firms' incentives to invest in capability building can be examined. In particular, the results of the analysis suggest that research on the issue of how competitive intensity affects firms' efforts to invest in strengthening their competitive capabilities is a priority. Such a study could determine whether a managed 'opening-up' of the economy, or 'shock-type' treatment, is the superior approach to industrial development policy in countries undertaking adjustment and reform.

The main policy implication derived from the framework model outlined in Figure 3.1 is the conclusion that a more complex view of 'competitiveness' in less developed countries undertaking structural reforms is required than that which is often implied by the conventional literature. The ability to achieve international competitiveness among manufacturing firms in LDCs is much more than getting prices right. It requires the need to address a whole set of factors that work synergistically together. The empirical analysis implies the need to distinguish which particular learning mechanisms have a significant impact on the development of specific firm-level capabilities. Not all types of learning mechanisms will strengthen all types of capabilities. Such a distinction would result in more efficient investment of resources in the appropriate knowledge accumulation channels.

APPENDIX 3.1

Table 3.4   Effort exerted by a firm on scanning activities – an example of one firm's scores

Scanning activities	Raw scores*	Weights	Weighted scores
Routine gathering of information from your customers	4	0.1	0.4
Explicit tracking of policies and market tactics of your competitors	2	0.2	0.4
Explicit profiling of final customers' preferences (customer review boards)	1	0.2	0.2
Conduct explicit market research studies	1	0.2	0.2
Benchmarking with other firms' operations	1	0.3	0.3
ROW SUM SCORE (SCAN1)	9	1.0	
WEIGHTED SCORE (SCAN2)	1.5		

Notes: * Raw scores were based on efforts exerted by firms, as measured on a Likert scale: 1 = none at all, 2 = very little, 3 = some efforts, 4 = considerable, 5 = a lot of effort.

Table 3.5   Sources of technical information and expertise used in solving operational problems: an example of one firm's scores

Sources of technical information and expertise	Scores*	Scores ≥4
Recruitment of qualified technical personnel	3	
Technical collaborations with overseas manufacturers and suppliers	1	
Technical consultants/private service firms	1	
Contacts with customers	5	5
Joint venture overseas partners/parent company	1	
Site visits to overseas plants	1	
Technical assistance from visiting overseas experts	1	
Ideas solicited from colleagues in other firms	3	
Thorough analysis of competitors products	4	4
Reverse engineering and copying other firms' products	4	4
From universities/technical colleges/technical centres	2	
Formal training courses overseas	1	
Total sum score across all sources (SEARCH1)	27	
Total sum score of sources with ≥ 4 (SEARCH2)		13

Notes: * Raw scores were based on the importance of each source of technical information for resolution of production problems, as ranked by sample firms on a Likert scale: 1 = unimportant → 5 = very important.

Table 3.6   Measurement of organisational innovation capabilities: an example of one firm's scores

Organisational innovation types that were selected to capture this capability	Scores*	Scores ≥4
Improvement proposal schemes	1	
Quality circles	4	4
Organisation of work in teams	2	
Smooth flow of work by close coupling of work stations	1	
Use of preventative maintenance programs	3	
Multi-skilling of production operatives	4	4
Multi-tasking of operatives	1	
Instituted cross-functional teams	2	
Reduction of layers of the organisational management structures	3	
Level of experimentation/informal modifications of production processes allowed to be done by production workers	1	
Installation of production information system	1	
Total sum score across the above outlined organisational innovations (ORGINVC1)	23	
Total sum of organisational innovations with scores ≥ 4 (ORGINVC2)		8

Notes: * firms were asked to rank implementation efforts along a Likert scale: 1 = none at all, 2 = very little, 3 = some, 4 = considerable, 5 = extensive implementation.

NOTES

1. Economic crises were often characterised by high inflation, chronic balance of payment deficit, high external debts, public sector deficits, capacity under-utilisation and large levels of unemployment.
2. Zambia started to undertake fast-track comprehensive reforms from the end of 1991, when a new government came to power. With a history of 'stop-go' approaches to reforms that had characterised the previous government, a sharp 'shock' type of SAP was seen to be desirable, both to break with the past as well as undertake a SAP that would be credible enough. By 1998, however, the sustainability of a fast-track SAP had again been brought into question because of the delayed privatisation of major components of Zambia's main copper mining parastatal – Zambia Consolidated Copper Mines Limited – which earns about 80 per cent of her foreign exchange. On South Africa's structural reforms as they relate to manufacturing, see Kaplinsky and Morris (1999).
3. Deindustrialisation can only properly apply to firms which would otherwise have had the possibility of surviving in the short to medium term, but are forced to close under a rapid liberalisation regime due to a hostile and non-supportive environment. The closure of high cost non-competitive firms is not considered as deindustrialisation. For a more technical definition of deindustrialisation, and the difference between positive and negative deindustrialisation, see Jalilian and Weiss (2000).

4. Standard benefits to the manufacturing sector that can be derived from opening up the economy have been placed into three main groups (Kirkpatrick, 1995; Lall and Latsch, 1998; Weiss, 1995): (i) Increased competition can force domestic firms to exert entrepreneurial efforts to lower their costs and improve the quality of their products; (ii) Allocative efficiency – reallocation of resources from inefficient to efficient subsectors, from inefficient to efficient firms, and from inefficient to efficient activities within firms; (iii) Dynamic efficiency – greater market size would lead to greater capacity utilisation and scale economies, import discipline would lead to greater specialisation, and accelerated technology transfer would induce learning benefits that strengthen the capacity to use and absorb the new technology/knowledge necessary to build up international competitiveness.

5. For some review on the 'technological capabilities' approach to industrial development, see among others: Bell and Pavitt (1993); Ernst *et al.* (1998); Herbert-Copley (1990); Lall (1992); Lall (1993).

6. Technological knowledge in our case refers to the knowledge stock embedded in the four components of productive technology outlined in Figure 3.1: Technoware, Infoware, Humanware and Orgaware. Technological knowledge is distinguished from other non-technical knowledge held by a firm (e.g., financial management, marketing know-how, purchasing know-how).

7. Kathuria (1998, p. 73) outlines six types of spillovers that can accrue to local firms from FDI: (i) Demonstration effects – local firms can imitate the technology used by MNCs' affiliates; (ii) Competitive effects – greater competition from MNC affiliates forces local firms to use their resources efficiently; (iii) Trained labour mobility – as employees in MNC affiliates move to take up positions in local firms; (iv) Local firms can be forced to acquire improved/new efficient technologies (rapid and frequent upgrading of their capital stock); (v) transfer of managerial practices that facilitate efficient organisation of production (i.e., Just-in-Time, Quality Circles, Kaizen, TPM, Total Quality Management, etc.); and (vi) export-related spillovers (i.e., exporting activities of MNC affiliates can lead to learning in local firms that subsequently spur their exporting activities).

8. One of the hidden costs of protection is when inefficient firms that manufacture intermediate inputs are also protected from price-competitive imported inputs. Local firms manufacturing final products are therefore forced to use high cost local inputs. Their internal inefficiencies are aggravated by inefficiencies located in the domestic supply chain, which further erodes their international competitiveness.

9. Some parts of the technological infrastructure are: restructuring consulting firms and technical extension services providers; testing and analysis centres, standards and metrology laboratories; institutes for technology transfer and research centres; quality control, quality assurance and reliability testing centres; industrial associations that offer technological services to member firms; technical services (e.g. information, library and design services providers); technical training centres (e.g., vocational training centre, technical colleges); engineering and management consulting services providers; maintenance and repairs services providers; packaging and advertising services providers; productivity centres.

10. According to Weiermair and Supapol (1993) dynamic efficiency underpins dynamic comparative advantage. Dynamic efficiency involves much more that the achievement of 'static' efficiency. It implies a firm's capability to respond to environmental turbulences/changes by maintaining organisational/managerial flexibility and adaptability.

11. For more detail on the Backward Elimination Method see Hair *et al.*, 1995.

12. The method for the calculation of ORGINVC1 is shown in Appendix 3.1.

13. Tolerance values (which range between 0 and 1) give an indication of the amount of variance in an independent variable that is not explained by other independent variables. A large tolerance value indicates low multicollinearity, while a smaller tolerance value indicates high multicollinearity. A commonly used cut-off threshold is a tolerance value of 0.10. Independent variables with values below 0.10 should not be used in the regression equation (Hair *et al.*, 1995, p. 127).

REFERENCES

Adei, S. (1990), Technological Capacity and Aborted Industrialisation in Ghana: The Case of Bonsa Tyre Company, *World Development*, Vol.18, No.11, pp. 1501–11.

Ahrens, J. (1997), Prospects of Institutional and Policy Reform in India: Toward a Model of the Developmental State?, *Asian Development Review*, Vol.15, No. 1, pp. 111–46.

Aw, B.Y. and G. Batra (1998), Technological Capability and Firm Efficiency in Taiwan (China), *World Bank Economic Review*, Vol. 12, No.1, pp. 59–79.

Baah-Nuakoh, A., C.D. Jebuni, A.D. Oduro and Y. Asante (1996), *Exporting Manufacturers from Ghana: Is Adjustment Enough?*, London, Overseas Development Institute.

Bell, M. (1984), 'Learning' and the Accumulation of Industrial Technological Capacity in Developing Countries, in Fransman, M. and King, K. (eds), *Technological Capability in the Third World*, London, Macmillan.

Bell, M. and K. Pavitt (1993), Accumulating Technological Capability in Developing Countries, in *Proceedings of the World Bank Annual Conference on Development Economics 1992*, Washington, World Bank, pp. 257–81.

Biggs, T., M. Shah and P. Srivastava (1995), *Capabilities and Learning in Africa Enterprises*, World Bank Technical Paper, No. 288, Washington, World Bank.

Biggs, T. and P. Srivastava (1996), *Structural Aspects of Manufacturing in Sub-Saharan Africa: Findings from a Seven Country Enterprise Survey*, World Bank Discussion Paper No. 346, Washington, World Bank.

Chandra, P. (1999), Competing through Capabilities: Strategies for Global Competitiveness of Indian Textile Industry, *Economic and Political Weekly*, Vol. 34 No. 9, March 5th, New Delhi, pp. M17–M24.

Cohen, W.M. and D.A. Levinthal (1990), Absorptive Capacity: A New Perspective on Learning and Innovation, *Administrative Science Quarterly*, Vol. 35, pp. 128–52.

Dodgson, M. (1991), Technology Learning, Technology Strategy and Competitive Pressures, *British Journal of Management*, Vol. 2, pp. 133–49.

Ernst, D., T.T.G. Ganiatsos and L.K. Mytelka (eds) (1998), *Technological Capabilities and Export Success in Asia*, London, Routledge.

Goldman, M., H. Ergas, E. Ralph and G. Felker (1997), *Technology Institutions and Policies – Their Role in Developing Technological Capability in Industry*, World Bank Technical Paper, No. 383, Washington, World Bank.

Hair, J.F., R.E. Anderson, R.L. Tatham and W.C. Black (1995), *Multivariate Data Analysis*, London, Prentice Hall.

Hall, R. (1993), A Framework Linking Intangible Resources and Capabilities to Sustainable Competitive Advantage, *Strategic Management Journal*, Vol. 14, pp. 607–18.

Herbert-Copley, B. (1992), Technical Change in African Industry: Reflections on IDRC-Supported Research, *Canadian Journal of Development Studies*, Vol. 13, No. 2, pp. 231–49.

Jalilian, H. and J. Weiss (2000), De-industrialisation in Sub-Saharan Africa: Myth or Crisis? in Jalilian, H., Tribe, M. and Weiss, J. (eds) (2000), *Industrial Development and Policy in Africa: Issues of De-industrialisation and Development Strategy*, Cheltenham, Edward Elgar.

Kaplinsky, R. and M. Morris (1999), Trade Policy Reform and the Competitive Response in KwaZulu Natal Province, South Africa, *World Development*, Vol. 27, No. 4, pp. 717–37.

Kathuria, V. (1998), Technology Transfer and Spillovers for Indian Manufacturing Firms, *Development Policy Review*, Vol. 16, pp. 73–91.

Kim, L. (1997), The Dynamics of Samsung's Technological Learning in Semiconductors, *California Management Review*, Vol. 39, No. 3, pp. 86–100.

Kirkpatrick, C. (1995), Does Trade Liberalisation Assist Third-World Industrial Development? Experience and Lessons of the 1980s, *International Review of Applied Economics*, Vol. 9, No. 1, pp. 22–41.

Lall, S. (1992), Technological Capabilities and Industrialisation, *World Development*, Vol. 20, No. 2, pp. 165–86.

Lall, S. (1993), Policies for Building Technological Capabilities: Lessons from Asian Experience, *Asian Development Review*, Vol. 11, No. 2, pp. 72–103.

Lall, S. (1995), Structural Adjustment and African Industry, *World Development*, Vol. 23, No. 12, pp. 2019–31.

Lall, S., G.B. Navaretti, S. Teitel and G. Wignaraja (1994), *Technology and Enterprise Development: Ghana Under Structural Adjustment*, Basingstoke, Macmillan.

Lall, S. and F. Stewart (1996), Trade and Industrial Policy in Africa, *Development – Journal of the Society for International Development*, No. 2, June, pp. 64–7.

Lall, S. and W. Latsch (1998), Import Liberalisation and Industrial Performance: The Conceptual Underpinnings, *Development and Change*, Vol. 29, No. 3, pp. 437–65.

Lall, S. and S. Wangwe (1998), Industrial Policy and Industrialisation in Sub-Saharan Africa, *Journal of African Economies*, Vol. 7, Supplement 1, pp. 70–107.

Lei, D.T. (1997), Competence-building, Technology Fusion and Competitive Advantage: The Key Roles of Organizational Learning and Strategic Alliances, *International Journal of Technology Management*, Vol. 14, No. 2/3/4, pp. 208–37.

Masuyama, S. (1997), The Evolving Nature of Industrial Policy in East Asia: Liberalisation, Upgrading, and Integration, in Masuyama, S., Vandenbrink, D. and Yue, C.S. (eds), *Industrial Policies in East Asia*, Tokyo, Nomura Research Institute and Singapore, Institute of South East Asian Studies.

Pack, H. (1993), Productivity and Industrial Development in Sub-Saharan Africa, *World Development*, Vol. 21, No. 1, pp. 1–16.

Pavitt, K. (1984), Sectoral Patterns of Technical Change: Towards a Taxonomy and a Theory, *Research Policy*, Vol. 13, No. 6, pp. 343–73.

Pietrobelli, C. (1994), Technological Capabilities at the National Level: An International Comparison of Manufactured Export Performance, *Development Policy Review*, Vol. 12, No. 2, pp. 115–48.

Proff, H. (1994), Structural Adjustment Programmes and Industrialisation in Sub-Saharan Africa, *Intereconomics*, Vol. 29, No. 5, September/October, pp. 225–33.

Riddell, R.C. (1990), A Forgotten Dimension? The Manufacturing Sector in Africa Development, *Development Policy Review*, Vol. 8, No.1, pp. 5–27.

Roessner, J.D., A.L. Porter, and H. Xu (1992), National Capacities to Absorb and Institutionalise External Science and Technology, *Technology Analysis and Strategic Management*, Vol. 4, No. 2, pp. 99–113.

Romijn, H. (1997), Acquisition of Technological Capability in Development: A Quantitative Case Study of Pakistan's Capital Goods Sector, *World Development*, Vol. 25, No. 3, pp. 359–77.

Sharif, N. (1995), The Evolution of Technology Management Studies, *Technology Management*, Vol. 2, pp. 113–48.

Steel, W.F. and L. Webster (1991), *Small Enterprises under Structural Adjustment in Ghana*, World Bank Technical Paper No. 138, Industry and Finance Series, Washington, World Bank.

Stein, H. (1992), Deindustrialization, Adjustment, the World Bank and the IMF in Africa, *World Development*, Vol. 20, No. 1, pp. 83–95.

Stiglitz, J. (1987), Learning to Learn, Localised Learning and Technological Progress, in Dasgupta, P. and Stoneman, P. (eds), *Economic Policy and Technological Performance*, Cambridge, Cambridge University Press.

Technology Atlas Team (1987), Components of Technology for Resources Transformation, *Technological Forecasting and Social Change*, Vol. 32, pp. 19–35.

Tribe, M. (2000), The Concept of 'Infant Industry' in a Sub-Saharan African Context, in Jalilian, H., Tribe, M. and Weiss, J. (eds) (2000), *Industrial Development and Policy in Africa: Issues of De-industrialisation and Development Strategy*, Cheltenham, Edward Elgar.

UNIDO (1996), *The Globalisation of Industry: Implications for Developing Countries Beyond 2000*, Vienna, United Nations Industrial Development Organization.

Wangwe, S.M. (ed.) (1995), *Exporting Africa: Technology, Trade and Industrialisation in Sub-Saharan Africa*, London, Routledge.

Weiermair, K. and A.B. Supapol (1993), Restructuring, Regrouping and Adjusting: Canadian Manufacturing in an Era of Free Trade and Globalisation, *Managerial and Decision Economics*, Vol.14, pp. 347–63.

Weiss, J. (1988), *Industry in Developing Countries: Theory, Policy and Evidence*, London, Routledge.

Weiss, J. (1995), *Economic Policy in Developing Countries: The Reform Agenda*, London, Harvester-Wheatsheaf.

Wong, J.K. (1995), Technology Transfer in Thailand: Descriptive Validation of a Technology Transfer Model, *International Journal of Technology Management*, Vol. 10, Nos. 7/8, pp. 788–96.

4. Policy reform and Ugandan export competitiveness: a constant market share (CMS) analysis

Nichodemus Rudaheranwa

1 INTRODUCTION

Trade deficits have been a major concern for developing countries, in particular sub-Saharan African countries, since the early 1980s. Efforts to alleviate trade deficits have comprised mainly policies to increase export earnings through increased volume and diversity (of composition and destination) of exports. Reducing the trade deficit has been an important objective, and expected outcome, of trade liberalisation. For an overview of the timing and types of the trade policy reforms see Greenaway (1998). However, for sub-Saharan Africa (SSA) the results of liberalisation have been mixed (Bennell, 1998).

The impact of liberalisation on the external sector in many SSA countries has been at best gradual (Duncan and Jones, 1993; Belshaw *et al.*, 1999). For example, Uganda adopted a comprehensive trade policy reform in 1987 that substantially reduced the bias against exports (Rudaheranwa, 1999) but after ten years the trade deficit remained high. Only a few major reforms were implemented before 1993. With the slow response of the export sector, SSA countries will find it difficult to reduce the growing debt burden. A study identifying factors impacting on the competitiveness of exports is therefore appropriate; that is the contribution of this chapter with an application to Ugandan exports.

The chapter is organised as follows. The concept of export competitiveness is discussed in Section 2. Section 3 reviews the constant market share (CMS) method used for the analysis, while the data are described in Section 4. Section 5 discusses the results and Section 6 relates the competitive position of Ugandan exports to the implicit taxation arising from transport costs. Section 7 concludes.

2 UNDERSTANDING EXPORT COMPETITIVENESS

The competitiveness of exports, interpreted as gains or losses of export market shares, is a relative concept, which may vary across commodity and geographical markets and over time. A country's export competitive position would be unfavourable, for example, if its export shares were declining over time and/or relative to those of its competitors. Two issues are discussed in the literature: (a) identifying those factors influencing export competitiveness and (b) the measurement of export competitiveness. Factors influencing export competitiveness may be grouped into two broad categories, namely price and non-price factors (Fleming and Tsiang, 1956/7; Geraci and Prewo, 1982). Price competitiveness encompasses the profitability (thus costs and prices) of exports of a given country relative to those of its competitors. Price indices however face well-known statistical and conceptual shortcomings (Leamer and Stern, 1970); for example, it is difficult to compare averages based on different commodity composition across countries.

A country might improve the competitive position of its exports if it is able to cut production costs either through cost-saving innovations or exploiting economies of scale in the production process. In this sense, increasing profits of export producers may be an indicator of improvement in export competitiveness. An example of devaluation suffices to illustrate how relative costs (hence profits) may influence the competitive position of exports. In the case of small open economies (price-taking exporters), following devaluation, a country's competitive position as measured by relative export prices may not improve because prices, in foreign currency, are adjusted. The devaluation would instead increase producer prices of exports (in local currency) and would act as an incentive for increased production for export sales. The resulting profit increase in the export sector may thus have a supply-related positive influence on export competitiveness and performance. However the benefit to exporters following the devaluation is offset to the extent that imported inputs are used.

Price competitiveness is measurable, but its use in assessing the export competitive position of a country relative to potential competitors encounters difficulties because it is difficult in practice to compare prices and costs across countries. The literature identifies non-price factors including, among others, export promotion activities, availability of product information, service facilities, delivery times, and the diversity and quality of export products. Non-price aspects of a country's export competitiveness are structural in nature, are difficult to measure in practice and reflect a country's dynamic comparative advantage. The difficulty in quantifying non-price factors has limited their application in empirical analysis.

Geraci and Prewo (1982) suggest the use of the ratio of an exporting country's potential output in manufacturing divided by the total potential output of the competitor countries to capture the role of non-price factors in export growth. They argue that any movements in this output ratio would indicate changes in the comparative level and growth rates of exporters' factor endowments that underlie non-price influences on export shares. This is similar to a constant market share (CMS) analysis (the focus of Section 3) typically used to decompose various sources of export growth. It is the approach that we employ in our analysis to identify sources of Ugandan export competitiveness.

3   THE METHOD OF CMS ANALYSIS

The literature attributes export growth of a given country to its export structure and/or its competitiveness. The competitiveness effect is the unexplained residual of the export growth that is not accounted for by the export structure (commodity and/or geographical market effects). The CMS analysis is a well-known decomposition technique that ascribes movements in export growth to either export structure or competitiveness (Narvekar, 1960; Leamer and Stern, 1970; Richardson, 1971a and 1971b). We decompose export growth into various sources in stages (under different assumptions).

The simplest form of CMS model assumes that exports are a single commodity destined for a single market. The export growth then results from increased exports due to the increased market size (say world exports) and the changing competitiveness defined as the difference between the actual export change and the structural effect. The level of world exports (hereafter *standard exports*) are a standard reference point or benchmark, defined to include only exports (commodities/geographical markets) from other sources that compete with exports of the focus country.

A formal relationship of the determinants of export growth is given by:[1]

$$\Delta x = \theta \Delta X + X \Delta \theta \qquad [1]$$

where θ is the export share of the focus country and, for a given year, equals the country's total actual exports divided by total standard exports. The lower-case x refers to total exports of the focus country while X refers to reference (standard) exports. The term on the left-hand side of equation [1] is total export growth. The first term on the right-hand side is the export growth associated with the growth in market size, and the last term is the unexplained residual (the competitive impact), which must be positive if export shares increased ($\Delta \theta > 0$). The former represents what export growth of the focus country would have been if it had maintained its export share while the competitive effect represents any factors contributing to an increase or decrease in the export share (an implicit measure of competitive-ness).

An alternative specification is to treat exports as a single commodity des-tined to various geographical markets (j). In this case we have the following relationship:

$$\Delta x = \theta\Delta X + (\Sigma_j\theta_j\Delta X_j - \theta\Delta X) + \Sigma_jX_j\Delta\theta_j + \Sigma_j\Delta X_j\Delta\theta_j \qquad [2]$$

where θ is the overall export share of the focus country (x/X) as in equation [1] and θ_j is the export share in destined-market j, (x_j/X_j). The term on the left-hand side and the first term on the right-hand side of equation [2] are similar to those in equation [1]. The bracketed term and last two components on the right side of equation [2] represent the geographical market and competitiveness effects respectively. One may instead assume a set of diverse export commodities each destined for a single market, that is, a world market for a particular export commodity group. In this case we get a relationship similar to equation [2] with the focus shifting to commodity composition (i) rather than geographical destination (j). Hence we have the following rela-tionship:

$$\Delta x = \theta\Delta X + (\Sigma_i\theta_i\Delta X_i - \theta\Delta X) + \Sigma_iX_i\Delta\theta_i + \Sigma_i\Delta X_i\Delta\theta_i \qquad [3]$$

where θ is the overall export share of the focus country (x/X) as in equation [1] and θ_i is the export share of commodity group i, (x_i/X_i). The term on the left-hand side and the first term on the right-hand side of equation [3] are similar to those in equation [1]. The bracketed term and last two components on the right side of equation [3] represent the commodity composition and competitiveness effects respectively. When exports are differentiated both across commodity (i) and market destination (j) we have (where the summa-tion over i alone stands for a commodity total over all markets):

$$\Delta x = \theta\Delta X + (\Sigma_i\theta_i\Delta X_i - \theta\Delta X) + (\Sigma_i\Sigma_j\theta_{ij}\Delta X_{ij} - \Sigma_i\theta_i\Delta X_i) + \Sigma_i\Sigma_jX_{ij}\Delta\theta_{ij} + \Sigma_i\Sigma_j\Delta X_{ij}\Delta\theta_{ij} \quad [4]$$
$$\quad\;\;(1)\qquad\quad(2)\qquad\qquad\qquad(3)\qquad\qquad\quad(4)\qquad\qquad(5)$$

Components (2) and (3) refer to commodity and market growth effects re-spectively. The two effects would be positive if the focus country's export structure is biased in favour of high-growing export (commodity and geo-graphical) markets. Components (4) and (5) are the unexplained part of export growth attributed to the competitive factor. A combination of changes in standard exports and export shares may impact on export growth. This has often been ignored in past studies, for example Richardson (1971a) only mentions it. This impact is captured by the last component in each of equa-

tions [2] through [4], for example component (5) in equation [4]. It is possible that the country's export competitiveness may improve, for example
because the country is increasing its export shares (high $\Delta\theta_{ij}$) in rapidly
growing commodities and markets (high ΔX_{ij}). A combination of these two
changes constitutes the interaction impact of the supply and demand conditions (defined below) on export growth.

A close observation of equations [2] through [4] suggests that some terms
cancel each other out, thus leaving simplified equations used in our estimation process:

$$\Delta x = \Sigma_j \theta_j \Delta X_j + \Sigma_j X_j \Delta\theta_j + \Sigma_j \Delta X_j \Delta\theta_j \qquad [2']$$

$$\Delta x = \Sigma_i \theta_i \Delta X_i + \Sigma_i X_i \Delta\theta_i + \Sigma_i \Delta X_i \Delta\theta_i \qquad [3']$$

$$\Delta x = \Sigma_i \Sigma_j \theta_{ij} \Delta X_{ij} + \Sigma_i \Sigma_j X_{ij} \Delta\theta_{ij} + \Sigma_i \Sigma_j \Delta X_{ij} \Delta\theta_{ij} \qquad [4']$$

The CMS, as an analytical tool for determining factors impacting on export growth, is subject to a number of problems (Richardson, 1971a), notably
regarding the definition and measurement of competitiveness. Relative prices
are often employed as indicators of relative competitiveness. Take an example of two commodity exports distinguished by sources of supply 1 and 2
competing in a given market. Commodity 1 would be said to have improved
its competitive position relative to commodity 2 if either the price of commodity 1 declined relative to the price of commodity 2 or the price of
commodity 2 increased relative to the price of commodity 1. Such an approach to valuing the competitiveness of exports based on relative prices has
several shortcomings. As noted in Section 2, it omits the role of non-price
factors like relative quality improvements, export services and delivery efficiency. Any differences in the efficiency of export-related institutions and
infrastructure facilities between the two competing suppliers may be critical
in impacting on the relative profitability of their export sales but may not be
captured in price changes.

The example given above further assumes a high elasticity of substitution,
defined as the percentage change in the relative quantity demanded divided by
the percentage change in the relative prices, between the two commodities
(Leamer and Stern, 1970: Chap. 3; Richardson, 1973). When commodities are
not homogeneous, as for high levels of commodity disaggregation or products
differentiated by source, relative prices are likely to be only one of the arguments that enter the demand function of exports. Income and price levels in the
importing country may be important as well. Richardson (1971a) points out
that when commodities are homogeneous, relative prices are locked into a
small range of variation and may not capture the impact of non-price factors.

The CMS analysis is sensitive to both the base period and commodity coverage. Thus, arbitrary selections of a base period and the level of disaggregation of the commodity and market groups complicate the interpretation of the competitiveness residual. The analysis is rigid in the sense that its implications may only apply to the specified time period with a particular breakdown of commodity and geographical markets. Different conclusions may emerge on the relative importance of the various factors impacting on export performance if another choice of time period and level of aggregation is made.

4   UGANDAN DATA

The crucial issue is to get information on Ugandan and 'standard' exports by commodity and geographical markets, for as long a period as possible. Data on Ugandan exports by commodity and geographical markets were obtained for the period 1993/94–1996/97. This is a short period, but other studies have used equally short time intervals.[2] Leamer and Stern (1970) used data between 1955 and 1959, Richardson (1971b) used data between 1960 and 1965, Narvekar (1960) used data between 1954 and 1958, and Mahmood (1981) employed data between 1972 and 1976. Data on Ugandan exports are available for 97 commodities at the harmonised coding system (HS) 2-digit level. We aggregate these commodities into fifteen main groups; details on commodities included in each group are given in Appendix 4.A1.

In principal, the CMS analysis can be done at any level of aggregation, although aggregating 97 commodities to 15 groups does not allow us to track the nature of export competitiveness for individual commodities. Instead, the competitiveness is analysed at an aggregate level on a restrictive assumption of uniform competitiveness for all export commodities in the group being considered. It is possible that minor and dominant commodities in a given group may experience different trends in competitiveness, but our results would only capture the general picture reflecting the competitiveness of the dominant commodity. There are Ugandan exports with no specified destination and these exports are allocated to markets according to the share of those markets in total Ugandan exports.

The CMS analysis faces a problem of defining the appropriate measure of standard (world) exports. In examining the export competitiveness of a given country, the appropriate standard exports are the sum of all competing exports from all sources to a given market.[3] Standard exports for the country are different for each commodity and geographical market, both of which may change over time. Standard exports are computed using data from FAO (1996) giving 1996 data as the latest information (at the time of computation). Most Ugandan exports are agricultural, and FAO, which publishes statistics on agricultural output, is an appropriate source of data.

Exports reported in FAO publications are classified at the SITC three-digit level. We reclassified the standard exports to match the Ugandan exports reported in the HS code system. Reconciling data from both sources encountered difficulties. For example, FAO sources did not report data on base metals, other manufactures and transport equipment sectors, hence they are dropped from our analysis (Ugandan exports of these goods are negligible). Similarly, for some countries importing from Uganda, there were no recorded imports available and they were dropped from the analysis (Appendix 4.A2). Generally these countries consume a small proportion of Ugandan exports, except for Rwanda, which seems to import more from Uganda than other Preferential Trade Area (PTA) countries.[4] Our results are only for markets whose import records were available.

In reconciling the SITC and HS data, it was difficult to match exactly the composition of each commodity group. In addition, Ugandan exports to overseas markets (Europe, America and Asia, etc.) transit through Kenya and may have been recorded as Kenyan imports from Uganda (or Ugandan exports to Kenya). For this reason Kenya was treated differently from other PTA countries. Treating Kenya as a separate market for Ugandan products produced export shares (in Kenya) far exceeding 100 per cent, which confirms our argument. Using export shares in each other market importing from Uganda, exports reported as destined to Kenya were redistributed to other markets including the PTA.

5 DISCUSSION OF RESULTS

The aim here is to track the source of the competitiveness for Ugandan exports across commodity and geographical markets. All calculations in this exercise are based on equations [2′] through [4′] with the exception of estimates reported in Table 4.1 that refer to total exports and are based on equation [4]. Tables 4.B1 through 4.B4 (and Table 4.B5, which gives export growth in value) in Appendix B report detailed results. In the text we focus on a summary of results only. First, we decompose total export growth into various sources (Table 4.1), namely overall market growth, effects due to export structure (commodity and destination) and competitiveness impact. It is clear that export performance is very sensitive to the competition influence, that is, just less than two-thirds (65 per cent) of export growth is due to competitive factors.

Ugandan exports performed poorly in terms of export diversification (either market destination or commodity composition depending on the order

Table 4.1   Sources of Ugandan export growth, 1993/94–1996/97

Sources	(US$m)	Share (%)	(US$m)	Share (%)
Market growth	0.43	13.98	0.43	13.98
Commodity composition	0.31	10.17	−0.17	−5.69
Geographical destination	−0.18	−5.98	0.30	9.88
Competitiveness effect	1.97	64.82	1.98	64.82
Interaction term	1.52	17.01	0.52	17.01
Total	3.05	100	3.05	100

Source and notes: Own computation by commodity composition followed by regional destination in columns 2 and 3. The order is reversed in columns 4 and 5. Computation based on
equation [4].

of computation). The growth of Ugandan exports is heavily dependent on
factors that tend to improve its competitive position; that is, its ability to
improve the export share in importing markets. Exports would benefit more if
efforts were focused on improving the country's competitive position (market
shares). The value of the commodity and geographical pattern effects are
expected to differ depending on which of the two is computed first (Leamer
and Stern, 1970), but the total impact of the two effects on export growth is
not affected by the order of computation (Richardson, 1971a). Indeed our
results indicate that the order of computation has a negligible overall effect.

Table 4.1 masks the impact of individual commodity and market-destined
groups on the growth of exports. Individual export commodities and/or destined markets tend to experience different growth rates and would contribute
differently to the country's export growth. Those commodities and destined
markets experiencing high growth would contribute positively to export growth.
We discuss the performance of individual geographical and commodity markets using results summarised in Tables 4.2 and 4.3 below. Table 4.2 reports
results on export growth when exports are disaggregated along the destined-
market lines and estimates in Table 4.3 are on export growth disaggregated
along the commodity-composition lines. In both tables we use the supply and
demand conditions to assess the relative impact of factors determining the
growth of exports. By demand conditions we mean those conditions that
influence the size of the destination market (captured by $\Delta X_{i(j)}$) and impact on
all competing exporters equally. Uganda, a small exporting country, is unable
to influence conditions in the export market and takes the demand conditions
as given.

The supply conditions simply refer to those factors that impact on export
shares ($\Delta \theta_{i(j)}$). The argument is that if a country is able to improve its supply

Table 4.2   Ugandan export growth 1993–97, by destination (%)

Market	PTA	ROA	UK	Belgium	Germany	ROE	ROW	Total
DD	0.24	0.36	2.76	4.28	1.24	6.97	2.26	18.12
SS	6.37	0.48	25.0	−0.31	−0.91	30.85	3.35	64.83
DDSS	1.01	−0.09	7.01	−3.56	−0.50	12.05	1.14	17.05
Total	7.62	0.74	34.8	0.41	−0.18	49.87	6.75	100

Notes: PTA (now COMESA) refers to member states of the Common Market for Eastern and Southern Africa, ROA and ROE stand for the rest of Africa and Europe respectively. UK and ROW refer to the United Kingdom and the rest of the world respectively. DD = demand conditions and SS = supply conditions. The computation is based on equation [2′] such that totals along each row are as follows: demand conditions (DD) = $\Sigma_j \theta_j \Delta X_j$, supply conditions (SS) = $\Sigma_j X_j \Delta \theta_j$ and the interaction term (DDSS) = $\Sigma_j \Delta X_j \Delta \theta_j$.

Source: Own computation.

conditions, export sales would increase. Increasing export sales however does not necessarily imply improved export shares; these depend also on the growth rate of the market overall. A country's export share may improve if the country managed to capture (displace) its competitors' export shares. Equally the country's export shares may not improve even though export sales might have increased, for example because of general improvement in overall import market demand. In all cases however, increases in export shares would imply that a focus country is able to increase its export sales in the importing market relative to its competitors. We assume that conditions in importing markets would impact on all exporters equally and therefore an individual country would increase its export share by improving its supply conditions.

The last column of Table 4.2 shows that supply conditions had the greater impact on Ugandan export growth (over 64 per cent) whereas demand conditions accounted for less than 20 per cent of growth. This suggests that export growth is more sensitive to changes in export share (supply conditions) than to changes in standard exports (demand conditions). Table 4.2 also provides an opportunity to track the relative impact of both the supply and demand conditions on export growth in each market. Supply conditions made a positive contribution in all but the Belgian and German markets. Demand conditions contributed positively in all markets. The results provide mixed evidence and no firm conclusions can be made on the underlying factors influencing conditions in each market. For example, the approach does not explain favourable supply conditions on exports to UK and ROE but less favourable conditions in Belgium and Germany.

Table 4.2 also highlights the relative importance of markets in impacting on Ugandan export growth. Europe (with the exception of Germany) contributes most (over 85 per cent) to export growth and the contribution from other markets is very small. This may be attributed to historical and commercial links between Uganda and European countries, for example the United Kingdom. Traditional agricultural exports, a high percentage of Ugandan exports, are destined for the European market, about 78 per cent in 1993 and 81 per cent in 1996 (Tables 4.B6 and 4.B7) so it is not surprising that a high source of Ugandan export growth originates from Europe. It is clear from Table 4.2 that both the demand and supply conditions in Africa (particularly PTA) and the rest of the world made a positive contribution (though small) to export growth.

Table 4.3 reports a summary of sources of export growth broken down by commodity type. Ugandan exports are mainly composed of agricultural commodities and a few manufactures. Exports are broken into sub-groups, namely traditional (TD) and non-traditional (NTD). Traditional exports refer to those commodities that have dominated Ugandan exports for a long time, such as coffee, cotton, tea and tobacco. Non-traditional exports refer to manufactures and relatively new emerging agricultural commodity exports, for example maize, beans, sesame seeds, vegetables, fruits and horticultural exports. As mentioned earlier, our analysis is done at a high level of aggregation mainly due to lack of data and therefore we are unable to assess the relative impact of demand and supply conditions on an individual commodity basis. We instead discuss the sources of the export growth under the TD, agricultural NTD and other NTD exports.

In broad terms, the greatest source of export growth is attributable to the supply conditions across all commodity sub-groups. The supply conditions accounted for about 38 per cent, 9 per cent and 18 per cent of TD, agricultural NTD and other NTD export growth respectively. Just less than two-thirds (about 65 per cent) of overall export growth was due to the improvement in the country's export shares (assumed to result from supply conditions). The demand conditions made small and positive contribution to all exports, particularly TD exports, once again suggesting that export growth was less sensitive to changes in market than supply conditions. The interaction of demand and supply conditions had a negative impact on the growth of agricultural NTD exports but a positive impact on growth of TD and other NTD exports such that their overall effect came closer to the effect of the demand conditions alone.

Individual commodities impacted differently on the growth of Ugandan exports. Among NTD agricultural exports, fish and food products had a positive contribution and animal products (including hides and skins) had a negative impact. The positive contributions more than compensated for the

Economic policy and manufacturing performance

Table 4.3   Ugandan export growth 1993–97, by commodity (%)

	Commodity	DD	SS	DDSS	Total
Agric.	Animal products (excl. 03)	0.20	−0.22	−0.24	−0.26
NTD	Fish and fish products (03)	0.68	4.81	0.63	6.12
	Food products	0.43	4.67	0.34	5.44
	Hides and skins	1.51	−0.66	−0.87	−0.02
	Sub-total	2.83	8.59	−0.14	11.28
TD	Coffee, tea, cotton, spices	13.16	31.15	9.78	54.10
	Mineral products	0.14	7.18	0.44	7.76
	Forestry products	0.05	−0.06	−0.02	−0.03
	Sub-total	13.35	38.27	10.21	61.82
Other	Manufactured foods	0.19	0.11	0.04	0.35
NTD	Chemicals	0.08	10.70	3.80	14.58
	Textile products	1.28	5.13	2.28	8.68
	Machinery	0.06	0.75	0.54	1.36
	Tobacco and beverages	0.34	1.27	0.32	1.93
	Sub-total	1.94	17.97	6.99	26.90
Total		18.12	64.83	17.05	100

Notes: TD stands for traditional export commodities and NTD refers to commodities other than TD. The computation is based on equation [3¢] such that totals along each column are as follows: demand conditions (DD) = $\Sigma_i \theta_i \Delta X_i$, supply conditions (SS) = $\Sigma_i X_i \Delta \theta_i$ and interaction term (DDSS) = $\Sigma_i \Delta X_i \Delta \theta_i$.

Source: Own computation.

negative influences, such that overall agricultural NTD exports contributed about 11 per cent to the export growth. The highest source of export growth among TD came from products such as coffee and tea, which is not surprising given that TD (mainly coffee) forms more than 80 per cent of total Ugandan exports (Morrissey and Rudaheranwa, 1998).

There are two significant features regarding other NTD exports. First, they comprise commodities that experienced positive export growth under all (demand and supply) conditions. Second, the impact on overall export growth due to other NTD was higher (just less than 27 per cent) compared to that due to agricultural NTD exports (about 11 per cent). Among other NTD exports, high export growth originated from chemicals (about 15 per cent) and textile products (about 9 per cent). Amongst agricultural NTD exports, supply conditions seem critical, probably because they involve small and/or relatively new exporters that face high transaction costs in penetrating export markets.

Overall, significant contributions to export growth are due to fish and food products (among agricultural NTD), coffee, cotton, and mineral products (among TD) and chemicals and textiles among other NTD exports (Table 4.B5). Food products encompass the emerging exports, specifically vegetable, fruits, horticultural, etc; other NTD are mainly manufactured exports. These exports seem promising, particularly if efforts are directed to improving supply conditions. Uganda is attempting to diversify its export structure, particularly the commodity composition. It is therefore encouraging that those commodities into which the economy intends to diversify seem to have been able to increase market share during the period analysed.

6   EXPORT COMPETITIVENESS AND IMPLICIT TAXATION DUE TO TRANSPORT COSTS

This section relates disprotection of exports due to transport costs to individual factors impacting on the competitive position of Ugandan exports. Freight charges increase costs of production, distribution and marketing of exports, thus making exports less profitable. Transport costs reinforce supply conditions in constraining trade and make exports less competitive. Intuitively, one would expect sectors encountering high implicit taxation arising from transport costs to be less successful in export sales. Milner *et al.* (2000) note that whilst Ugandan trade reforms reduced protection of importables, and disprotection (taxation) of exports, considerably, non-policy barriers to trade, especially transport costs, remained very high. When trade barriers are reduced, non-policy barriers assume greater significance.

Table 4.4 summarises the correlation coefficients for the relationship between the degree of competitiveness of Ugandan exports and the implicit taxation arising from transport charges. The correlation coefficients are computed for exports to COMESA and non-COMESA markets. A few commodity exports are destined overseas while others are destined to regional markets (Table 4.B6), in which case marine transport does not apply. We discuss the link between the relative competitive position of exports in regional (COMESA) markets to transport barriers using overland transport costs. For non-COMESA markets surface (land and sea) transport costs are used.

The correlation coefficients (albeit very low) exhibit the expected negative relationship between the competitiveness (supply conditions or COM3) of Ugandan exports and the implicit taxation arising from costs of land transportation. High implicit taxation of exports from transport costs is generally associated with low competitiveness in the non-COMESA market, but only

Table 4.4   Export competitiveness and implicit taxation of exports

Variable	(a) COMESA (land transport)			(b) non-COMESA (surface transport)		
	Mean (%)	STD	Corr.	Mean (%)	STD	Corr.
Transport	27.88	18.6	1	56.64	37.74	1
COM1	0.703	1.123	0.031	8.39	15.87	−0.263
COM2	0.936	0.312	0.267	1.54	2.96	−0.174
COM3	0.588	1.037	−0.078	5.45	9.33	−0.283
COM4	0.023	0.866	0.382	1.51	3.92	−0.295

Notes: Part (a) shows the correlation between implicit taxation arising from land transport and competitiveness of Ugandan exports destined for the COMESA market. Part (b) shows the correlation between Ugandan exports destined for markets outside COMESA and the taxation due to surface transportation. Mean values, standard deviations (STD) and simple correlations (corr.) are provided. Export growth is classified as follows: COM1 = due to supply and demand conditions plus their interaction, COM2 = due to the interaction of demand and supply conditions, COM3 = due to supply conditions, and COM4 = due to demand conditions (for definitions of demand and supply conditions see Tables 4.2 and 4.3).

Source: Own computation with information from Tables 4.B1–4.B4 and implicit taxation data from Milner *et al.* (2000).

appears for COMESA markets in respect of supply conditions. Only food products (maize and beans) encounter low taxation due to transport costs and may be regarded as competitive in the COMESA region. Given the proximity to the market, it is a surprising outcome that some products encountering low implicit taxation due to transport costs are less competitive. The explanation may be that transport costs do little to help explain competitiveness (however one has to note that the transport measure is a 1994 snapshot whereas COM3 represents a change over time). Alternatively it might be that these products are effectively 'importables' sectors and/or COMESA countries produce similar goods themselves.

An alternative explanation is that other costs of marketing within the region that are not reflected in transport costs may be responsible. Costs arising from policy and non-policy trade barriers such as inadequate infrastructure and inefficient institutions (inefficiency in handling and clearing procedures, costs of information, high costs of credit, high non-tariff barriers) are likely to make exports less profitable in the regional market. Multinational companies that are able to internalise some or most transaction costs (particularly given their access to credit and information) tend to encourage trade outside the region. Implicit taxation of exports due to land transport costs would (weakly) reinforce the supply conditions and reduce the profitability (hence competitiveness) of Ugandan exports to COMESA. The correlation coefficient, though small, is negative. Textiles, clothing and footwear products appear relatively competitive even though they face relatively high implicit taxation from freight costs (Rudaheranwa, 1999).

The correlation coefficients for Ugandan goods destined for overseas markets are also reported in Table 4.4. Coffee, cotton and tea exports (and to some extent fish products) are associated with low implicit taxation arising from transport costs and high competitiveness. This would be expected as these products dominate the country's export value (Tables 4.B6 and 4.B7). Other commodity exports face high implicit taxation due to freight charges and are associated with low competitiveness in overseas export markets. The correlation coefficients are –0.26 and –0.28 between implicit disprotection and competitiveness of exports respectively due to overall factors and due to supply conditions only. This reflects the reduction in competitiveness due to the implicit taxation of exports arising from transport costs.

7 CONCLUSION

A few issues emerge from our discussion. First, supply conditions constrain the competitive position of Ugandan exports, particularly those into which the economy is attempting to diversify. Second, transport costs are a contributory factor in reducing the profitability of some Ugandan exports. This relationship in the case of trade within the COMESA region is weak, probably due to other transaction costs impacting on exporters. Third, we find no evidence to suggest that the growth in market size (demand conditions) is responsible for the low overall growth of Ugandan exports. Instead our analysis indicates that the competitiveness of Ugandan exports is sensitive to supply conditions. More importantly, the results suggest that the limited improvement in Ugandan export performance, including manufactures, was largely attributable to Ugandan reforms (supply side conditions). This is evidence for a potentially beneficial effect of liberalisation, even if export response is slow. It is clear that Uganda will find it difficult to increase the volume and diversity (composition and destination) of exports without adopting a strategy that reduces costs arising from inefficient transport and associated infrastructure facilities.

Using a simplified CMS model, this analysis identified factors impacting on the competitiveness of Ugandan exports both by commodity and destined markets. The analysis covers the greater part of Ugandan exports and competing products (competing goods produced within importing countries were not included in standard exports). Results generally show that the growth of exports was more sensitive to supply (competitive factor) than demand conditions. That is, increasing market share was a more important source of export growth than increasing the size of market. This is consistent with evidence in the literature (Love, 1984; Balassa, 1990; Svedberg, 1991) that domestic rather than external market conditions are more important in constraining export performance. Our analysis also indicates that diversifying into non-traditional exports appears promising and encouraging for the growth of Ugandan exports. Policies that promote increased efficiency in the economy generally, and manufacturing specifically, such as improved infrastructure, communications and utilities, can also benefit exporters.

Past studies using the CMS approach ignored the interaction effect of changes in export shares and 'standard' exports on the growth of exports. The omission of the interaction effect seems to suggest that the factors impacting on export growth are not fully accounted for. The interaction effect of demand and supply conditions on export growth may not be negligible in some cases, for example it explained about 17 per cent of total export growth, which is close to the contribution originating from demand conditions alone. The evidence on the relationship between the degree of competitiveness and the implicit taxation of exports from transport costs is rather mixed. Some commodity exports (textile products and chemicals) are highly taxed from transport costs yet appear competitive while others (such as machinery) are less competitive yet encounter low taxation. The main exports (coffee, cotton, and fish products) face relatively low implicit taxation due to freight costs and seem competitive. This implies that even those products that are competitive would benefit more if the implicit taxation arising from an inefficient trade-related infrastructure system were reduced.

APPENDIX 4.A1   COMMODITY (HS CODE) AND MARKETS DESCRIPTION

Animal products (01–02, 04–05), Vegetable products (06–08, 10–15), Coffee, tea, and spices (09), Manufactured foods (16–21, 23), Tobacco and beverages (22, 24), Mineral products (25–27, 68–71), Chemical products (28–38), hides and skins (41–43). Forestry products (44–49), Textile, textile articles (50–53), Footwear and headgear (54–67), Base metals and articles thereof (72–83), Machinery (84–85), Transport equipment (86–89), Miscellaneous products (39–40, 68–71, 90–97).

APPENDIX 4.A2   COUNTRIES THAT TRADE WITH UGANDA

PTA refers to the Preferential Trade Area of Eastern and Southern Africa (now COMESA), ROA refers to the rest of African countries outside the PTA region. ROE refers to the rest of Europe apart from the United Kingdom, Belgium and Germany, and ROW stands for the rest of the world. Due to lack of recorded standard imports, 41 countries and cities to which Uganda exports were excluded in the current exercise. They include: Afghanistan, Allen Road (town), Andorra, Antigua and Barbuda, Belize, Botswana, British Virgin Islands, Brunei Darussalam, Bulgaria, Bungoma (town), Burma, Burundi, Yemen Republic, Djibouti, Dubai, East Timor, French ST, Gibraltar, Grasmark (town), Guinea Bissau, Heard and McDonald Islands, Homa Bay (town), Kitate (town), Lausanne (town), Lesotho, Montserrat, Mozambique, Namibia, Nepal, Netherlands Antilles, Neuchâtel (town), Niger, Rwanda, Saint Vincent and the Grenadines, San Marino, Shatin (Town), Swaziland, Taiwan, and the Turks and Caicos Islands.

APPENDIX 4.B FULL RESULTS

Table 4.B1 Impact of market size (market shares constant) (%)

Market	PTA	ROA	UK	Belgium	Germany	ROE	ROW	Total
Animal products	0.00	–	0.00	–	0.00	0.01	0.20	0.20
Fish products (03)	0.02	0.00	0.32	0.09	0.03	-0.02	0.24	0.68
Food products	-0.18	–	0.12	0.07	0.02	0.35	0.05	0.43
Coffee, tea and spices	0.07	0.04	0.28	3.96	1.08	6.13	1.59	13.16
Manufactured foods	0.11	0.00	0.01	0.01	0.00	0.04	0.01	0.19
Tobacco and beverages	0.02	0.00	0.04	0.14	0.07	0.04	0.03	0.34
Mineral products	-0.04	–	0.15	0.00	0.00	0.00	0.03	0.14
Chemicals	0.04	0.00	0.00	0.00	0.00	0.02	0.01	0.08
Hides and skins	0.00	0.28	0.90	0.00	0.00	0.30	0.04	1.51
Forestry products	0.04	–	0.00	0.00	0.00	0.00	0.00	0.05
Textile products	0.16	0.00	0.99	0.00	0.00	0.08	0.05	1.28
Machinery	0.01	0.03	-0.06	0.00	0.03	0.04	0.01	0.06
Total	0.24	0.36	2.76	4.28	1.24	6.97	2.26	18.12

Table 4.B2 Effect of changes in export shares (Xij constant) (%)

Market	PTA	ROA	UK	Belgium	Germany	ROE	ROW	Total
Animal products	0.16	–	–	–	–	-0.03	-0.35	-0.22
Fish products (03)	-0.08	0.03	-0.77	1.57	0.05	2.34	1.67	4.81
Food products	3.32	0.22	1.82	-0.06	-0.05	-0.93	0.36	4.67
Coffee, tea and spices	0.42	0.04	24.34	-7.77	-1.30	16.24	-0.82	31.15
Manufactured foods	-0.02	-0.02	0.09	0.02	0.01	-0.05	0.08	0.11
Tobacco and beverages	0.06	0.29	0.05	–	0.38	0.54	-0.05	1.27
Mineral products	0.11	–	-0.35	5.80	0.00	0.94	0.68	7.18
Chemicals	0.43	0.01	0.10	0.14	-0.01	9.96	0.07	10.70
Hides and skins	0.00	-0.09	-1.38	0.00	–	-0.16	0.97	-0.66
Forestry products	-0.05	–	0.00	–	0.00	-0.01	0.00	-0.06
Textile products	1.57	0.01	1.07	0.00	0.00	2.02	0.46	5.13
Machinery	0.45	-0.02	0.04	–	–	0.00	0.29	0.75
Total	6.37	0.48	25.01	-0.31	-0.91	30.85	3.35	64.83

Table 4.B3 Impact of both changes in market size and shares (%)

Market	PTA	ROA	UK	Belgium	Germany	ROE	ROW	Total
Animal products	-0.11	–	–	–	–	0.00	-0.13	-0.24
Fish products (03)	-0.02	0.01	-0.30	0.50	0.02	-0.07	0.48	0.63
Food products	-0.13	0.09	0.45	-0.03	-0.01	-0.20	0.17	0.34
Coffee, tea and spices	0.11	0.02	7.15	-3.94	-0.58	8.00	-0.98	9.78
Manufactured foods	-0.01	0.00	0.02	0.00	0.00	-0.02	0.05	0.04
Tobacco and beverages	0.02	0.07	0.02	–	0.06	0.15	-0.01	0.32
Mineral products	-0.02	–	-0.13	-0.10	0.00	0.15	0.55	0.44
Chemicals	0.07	0.00	0.05	0.00	0.00	3.65	0.04	3.80
Hides and skins	0.00	-0.27	-0.82	0.00	–	-0.07	0.30	-0.87
Forestry products	-0.02	–	0.00	–	0.00	0.00	0.00	-0.02
Textile products	0.99	0.01	0.60	0.00	0.00	0.46	0.22	2.28
Machinery	0.14	-0.02	-0.03	–	–	0.00	0.45	0.54
Total	1.01	-0.09	7.01	-3.56	-0.50	12.05	1.14	17.05

Table 4.B4   Overall export growth (%)

Market	PTA	ROA	UK	Belgium	Germany	ROE	ROW	Total
Animal products	0.04	–	–	–	–	-0.03	-0.28	-0.26
Fish products (03)	-0.08	0.04	-0.74	2.17	0.10	2.24	2.39	6.12
Food products	3.01	–	2.39	-0.02	-0.04	-0.79	0.57	5.44
Coffee, tea and spices	0.60	0.10	31.77	-7.75	-0.79	30.37	-0.20	54.10
Manufactured foods	0.08	-0.02	0.12	0.03	0.02	-0.03	0.14	0.35
Tobacco and beverages	0.09	0.37	0.11	–	0.51	0.74	-0.02	1.93
Mineral products	0.05	–	-0.33	5.70	0.00	1.09	1.25	7.76
Chemicals	0.53	0.01	0.15	0.14	0.00	13.63	0.12	14.58
Hides and skins	0.00	-0.08	-1.30	0.00	–	0.07	1.30	-0.02
Forestry products	-0.03	–	0.00	–	0.00	-0.01	0.00	-0.03
Textile products	2.72	0.02	2.66	0.00	0.00	2.55	0.73	8.68
Machinery	0.60	0.00	-0.05	–	–	0.03	0.76	1.36
Total	7.62	0.74	34.78	0.41	-0.18	49.87	6.75	100.00

Table 4.B5   Overall export growth (US$)

Market	PTA	ROA	UK	Belgium	Germany	ROE	ROW	Total
Animal products	1 275	–	–	–	–	–786	–8 577	–8 022
Fish products (03)	–2 343	1 146	–22 735	66 241	3 071	68 532	73 091	187 003
Food products	92 073	–	73 195	–561	–1 317	–24 064	17 539	166 267
Coffee, tea, etc.	18 392	3 147	971 392	–237 076	–24 196	928 401	–6 197	1 653 864
Manufactured foods	2 461	–483	3 693	1 053	615	–939	4 163	10 562
Tobacco and beverages	2 657	11 179	3 409	–	15 634	22 572	–647	59 065
Mineral products	1 430	–	–9 955	174 140	0	33 360	38 270	237 245
Chemicals	16 356	314	4 644	4 409	–146	416 642	3 573	445 790
Hides and skins	–8	–2 490	–39 773	23	–	2 005	39 690	–530
Forestry products	–776	–	–84	–	22	–228	73	–956
Textile products	83 035	690	81 190	8	94	78 092	22 373	265 482
Machinery	18 414	–151	–1 617	–	–	951	23 088	41 506
Total	232 968	22 753	1 063 397	12 536	–5 354	1 524 539	206 438	3 057 277

Table 4.B6 Ugandan export structure in 1993 (% of total Ugandan exports)

Market	PTA	ROA	UK	Belgium	Germany	ROE	ROW	Total
Animal products	0.01	–	0.01	–	0.01	0.10	1.22	1.35
Fish products (03)	0.22	0.00	1.83	0.63	0.22	1.76	1.81	6.47
Food products	9.93	–	1.08	0.34	0.18	3.57	0.22	15.32
Coffee, tea and spices	0.59	0.25	2.11	17.27	5.40	27.53	2.95	56.11
Manufactured foods	0.36	0.03	0.18	0.10	0.03	0.26	0.03	0.99
Tobacco and beverages	0.14	0.01	0.25	2.58	0.87	0.32	0.34	4.50
Mineral products	0.40	–	0.92	0.02	–	0.03	0.07	1.44
Chemical products	0.54	0.00	0.00	0.07	0.02	0.13	0.05	0.81
Hides and skins	0.00	0.20	3.33	0.01	0.01	1.47	0.26	5.27
Wood products	0.21	–	0.01	0.01	0.00	0.03	0.03	0.28
Textiles and footwear	0.55	0.00	3.89	0.00	0.04	0.73	0.23	5.44
Base metals and articles thereof	0.17	0.01	0.13	–	–	0.00	0.03	0.35
Machinery	0.08	0.06	0.14	0.00	0.25	0.13	0.02	0.69
Transport equipment	0.33	0.01	0.20	0.04	0.00	0.05	0.13	0.76
Miscellaneous products	0.12	–	0.06	0.00	0.01	0.01	0.01	0.21
Total	13.66	0.59	14.14	21.08	7.05	36.10	7.39	100.00

Table 4.B7 Ugandan export structure in 1996 (% of total Ugandan exports)

Market	PTA	ROA	UK	Belgium	Germany	ROE	ROW	Total
Animal products	0.03	–	–	–	–	0.01	0.19	0.23
Fish products (03)	0.01	0.03	0.06	1.68	0.14	2.08	2.19	6.18
Food products	5.12	0.21	1.97	0.09	0.03	0.56	0.46	8.44
Coffee, tea and spices	0.59	0.15	22.36	0.04	1.13	29.25	0.77	54.28
Manufactured foods	0.17	–	0.14	0.05	0.02	0.06	0.10	0.54
Tobacco and beverages	0.10	0.25	0.15	–	0.62	0.60	0.09	1.82
Mineral products	0.16	0.01	0.06	3.90	–	0.75	0.88	5.75
Chemical products	0.53	0.01	0.10	0.12	0.00	9.35	0.10	10.21
Hides and skins	0.00	0.01	0.14	0.00	–	0.50	0.97	1.61
Wood products	0.05	0.01	0.00	0.00	0.00	0.00	0.01	0.07
Textiles and footwear	2.03	0.02	3.02	0.00	0.01	1.97	0.57	7.61
Base metals and articles thereof	0.20	–	0.03	–	0.02	0.00	0.05	0.30
Machinery	0.44	0.02	0.01	–	–	0.06	0.52	1.04
Transport equipment	0.19	0.06	0.02	0.01	0.00	0.17	0.91	1.36
Miscellaneous products	0.44	0.01	–	–	0.00	0.02	0.06	0.53
Total	10.07	0.77	28.05	5.90	1.97	45.38	7.86	100.00

NOTES

1. This discussion uses a discrete time version of the continuous time specification outlined in Richardson (1971a).
2. As the data are inadequate for any time series estimation, CMS is possibly the only rigorous technique available for this analysis.
3. Products are exports as viewed by exporters but importers view them as imports. Standard exports used in our analysis are imports of competing products into a market, and therefore exclude competing products produced within the importing country.
4. The PTA was established in 1978 and transformed into a Common Market for Eastern and Southern Africa (COMESA) in 1994. According to the United Nations Economic Commission for Africa (ECA) (1995), COMESA member states are: Angola, Burundi, Comoro, Djibouti, Ethiopia, Kenya, Lesotho, Malawi, Madagascar, Mauritius, Mozambique, Namibia, Rwanda, Sudan, Swaziland, Uganda, Tanzania, Zambia and Zimbabwe. NPTA refers to all other countries.

REFERENCES

Balassa, B. (1990), 'Incentive policies and export performance in Sub-Saharan Africa', *World Development*, **18**, 383–91.

Belshaw, D., P. Lawrence and M. Hubbard (1999), 'Agricultural tradables and economic recovery in Uganda: The limitations of structural adjustment in practice', *World Development*, **27**, 673–90.

Bennell, P. (1998), 'Fighting for survival: Manufacturing industry and adjustment in sub-Saharan Africa', *Journal of International Development*, **10**, 621–37.

Duncan, A. and S. Jones (1993), 'Agricultural marketing and pricing reform: A review of experience', *World Development*, **21**, 1495–1514.

ECA (1995), *Survey of Economic and Social Conditions in Africa*, New York: United Nations, Economic Commission for Africa.

Fleming, J.M. and S.C. Tsiang (1956/57), 'Changes in competitiveness strength and export shares of major industrial countries', *IMF Staff Papers*, **5**, 218–48.

Geraci, J.V. and W. Prewo (1982), 'An empirical demand and supply model of multilateral trade', *Review of Economics and Statistics*, **64**, 432–41.

Greenaway, D. (1998), 'Does trade liberalisation promote economic development?', *Scottish Journal of Political Economy*, **45**, 491–511

Leamer, E.E. and R.M. Stern (1970), *Quantitative International Economics*, Boston: Ally and Bacon Inc.

Love, J. (1984), 'External market conditions, competitiveness, diversification and LDCs' exports', *Journal of Development Economics*, **16**, 279–91.

Mahmood, Z. (1981), 'Changes in export shares and competitive strength in Pakistan', *The Pakistan Development Review*, **20**, 399–415.

Milner, C., O. Morrissey and N. Rudaheranwa (2000), 'Policy and non-policy barriers to trade and the implicit taxation of exports in Uganda', *Journal of Development Studies*, **37**, 67–90.

Morrissey, O. and N. Rudaheranwa, (1998), 'Ugandan trade policy and export performance in the 1990s', University of Nottingham: *CREDIT Research Paper No. 98/12 (CDP006)*.

Narvekar, P.R. (1960), 'The role of competitiveness in Japan's export performance, 1954–1958', *IMF Staff Papers*, **8**, pp. 85–100.

Richardson, J.D. (1971a), 'Constant-Market-Share analysis of export growth', *Journal of International Economics*, **1**, 227–39.

Richardson, J.D. (1971b), 'Some sensitivity tests for a 'Constant-Market-Shares' analysis of export growth', *Review of Economics and Statistics*, **53**, 300–304.

Richardson, J.D. (1973), 'Beyond (but back to?) the elasticity of substitution in international trade', *European Economic Review*, **4**, 381–92.

Rudaheranwa, N. (1999), *Transport Costs and Export Trade of Landlocked Countries: Evidence from Uganda*, unpublished PhD Thesis, The University of Nottingham.

Svedberg, P. (1991), 'The export performance of Sub-Saharan Africa', *Economic Development and Cultural Change*, **39**, 549–66.

5. Becoming an exporter of manufactures: the case of Indonesia

John T. Thoburn*

During the 1980s Indonesia moved from being a negligible exporter of manufactures to a significant supplier. In 1980 manufactures generated less than 3 per cent of total exports; by 1992 they were nearly 50 per cent (Hill, 1996: 81). This expansion followed a series of trade reforms as Indonesia – a major oil exporter – coped with the collapse in the price of oil (and other primary commodities). The present chapter focuses on the three main manufacturing export sectors: textiles and garments, footwear and electronics.[1] It looks at the role of foreign investment and the relation between export-oriented production and the legacy of industries developed under Indonesia's earlier programme of import-substituting industrialisation. A particular focus is on the operation of the export-promoting trade regime in relation to the needs of each sector, and in relation to the possibilities for economically efficient backward integration by the export sectors.[2] In the 1990s, previously exceptionally high rates of non-oil export growth started to slow. From 1994 until the 1997–98 Asian financial crisis, textile, garment and footwear exports never regained their previous momentum, although electronics exports continued to grow rapidly. The period 1992 to 1994 represents something of a watershed in Indonesia's remarkably rapid development of manufactures exports, and the country's progress up to then may provide lessons for other countries wishing to move in a similar direction. The year 1994 is taken as our point of reference. Material is derived from 30 interviews with companies and trade associations in textiles, garments, footwear and electronics in Indonesia. The narrative is updated to more recent years, but the many institutional details, such as tariffs on particular items, are left as they were in 1994, and serve as illustrations of how the trade regime affects export patterns. The chapter does not attempt any analysis of the likely longer-term effects of the 1997–98 Asian crisis on exports. This is in the belief that it is too early to say

* This chapter is based on material from a consultancy with the Harvard Institute for International Development in Indonesia in 1994. However, neither HIID, nor any Indonesian government agency, is responsible for any view expressed here, and any errors are mine alone.

whether the crisis represents a structural break in Indonesia's development path or a temporary setback.

1   THE TRADE REFORMS

The 1980s trade reforms have already been well documented by other writers, and can be introduced here quite briefly.[3] Successful exchange rate management was a feature of Indonesian economic policy from soon after the New Order regime came to power in 1966 until the onset of the 1997–98 Asian crisis.[4] Following the collapse of world oil prices in the early 1980s, substantial devaluations of the Indonesian rupiah were undertaken in 1983 and 1986. With a lack of domestic demand pressure, these translated into real depreciations. A policy was then adopted of floating the rupiah and managing the float so as to maintain a constant real exchange rate, initially against the US dollar and subsequently (in the early 1990s) against a weighted average of currencies.

In the early 1980s, however, and despite a relatively open capital account on the balance of payments, the domestic economy was heavily protected against import competition. Effective protection on importables was estimated as high as 200 per cent on average, with great variability between sectors (Hill, 1996: 112). In order to reduce anti-export bias by giving exporters access to a free trade regime to buy inputs on the world market, a duty drawback and exemption scheme was introduced in May 1986. Initially known as P4BM, and later as Bapeksta, this arrangement was administered in a relatively corruption-free manner, and would prove a vital inducement to foreign investors to establish export production. Although the trend towards increasing protection against imports had been reversed by the late 1980s, particularly with regard to non-tariff barriers, substantial tariffs remained in place throughout the years of rapid export growth.

Besides Bapeksta, Indonesia also operated export processing zones (often referred to as 'bonded zones' by commentators on the Indonesian economy). The EPZ facility in Indonesia antedates Bapeksta by more than a decade (Warr, 1983). In addition, individual firms were later given the right to have direct access to duty free imported inputs under the EPTE (*Entrepot Produksi untuk Tujuan Ekspor*) scheme, introduced in February 1993 (Pangestu and Azis, 1994: 26). Also, in 1994 there was the recently introduced EPTE.PE (*EPTE, Perusahan Engineering*) arrangement, which was a helpful way of combining EPTE export privileges with some production for the domestic market (to our knowledge, however, by late 1994 only one firm had been granted access to this scheme).

The third strand in the reforms that facilitated exports was the revision and liberalisation in 1987 and 1988 of the laws governing foreign direct investment (FDI). In addition, special measures were enacted to give priority to inward investment from Japan and the four Asian newly industrialising countries (Korea, Taiwan, Hong Kong, and Singapore). These measures were intended to facilitate relocation to Indonesia of labour-intensive industries losing their comparative advantage in those countries, and included bilateral investment guarantees and tax treaties. The minimum size of FDI projects was also reduced so as to encourage relocation by small and medium enterprises. The late 1980s saw a rapid build up of inward foreign investment. In 1990, 58 per cent of all inward investment projects were from the four Asian newly industrialising countries (NICs); the figure rises to 76 per cent if Japan is included. Some 84 per cent of the Asian NIC inward investment projects and 57 per cent of Japanese projects were export-oriented. Korea and Taiwan were relatively new investors. Singapore and Hong Kong had a longer history, but it was Japan that was Indonesia's largest inward investor, accounting for over 40 per cent of total cumulative inward investment from 1967 to 1989 (Thee, 1991). Japan also had a long history of being the largest source of foreign investment in Indonesian textiles. However, by the late 1980s some three-quarters of *new* textile and garment inward FDI approvals were from Hong Kong, Taiwan and Korea, of which Korea was the most important in terms of the number of projects (Hill, 1991: 101).

2 THE BUILD UP OF MANUFACTURING EXPORTS

By 1993–94 manufacturing exports (excluding plywood and other wood products) constituted 53 per cent of Indonesia's non-oil exports. The most important manufactures exports were garments (11.6 per cent of total non-oil exports), textiles (9.1 per cent), electronics products (6.6 per cent) and footwear (6.1 per cent). The early 1990s were a watershed in Indonesia's manufacturing export development in textiles, garments and footwear – the end of a period of unprecedented export expansion.

Textile and garment production had developed up to the 1970s on the basis of import substitution. The sectors began to export significant amounts in the 1980s. Over the five years 1988–92, textile and garment exports rose at an annual compound rate of 33.2 per cent measured in constant dollars,[5] with textiles growing marginally faster than garments. The speed of expansion in the early 1990s is understated by the gross export figures; Indonesia was both importing and exporting textiles (garment imports were minimal). From 1990 to 1992 the ratio of imports to exports of textiles fell from nearly two-thirds to just over one-third; so while gross exports of textiles and garments doubled, *net* exports almost tripled. Growth slowed sharply from 1992 to 1993, and looks only marginally better if expressed in terms of net exports;

the growth rate of gross exports was 2.3 per cent, and that of net exports 5.5 per cent.

Footwear exports also exhibited startling growth from the late 1980s to the early 1990s. Starting from a low base of $8 million in 1986, they had risen by 1993 to over $1.6 billion, accounting for 12 per cent of total manufacturing exports. Over the five years 1989–93 footwear exports rose at an average annual compound rate of 47 per cent measured in constant dollars. The year 1993 registered a 26 per cent growth in shoe exports compared to 1992.

Electronics[6] exports came late to Indonesia's manufacturing export boom. Exports approximately doubled in each year from 1989 to 1992. From 1992 to 1993, when many other export industries were experiencing difficulties, electronics exports rose by another 43 per cent. However, the import content of Indonesian electronics exports was very high. Electronics was not yet a major net earner of foreign exchange like textiles and garments, although it had the potential to become one.

The slowdown in non-oil export growth in 1993 and 1994 occurred despite the highest growth in global trade volumes for the previous 20 years. Textile exports fell in 1993 and 1994, while garment exports slowed in 1993 and fell in 1994. The growth rate of footwear exports almost halved in 1994 to 13.7 per cent, although it had picked up again in early 1995 (James, 1995: 20–6).

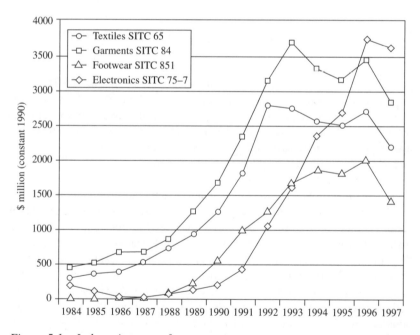

Figure 5.1   Indonesian manufactures exports

Although overall non-oil export growth was 17.1 per cent by the fiscal year 1995–96, it slowed to 6.7 per cent in 1996–97. Textiles and garments were once more in difficulty, and footwear exports also slowed sharply. Again, though, the electronics/electrical sector continued to expand. Electrical goods export values rose 28 per cent, and within that category electronics and computer equipment rose 35 per cent. The slowdown in non-oil exports was not confined to Indonesia; Malaysian and Thai exports also slowed. Much of the export slowdown was due to slacker growth in Japan and the East Asian NICs, presaging the Asian crisis (Lindblad, 1997: 16).

Figure 5.1 gives an overview of Indonesia's export development, using annual data from the UN *International Trade Statistics Yearbooks*, converted to constant 1990 dollars with the UN index of manufactured export dollar unit values as deflator. The peaks and subsequent slowdowns in textile and garment exports successively are striking. A temporary slowdown in foot-wear comes later,[7] while electronics exports continued to rise. The fall in exports at the time of the 1997 financial crisis is even more dramatic.

In the remainder of this chapter, we consider the trends in the major export products in more detail and seek an explanation for the slowdown described here.

3 FACTORS IN THE BUILD UP OF MANUFACTURING EXPORTS

Indonesia's entry into global manufacturing markets from the late 1980s is to a large extent due to FDI in labour-intensive products, gaining access to the country's low wage labour and (in the case of textiles and garments) unused Multi-Fibre Arrangement export quotas. However, prior to the manufacturing export boom, Indonesia had also attracted import-substituting foreign invest-ment. These investors also shifted towards export orientation, particularly in textiles and to some extent in electronics. In footwear, inward investment created more of a dualistic economic structure, with older established firms continuing to serve mainly the domestic market (Chapman, 1992).

In textiles and garments, and to some extent in footwear, Indonesia's comparative advantage has proved fragile, both in the face of competition in world markets and with regard to the competition for foreign investment. In garments and footwear, FDI is strongly driven by the sourcing decisions of international buyers. Such buyers source from a range of countries to mini-mise risk, and are constantly seeking lower cost sources of reliable supply. The buyers typically do not invest themselves, but work through firms from Asian newly industrialising countries, which undertake the investment.[8] The competitive position of all Indonesia's labour-intensive export industries is also sensitive to the trade regime, and particularly to the country's export promoting trade arrangements. However, the degree of sensitivity differs between industries as a result both of the structure of protection against imports and as a result of industry-specific characteristics.

3.1   Textiles and garments

Textiles and garments have a complicated structure of production that can be highly trade dependent. This makes the pattern of exports and the degree of backward integration from garments to textiles highly sensitive to the trade regime, as indeed is the competitiveness of the sector. Textile products can be exported at each stage of the commodity chain from fibres, yarn, and unfinished fabric, to finished fabric and garments. Spinning and weaving[9] require long-term planning and are rather inflexible operations needing long production runs. These features do not tie in closely with the short production runs and frequent style and raw material changes necessary in export garment production. Short production runs have increasingly become a feature of the world garment production industry, and in Western countries this development has brought about closer co-operation between garment makers and textile manufacturers. Short runs are more a feature of upmarket garments, but Indonesian garment exporters by 1994 were finding moves to smaller, variegated orders becoming more pronounced even in the middle ranges.

The relation between exports of textiles and exports of garments can be illustrated by the experience of companies in Indonesia that are vertically integrated from the spinning of yarn and the weaving of fabric, on to the production of garments. These companies often do not use all the fabric they produce in their garment production, and their garment operations often buy in fabric. For vertically integrated companies, the decision whether to export textiles or to use them in garments depends on world textile prices in relation to domestic production costs and domestic prices. The export of fabrics as well as garments allows the use of a wider range of quotas. Companies may make both textiles and garments, intending to export each separately. Using local fabrics in export garments would not generally raise export earnings if the fabrics were diverted from being directly exported.

There is little similarity among major world textile and garment exporters in the balance between textile and garment net exports; there was not a clear model for Indonesia to follow. Taiwan and Korea are large exporters of textiles as well as of garments; and both have substantial textile imports too, with a large overall textile export surplus. This is similar to Indonesia's pattern of trade. In contrast, Japan is a large gross and net exporter of textiles, but exports almost no garments; this probably reflects the higher labour intensity of garment production compared to textiles. China is not a large *net* exporter of textiles, though its gross textile exports are as great as Taiwan's. In Taiwan and Korea's case, exports of textiles reflect the economies of scale which can be achieved in synthetic fabric production, and the gains from international specialisation in the production of different types of fabric. Also, while Multi-Fibre Arrangement restrictions on textile trade remain (that is, up to 2005, when the MFA will have been phased out), exporting fabrics as well as garments gives wider market access.

Fibres and yarns

Indonesia's production of fibre and yarn has been a significant contributor to indirect exports, and a generator of some direct exports too. Spinning capacity in Indonesia is the largest in ASEAN. Japanese FDI has been important since the 1970s in the build up of synthetic fibre and yarn capacity. The industry in the early 1990s was operating efficiently at close to world market prices. Two-thirds of Indonesia's exports of fabrics are cotton or cotton-based, and one-third are based on artificial fibres (which may be mixed with cotton). In the case of garments, the shares are approximately a half each. In synthetic fibres, almost two-thirds of production is of filament yarn rather than staple fibre (a higher proportion than in other East Asian producers). The use of filament yarn allows the spinning stage of textile production to be by-passed.

There is little production of cotton in Indonesia, and almost all cotton for the textile industry is imported. Cotton made up 30 per cent of total textile and garment imports in 1992. Indonesia already sources almost all of its artificial fibre needs locally. There is only a 10 per cent tariff on imports of polyester staple fibre and filament yarn. However, most inputs into polyester production were imported duty free, so the effective rate of tariff protection was over 20 per cent.[10] Despite this protection, fierce import competition in the early 1990s kept prices low.

In the case of polyester filament yarn, which makes up half of Indonesian artificial fibre output, domestic production is enough to meet domestic needs; there are minimal imports, and an export surplus. In polyester staple fibre, which provides a third of the domestic textile industry demand for artificial fibre, domestic production meets some 85 per cent of domestic needs. The domestic polyester industry in 1993 was hit by a world surplus caused by China temporarily halting its imports. Korean polyester exports to Indonesia rose sharply, causing prices of polyester filament yarn almost to halve during the course of 1993, and in 1994 prices were slow to rise to their former level. Profits of polyester firms in the domestic industry were sharply reduced.

Fabrics

Fabric exports were almost evenly divided in volume terms between those exported directly and those exported indirectly as garments. Domestic sourcing of fabrics was inhibited by the poor quality of many local cotton fabrics, and it was also made difficult by problems in reclaiming VAT (discussed below). Direct exports of fabrics in the early 1990s were being sold predominantly to non-quota markets; less than a third was sold to the US and Europe, and about a quarter to ASEAN. Exports of grey cloth (i.e. unfinished fabric) were being driven in the 1990s by low prices on the Indonesian domestic market; these low prices were caused by domestic overproduction and lack of domestic finishing capacity rather than by import competition. Although woven fabric exports rose rapidly in the 1980s, exports had been a major source of growth for the subsector as far back as the mid-1970s (Hill, 1991: 106).

Despite import duties on fabrics of 25–35 per cent, there was no consistent relation between domestic prices and import prices (according to interviewees). The relation between domestic and world prices would fluctuate according to the state of the world market and domestic supply, such that at times higher prices could be obtained on the export market. A wide range of interviewees suggested that the protection had not raised the domestic fabric prices they paid by the full amount of the tariff (that is, by 25–35 per cent).[11] The relation between world price and domestic price varied over time, and between fabrics, according to the state of domestic and world market competition. World prices for low-end market synthetic fabrics were kept down by Korean and Taiwanese competition in world markets; this influenced the price at which domestic producers could sell to exporters. Domestic fabric prices were also kept down by oversupply from domestic mills following the great expansion of the industry in the early 1990s, and allowing imports might well not have lowered them further.

Producers also preferred to export because overseas customers pay more promptly, using letters of credit; domestic customers require long periods of credit, the cost of which the supplier normally adds to the price. The greater ease of obtaining payment on the export market has not only been a strong incentive to export grey cloth, where domestic prices were already low in relation to world prices, but also to export finished fabric, where domestic prices held up better in relation to world prices. Most finished fabrics sold to the domestic market were cotton prints, whereas Indonesia's export position was stronger in fabrics of cotton/polyester mixes. Indonesia finds it difficult to compete with China and Pakistan in pure cotton fabric, and most of the cotton fabrics sold on the domestic market would not be of high enough quality for export. For fabric producers, there was access to most inputs at prices close to world prices. Synthetic yarns carried a low (10 per cent) duty, but imports were sometimes sold at below the cost of local producers (who claimed 'dumping'). This was a powerful force keeping prices low.

The year 1993 was a bad year for fabric exporters, even for good quality fabrics (where polyester/cotton mixes are most common). One producer explained that there had been strong competition from China at prices that he felt were inexplicable by normal economic criteria.

Garments

The garment industry has been helped in its expansion by foreign investment, particularly from Hong Kong. These are firms which have close contacts with international buyers, and who have reputations for being able to provide quality and keep to delivery schedules. As costs have risen in Hong Kong, Indonesia has increased its exports.

Many garment exporters interviewed in 1994 regarded Indonesian garment production as facing serious difficulties, despite its previously rapid export expansion. Some exporting companies had closed. Hong Kong investors said that their garment factories in China were making profits while their Indonesian operations were struggling to survive. International buyers had been reducing their purchases in Indonesia. One well-known buying group said they had downgraded Indonesia from their number two Asian supplier of garments to their number three, in favour of Sri Lanka; they sourced most from China, despite worries about China's political instability in future. Lower wage countries such as Bangladesh and Sri Lanka were becoming significant players in world textile exports, though both had problems of political instability.

International buyers of garments in 1994 were worried because:

- In comparison to China, Indonesian labour productivity was low in relation to real wages. A Hong Kong investor said that in his factory a worker with the same equipment could make eight or nine pieces of a garment in a day, whereas in China his company's factories got about 15 pieces per worker per day. Real wages were broadly similar between southern China and Indonesia. However, producers did like the Indonesian government's system of pre-announcing increases of the minimum wage at known times. This system allowed them to predict increases in cost.
- There were complaints by producers that MFA export quotas were allocated on the basis of influence rather than capacity to export. Some quota recipients were said to have had no productive capacity, and simply obtained quotas to resell. It was recognised, though, that the situation had eased from 1993.
- There were complaints from producers that electricity prices had risen. However, electricity in fact was only a very minor cost item.
- More important, their suppliers were having serious problems with Bapeksta.

Export promoting trade arrangements for garments   For garment producers, access to imported inputs at world prices was important, since fabrics carried an import duty of 25–35 per cent. For fabric and yarn producers, access to imported inputs was far less of a problem. Inputs for yarn and fabrics generally carried low or zero rates of import duty. Even where there were import duties, domestic competition often kept domestic prices near to world prices.

There was considerable dissatisfaction among garment firms about the operation of Bapeksta's import duty exemptions and drawbacks, and the inspections associated with them. Interestingly though – and in contrast – most export shoe companies interviewed thought Bapeksta was working satisfactorily. Garment interviewees thought the difference between them and the shoe producers was probably due to the more frequent input changes in garments, which varied with each order and were impossible to specify in advance. Exporters were aware that the government had to counter 'fictitious exports', but many commented to the effect that 'government penalises honest exporters'.

For exporters having difficulties with Bapeksta, EPTE status became an alternative from 1993. However, some exporters felt it would be difficult to obtain. Others feared EPTE status, since the EPTE scheme is administered by Customs, although there were no complaints from any EPTE company. Bonded zones were perceived by firms outside them as having locational disadvantages such as difficulties in obtaining labour, high land costs, and high official (and unofficial) fees.

Where fabrics in Indonesia were available in export quality – denim often was given as an example – domestic sourcing was seriously impeded by difficulties with VAT. In principle, a company could reclaim VAT paid on a domestic input into an exported good. In practice, obtaining a refund was taking a year or more. For a manufacturer of, say, jeans, where fabric costs are equivalent to almost half of the export price, such delays were a heavy drain on working capital, which was financed at high interest rates in Indonesia. It would have been useful if export-oriented firms using Bapeksta could have been given the same exemption from VAT on domestic purchases as given to firms with EPTE status and those in bonded zones. For indirect exporters, import duty drawbacks were available in principle; in practice they were virtually impossible to claim. This exemption was less important for domestic producers of fabric since cotton imports were duty free and synthetic yarn imports subject to only 10 per cent duty.

In sum, the Indonesian government needed to provide garment export companies with a more competitive environment in which to work. Companies needed to be given better access to traded inputs at world prices, and they needed to be able to choose between sourcing inputs locally or through imports, without their decisions being distorted by institutional problems such as VAT refunds. They also needed a competitive exchange rate to be maintained; the appreciation of the rupiah in relation to the US dollar in the mid-1990s, where competitors' currencies were not appreciating similarly, was damaging export competitiveness.

3.2 Footwear

Sports shoes comprised the bulk of Indonesia's footwear exports: 74 per cent of the dollar value of shoe exports in 1993, little changed from a 1989 figure of 77 per cent. The US remained overwhelmingly the most important market, as it had been since the late 1980s, as production shifted towards the more expensive brands popular in the USA such as Nike, Reebok and Adidas. The top ten brands probably accounted for over two-thirds of sports shoe sales. Indonesian production was highly export-oriented, despite a large, though low income, population to provide a market.

Indonesia's rapid expansion of shoe exports had raised it to the world's seventh largest exporter by 1993, although it lagged far behind China and Italy in total world exports of shoes, with world market share of only 4 per cent. The world footwear market is highly segmented, however. Italy, producing upmarket fashion shoes, is not a competitor to Indonesia; nor at present are Brazil, Spain and Portugal, which make leather shoes. Indonesia's main competition comes from China. In the top end sports shoe market, Indonesia and China each accounted for nearly a third of world sales. We focus here mainly on the top-end branded sports shoe sector, the most important for Indonesian exports.

The rapid growth in Indonesia's exports of top-end sports footwear has been the result of a rise in Indonesia's share of international buyers' worldwide sourcing of major brand-name sports shoes. This sourcing is mainly from Asia. China, Indonesia and Thailand are the main suppliers, though there is also still some purchasing from Korea and Taiwan. The growth of the industry in Indonesia, as in other Asian countries, has been driven by the migration of shoe manufacturers from Korea and, to a lesser extent, from Taiwan. Korean and Taiwanese joint ventures in Indonesia are the core of this export industry.

Buyers are influenced in their sourcing decisions not only by cost but also by the wish to diversify to avoid risks from political instability and protectionist threats against particular countries. In the top-end market this has led to some diversion away from China. Buyers in the early 1990s feared political instability in China after the death of Deng Xiaoping, even though, in the event, these fears proved unfounded. Indonesia was the main beneficiary of these fears, and was built up to equal China as the buyers' largest source of branded sports shoes. There were signs by 1993–94 that this expansion was reaching a peak. One top end buyer in 1994 said Indonesia's share of its worldwide supply was already at a maximum at about one-third, and they were looking for growth of supply elsewhere. For many buyers, the third largest supplier was Thailand, and little growth was planned from there because of its high wage levels compared to other countries in the region.

In the top end brands, then, Indonesia was starting to face a situation where it could not increase its share of the world production. It was in the hands of the buyers of the major brands, and had to depend on the growth of world demand together with any increases in market share the top brands could achieve. The really high value production of Korea and Taiwan was unlikely to migrate to Indonesia quickly. This high grade production was seen by the Taiwanese and Koreans as a way of maintaining their technological lead. These models require frequent investment in tooling to make high-tech items like transparent air soles. Taiwan keeps its costs down by buying in uppers ready stitched from China, which halves the labour requirements per shoe compared to an Indonesian factory.

At the same time as top-end sports shoe exports boomed, Indonesia was losing market share in lower- and medium-grade footwear exports. International buyers of these cheaper products (such as large discount retail chains) had switched to lower-cost sources, particularly to China. Here, cost differences are more important than in the more expensive ranges, where there are large mark-ups. The footwear industry has thus experienced simultaneously an expansion based on a relatively small number of firms – the two largest top-end buyers have less than 25 Indonesian suppliers between them – and many factory closures.

Exports by companies oriented towards the local market

The Indonesian shoe industry was dualistic in the sense that most of the companies making top-end sports shoes for export did not sell to the domestic market, and most companies selling in the protected domestic market (tariffs were 30–40 per cent) did not export. Most of the exporting companies, especially at the top end, were foreign investors. Even the better known Indonesian domestic brands had difficulty in establishing themselves overseas. Firms who succeed in moving from the domestic market to exports would depend on orders for buyers' brands. Buyer contacts are important sources of improving product design. Local firms were helped, however, by the availability on the open market of Taiwanese and Korean managers and supervisory staff, who had migrated to Indonesia as their home shoe factories closed. These people could help local firms use best practice technology and achieve international standards of quality control.

Local supply of footwear components

Most firms producing for the local market used local components. Protection on the wide range of shoe components averaged at least 15 per cent in 1994. The degree of domestic competition in components appeared to be less than in footwear, and there was less tariff redundancy. Domestic component producers often could not produce components of a quality suitable for export, however. Economic reform in the component industry was thus an important factor in increasing competitiveness.

Increasing the proportion of materials sourced in Indonesia could raise value added in export shoe production considerably. For a typical top-end export sports shoe, materials and components are about 60 per cent of the ex-factory price. In 1994, some 70–80 per cent of these inputs were imported, equivalent to almost half of the export value of the shoe.

For a sports shoe exporter, local sourcing of materials would have many potential advantages:

- It speeds turnaround time. This is important in an industry where the time from order to dispatch is about three months;
- It aids product development if suppliers are near at hand to consult;
- It saves on cost of transport;
- It avoids customs delays for crucial items and the accompanying unofficial payments.

International buyers, in both the top and medium ranges of the sports shoe market, exercise tight control over materials sourcing. Exporters are often instructed to buy particular items from particular companies. This is important in quality control. Top-end buyers in 1994 claimed that they were encouraging local sourcing by their shoe suppliers, and urging them to form strategic alliances with component makers.

The experience of China in component supply for sports shoes is instructive. According to a top-end international buyer, local sourcing of materials and components rose within a five year period from only 5 per cent of materials supplied (simple items like boxes and shoelaces) to 70–80 per cent. Like the expansion of Chinese sports shoe exports, export-quality component supply in China was developed by inward Taiwanese investment. Component suppliers followed their customers. In Indonesia, a similar trend was starting in the early 1990s. The labour cost differential between Taiwan and China (or Indonesia) was less of an incentive to migrate than in footwear, since component production is less labour-intensive, but the differential is not insignificant. One Taiwanese component investor in Indonesia making moulds, explained that, with low wages in Indonesia, he could manufacture for less than a third of the cost of Taiwan. He felt that component manufacture in China had developed to the point where competition had pushed component prices so low that he could make more profit in Indonesia. He had been encouraged by the knowledge that some of his old customers from Taiwan had set up in Indonesia, and he expected orders. This company was making moulds, a crucial capital replacement input in shoe manufacture. A customer said at interview that they were proposing a joint venture with him, with their buyer's encouragement. Similar stories have emerged from interviews with Korean shoe manufacturers, who said 10–20 Korean component makers were in the process of locating in Indonesia. Foreign investment approvals showed that shoe component investment was gathering momentum in Indonesia: 1993 approvals were $17.8 million, an amount equal to three-quarters of the size of the foreign investment approvals in footwear.

Many firms interviewed spoke of the deterrent to buying inputs locally which resulted from difficulties in reclaiming the VAT paid on domestic purchases. Where an exporter has substantial local sales, VAT paid on domestic components could be set against VAT liabilities on domestic sales; but firms orientated mainly to export sometimes experienced delays in VAT reclaims of a year or more. This imposed significant costs in terms of working capital. EPTE status, by exempting firms from VAT, encouraged local sourcing.

Export promoting trade arrangements for footwear

Indonesia's shoe exports, like those of other sectors, had been stimulated by offering the exporters free trade access to imported inputs via duty drawbacks/exemptions through Bapeksta, Export Processing Zones (EPZs) and EPTEs. The footwear companies interviewed had mainly been using Bapeksta. In general they felt satisfied with its operation, particularly those with 'white list' (duty exemption) status. The Footwear Manufacturers Association, APRISINDO, was praised by manufacturers for its effective representations to Bapeksta on their behalf.

3.3   Electronics Exports

While Indonesia was developing its electronics exports in the early 1990s, electronics in the world economy had been the fastest growing industrial sector. Value added in world electronics production was growing in the early 1990s at about 6 per cent a year, almost double the rate of growth of real GDP (3.1 per cent), and much faster than the growth in manufacturing value added (3.8 per cent). The growth in world electronics production was associated not only with the growth of demand for consumer electronics, but with the increased application of electronics to manufacturing production and to information processing. The increased use of electronics in automobiles has been an important source of demand (Wellenius, Miller and Dahlman 1993).

Indonesia's export opportunities in electronics products were heavily con-ditioned by rapid changes in the world electronics industry. These changes included increased worldwide sourcing of components, shortening product cycles, increased capital intensity of production, and increased quality re-quirements even for low-end products. Indonesia came late to electronics exporting, and its electronics industry was therefore likely to develop in a somewhat different way from those of other South East Asian countries which started earlier.

Indonesia's electronics industry has lagged considerably behind that of other ASEAN countries. Its shares of electronics in production value added and in exports were lower than the other countries. In addition, in the early 1990s Indonesia was the only country in ASEAN (other than Brunei) to have had gross export earnings in electronics which were smaller than its gross imports. A gross export surplus in electronics is not necessarily desirable. A country might be a world-class exporter of, say, televisions, and import telecommunications equipment; such an intra-industry trade pattern would give it gains from specialisation. Nevertheless, other ASEAN countries have developed an export surplus by reducing the import content of consumer and industrial electronics and increasing the range of their consumer and indus-trial electronics exports, and Indonesia looks set to follow a similar path.

Consumer electronics accounts for a larger proportion of Indonesia's ex-ports than in the rest of ASEAN. The share of industrial electronics in total electronics exports is smaller in Indonesia, and the share of components is very much smaller. Indonesia's exports have grown out of its earlier pattern of import substitution. In 1992 televisions were the largest single export item, generating 13 per cent of electronics export earnings. By 1994, however, VCRs had overtaken TVs, and there has also been a growth in telecommuni-cations equipment. Consumer electronics represents a more usual point of entry for countries new to the industry, and in principle, exports could build on the experience of producing for the domestic market. In practice, however, there were several problems apparent in the early 1990s:

- Years of high effective protection had left the Indonesian domestic industry with high costs and often outmoded equipment.
- A related issue was that overseas consumers were demanding high quality even in low-end products, low price no longer being a substi-tute for good quality. Indonesian domestic producers required new investment to reach these standards.
- Technical change had reduced labour requirements, while Indonesian production was rather labour-intensive.
- Indonesia lacked domestic firms capable of supplying parts to final producers. Although no country can expect to operate a fully integrated

electronics industry, the lack of a domestic supplier base impedes efficient manufacturing based on just-in-time delivery and close buyer-supplier relations. A hopeful sign was a strong indication, according to the KIET (1994) survey, that component producers in Korea were showing interest in relocating overseas to follow major producers of consumer electronics who relocated in the 1980s.

- There still appeared to be negative effective protection on some components, which discouraged the development of their production locally. This resulted from the fact that official policy to give component makers exemption from import duties on their raw materials was not being universally applied.

Export promoting trade arrangements for electronics producers
For exporters of final electronics products, difficulties with Bapeksta in 1994 were causing major problems because of the large number of components and the short turnaround times required for orders. Exporters in 1994 were paying import duties averaging only 5 per cent on components, though some duties had already been reduced to zero. However, the delays caused by reclaiming even low duty payments damaged electronics export prospects, and such damage counted strongly against any revenue obtained from duties on components destined for products sold domestically. EPTE status was appreciated by the companies that secured it. Although it was early to judge in 1994, the new EPTE.PE arrangement appeared to be an effective way of encouraging domestic sourcing of inputs and helping firms oriented to the domestic market to develop exports.

4   THE EXPORT SLOWDOWN

Some slowdown in textile, garment and footwear exports was to be expected after the explosive growth of the late 1980s and early 1990s, but the slowdown which started in 1992–93 also reflected a more fundamental loss of export competitiveness, particularly in textiles and garments. Policy changes, to be discussed in the next section, could have redressed this to some extent. There were three special reasons for the slowdown which were outside Indonesia's control:

- Unfilled MFA quotas had allowed rapid expansion of textile and garment exports. This growth necessarily slackened once those quotas were filled, which they were by the early 1990s. The sharp slowdown in 1993 was mainly a result of falling prices caused by increased competition, though stagnation in export volumes also played a role.

- Export growth was facilitated in the late 1980s by the relocation of Taiwanese, Korean and Hong Kong producers, as a result of their rising wages and loss of Generalised System of Preferences (GSP) privileges,[12] and following the appreciation of the Taiwanese and Korean currencies. These relocations were approaching completion by the mid-1990s, although in footwear there was still scope for the relocation of Korean and Taiwanese component production.
- The world recession in the early 1990s slowed the growth of demand.

During the recession, not only did Indonesia's export growth slacken, but the country lost market share, at least in textiles and garments. Although exports of textiles, garments and footwear from Malaysia and Thailand also slowed to the growth rate (5–6 per cent) of Indonesia's in 1993, they were relatively high wage countries, which could have been expected to lose their comparative advantage in such labour-intensive products. As growth in the world economy accelerated in 1994, Indonesian textiles and garment makers did not experience the growth in orders that economic recovery in America and Europe would have led them to expect. In contrast, China's textile and garment exports grew rapidly.

In 1994, then, there was a danger that foreign investors and international buyers in textiles and garments would reduce their involvement in Indonesia in favour of locations where the total costs of operation were lower. Although Indonesia was likely to move away from textile and garment exporting in the longer term in favour of higher value-added exports, what was at risk was the premature loss of those exports. The loss of textile and garment foreign exchange earnings could not have been replaced by sufficient expansion in other exports, even electronics. The loss of such labour-intensive exports would also have damaged employment. Increases in export quotas in the US and Europe during the phasing out of the Multi-Fibre Arrangement would increase the competition faced by Indonesia in quota markets. In non-quota markets competition was already intense, and these markets were where Indonesia was losing market share.

Footwear exports were not so much in danger as textiles and garments, although their growth had slowed. Indonesian exporters were well established and highly competitive in top-end sports shoes, which constituted the bulk of shoe exports. There was a risk, though, of further loss of market share in low-end shoe exports, where there was strong competition from China. Although Indonesia's share of the world market for top-end sports shoes was near its peak, it was still possible that the *net* exports of footwear could achieve high average annual growth through a rise in domestic content.

Electronics exports in late 1994 had grown at 47 per cent during the previous 12 months, and were expected to continue to achieve rapid growth.

However, their import content was very high, and much more could be done to raise their net export earnings. This was especially important if textiles and garments were to continue to perform poorly.

5   POLICY ISSUES

Although, as mentioned, some reasons for the slowdown were global, other problems could have been resolved by policy interventions. These related mainly to trade taxes and mechanisms for refunding duty paid.

5.1   Difficulties Experienced by Exporters and Indirect Exporters in Obtaining Duty Free Access to Imported Inputs

It would have been desirable to restore the former function of facilitating exports to the duty drawback and rebate system administered through Bapeksta, and to reduce its role in auditing to prevent fraud (diverting to the domestic market goods imported duty free as inputs for exports). Auditing needed to be done far more selectively. Auditing for EPTE and bonded zone firms also needed to be selective. It would also have been desirable to offer Bapeksta facilities to indirect exporters, which in practice they could not obtain in the early 1990s.

5.2   Distortions in the Choice Between Domestic and Imported Inputs Caused by Delays in Securing Refunds of VAT on Domestically Purchased Inputs

It would have been desirable to extend to all exporters the VAT exemption given only to firms in bonded zones and with EPTE status.

5.3   Distortions in the Tariff Structure

It would have been desirable to remove the tariffs on imports of exportable products over (say) a five-year period. These tariffs were reducing the incentives to improve product quality, although this protection in the past had had some positive effects on exports.[13] It would have been desirable to remove progressively (say over five years) the tariffs on imported inputs for textiles, garments and footwear. Tariffs on imports of electronic components, where import duty payments averaged about 5 per cent, could have been removed immediately. It would have been useful to remove duties on raw material inputs into electronic component manufacture. These duties were discouraging investment in the production of components. The evidence from interviews was that not all eligible companies were obtaining exemption.

5.4 Various Cost Issues

These included wages growing faster than labour productivity, exchange rate appreciation, and the imposition of unofficial payments. The solution to low labour productivity lay mainly in the hands of exporting companies themselves, but the government could help in the longer term by improving education and training. Stopping increases in the minimum wage was not the answer to Indonesia's export problems, but increases should be kept in line with productivity gains. Keeping the exchange rate competitive was important. Although Indonesia's real effective exchange was depreciating in 1994 and into 1995, from then on, until the start of the 1997 Asian crisis, it appreciated somewhat (IMF, 1997: 8). As Indonesia was becoming a more open economy, with more traders operating on very competitive markets, the issue of unofficial payments was important too. Steps to reduce these payments would have increased the competitiveness of export companies.

6 CONCLUSIONS

This chapter has traced the rapid rise in Indonesian manufacturing exports between the mid-1980s and the early 1990s, using 1994 as a reference point. Indonesia's manufactures exporting started with labour-intensive products – garments and footwear – together with textiles, which are somewhat less labour-intensive. Electronic assembly followed soon after. This is a typical pattern through which developing countries have participated in globalisation, but what is striking is the sheer speed of the transformation.

Footwear exports represent the grafting of an export-oriented sector on to the Indonesian economy through inward investment. It is an archetypal case of the so-called *flying geese* pattern of development in Asia, whereby countries losing comparative advantage in a labour-intensive industry transfer that industry to a country with lower wages (Blomqvist, 1996). In this case, the investment came mainly from Korea and Taiwan. Such export production is highly dependent on international buyers – in this case the companies which market branded sports shoes – which spread sourcing over several countries to reduce risk. Once the relocation to Indonesia had taken place to the extent suggested by the international buyers, export expansion would naturally reach a plateau, where further growth would depend on total market expansion. Even the existing level of exports would then depend on the buyers' continued willingness to source from Indonesia. China has been Indonesia's main

competitor for footwear (and most other labour-intensive industry) investment, and Indonesia would run the risk of the investment moving out of the
country if labour costs rose, or if the investment climate deteriorated (as it did
sharply during the Asian crisis). The efficiency of the export-promoting trade
regime is an important part of that climate.

At first sight, garment exporting from Indonesia seems like a grafted-on
sector, similar to footwear. However, unlike footwear, where there was little
foreign investment in the domestic sector and where the domestic sector did
little exporting, Indonesia had had substantial foreign investment in textiles
for domestic production. Such import-substituting investment laid the basis
for the subsequent exporting of textiles. Similarly, electronics exporting also
grew partly out of a move to export orientation by previously import-substituting foreign investors. As of 1997, prior to the start of the Asian crisis, the
expansion of electronics exports had not reached a plateau similar to that of
the other export industries.

One of the most important factors in Indonesia's export boom – besides the
establishment of a realistic real exchange rate and the liberalising of inward
investment regulations – was the efficiency of the country's export promoting
trade regime. Although Indonesian EPZs had already been established for more
than a decade, it was the setting up in 1986 of what became Bapeksta that was
the key to the export expansion. In the early 1990s, EPZs were perceived by
exporters as having many cost and administrative problems. This helps to
explain why the EPZs' earlier presence did not kick start a manufactures export
drive, although the development in the 1990s of the Batam EPZ does seems to
have facilitated electronics exporting (Lindblad, 1997: 16). An alternative export facilitating arrangement EPTE which was given to individual firms, provided
some competition for Bapeksta, in a similar fashion to that in which EPZs had
to compete with Bapeksta to attract firms to use their facilities. This competition improved efficiency, especially since Bapeksta and the EPTE facility were
run by different agencies. One reason for the export slowdown over the 1992–
94 period in garments was that Bapeksta was starting to shift its function from
export facilitating to auditing against fraud (inputs imported duty free being
resold on the protected domestic market). An interesting contrast is China,
which also had a very successful export promoting trade regime, based on
export processing arrangements made available to individual exporting companies. China seemed to be more concerned with export facilitation rather than
auditing for fraud. One consequence was China's rapid expansion of exports –
becoming the world's largest exporter of garments, for example – but another
was that actual import duty collection was only a small fraction of the notional
duty on imports (World Bank, 1994).

Export processing facilities, like EPZs and Bapeksta, necessarily encourage exporting firms to buy inputs on the international market rather than

locally. This counteracts the anti-export bias generated by the price of those inputs being high on the local market because they receive tariff protection, and generates pressure on local suppliers to cut prices if they wish to supply the export sector. However, in Indonesia, a shift in VAT rebates from Bapeksta to the tax authorities caused delays in VAT refunds on domestic purchases, and so distorted exporters' choice away from local purchases of inputs. In the case of garments, inputs in the form of fabric could also be exported directly, so a 'deepening' of the garment production structure (that is, increased local purchases) would not necessarily have raised total export earnings. In the case of footwear, local components suppliers were often both unable and unwilling to service the export sector, but by 1994 a trend was strongly in evidence that small suppliers of components from Korea and Taiwan were starting to relocate themselves to Indonesia.

The Asian crisis caused a sharp fall in Indonesia's main manufacturing exports (see Figure 5.1). Although exporters benefited from the large depreciation of the rupiah at that time, which raised the domestic currency price of their exports, they faced higher costs for imported inputs. A major reason for the decline appears to have been difficulties faced by exporters in getting credit for imported inputs. Manufacturing exports fell further in 1998, although there was some recovery in 1999 (Booth, 1999: 15–16). One recent change was the abolition of import duty exemptions (Fane, 2000: 27), thus weakening the export facilitating function of Bapeksta, and forcing exporters into seeking drawbacks instead.

The Asian crisis, it appears, compounded a slowdown in export growth that had already begun. The analysis of the slowdown presented here illustrates the importance of keeping government export promotion arrangements running smoothly.

NOTES

1. The chapter does not consider plywood, another major non-oil export, and from now on we do not define it as a manufacture. Plywood is something of a special case, and exports were developed in part in response to an export ban on logs. Hill (1996: 81), cited previously in the text, presumably does include plywood as a manufactured export.
2. Such backward integration would increase foreign exchange earnings in an industry by raising the ratio of net to gross exports.
3. See Hill (1990) and Hill (1996, chs 5 and 6). A useful short summary is given by Bevan *et al.* (1999: 272–9). The account here draws heavily on Hill (1996).
4. From now on, to avoid repetition, all generalisations will refer to the period *before* the onset of the 1997–98 Asian crisis, unless otherwise stated or obvious from the context.
5. Using the UN index of manufactured export (dollar) unit values of industrial countries as the deflator. This gives a measure of the real purchasing power of Indonesia's exports.
6. There is no generally accepted definition of 'electronics'. The broad category of Electrical Machines and Appliances (SITC 75–77) is sufficient for our purposes.

7. Note that the slowdown in footwear exports is apparent only when the series is deflated. Footwear exports continued to rise in terms of *current* dollars.
8. See Gereffi (1992) on footwear global commodity chains, and Gereffi (1994 and 1999) on garment chains.
9. Some 85 per cent of fabric in Indonesia is produced by weaving. The rest is knitted. See *Indonesian Commercial Newsletter*, 26 July 1993.
10. According to one producer, tradeable raw materials represent at least half of output value. To the extent that tradeable inputs are significantly greater than 50 per cent, the ERP will be greater than 20 per cent, with a 10 per cent tariff on output and no tariffs on inputs.
11. That is, there was tariff redundancy. Also, it is probable that fabric producers offered lower prices to exporters, who had duty free import privileges, than to domestic customers, in the belief that the exporters were unlikely to resell on the domestic market in sufficient quantities to damage the fabric producers' sales.
12. The issue here is that Asian NICs were deemed to have 'graduated' out of the developing country status necessary to receive import preferences under developed countries' Generalised System of Preferences schemes.
13. This issue is discussed briefly with regard to Indonesian textile exports, compared to textile exports from Zimbabwe and Nigeria, in Thoburn (2000).

REFERENCES

Bevan, D., P. Collier and J. Gunning (1999), *The Political Economy of Poverty, Equity and Growth: Nigeria and Indonesia*, New York: Oxford University Press for the World Bank.

Blomqvist, H. (1996), 'The "flying geese" model of regional development: a constructive interpretation', *Journal of the Asia Pacific Economy*, **1**(2), pp. 215–31.

Booth, A. (1999), 'Survey of recent developments', *Bulletin of Indonesian Economic Studies*, **35**(3), pp. 3–38.

Chapman, R. (1992), 'Indonesia trade reform in close-up: the steel and footwear experiences', *Bulletin of Indonesian Economic Studies*, **28**(1), pp. 67–84.

Fane, G. (2000), 'Survey of recent developments', *Bulletin of Indonesian Economic Studies*, **36**(1), pp. 13–44.

Gereffi, G. (1992), 'New realities of industrial development in East Asia and Latin America: global, national and regional trends', in R. Applebaum and J. Henderson (eds), *State and Development in the Asia Pacific Rim*, London: Sage.

Gereffi, G. (1994), 'The organisation of buyer-driven global commodity chains and how US retailers shape overseas production networks', in G. Gereffi and M. Korzaniewiez (eds), *Commodity Chains and Global Capitalism*, Westport, CT: Praeger.

Gereffi, G. (1999), 'International trade and industrial upgrading in the apparel commodity chain', *Journal of International Economics*, **48**, pp. 37–70.

Hill, H. (1990), 'Indonesia: export promotion after the oil boom', in C. Milner (ed.), *Export Promotion Strategies: Theory and Evidence from Developing Countries*, London: Harvester Wheatsheaf.

Hill, H. (1991), 'The emperor's new clothes can now be made in Indonesia', *Bulletin of Indonesian Economic Studies*, **27**(3), pp. 89–127.

Hill, H. (1996), *The Indonesian Economy since 1966: South East Asia's Emerging Giant*, Cambridge: Cambridge University Press.

IMF (1997), *World Economic Outlook, Interim Assessment*, December, Washington, DC: International Monetary Fund.

James, W.E. (1995), 'Survey of recent developments', *Bulletin of Indonesian Economic Studies*, **31**(3), pp. 3–38.

KIET (1994), *Investment Demand of the Asian Electronics Industry*, Korea Institute of Industrial Economics and Trade.

Lindblad, J.T. (1997), 'Survey of recent developments', *Bulletin of Indonesian Economic Studies*, **33**(3), pp. 3–33.

Lindblad, J.T. (2000), 'Korean investment in Indonesia: survey and appraisal', *Bulletin of Indonesian Economic Studies*, **36**(1), pp. 167–84.

Pangestu, M. and I.J. Aziz (1994), 'Survey of recent developments', *Bulletin of Indonesian Economic Studies*, **30**(2), pp. 3–47.

Thee, K.W. (1991), 'The surge of Asian NIC investment into Indonesia', *Bulletin of Indonesian Economic Studies*, **27**(3), pp. 55–88.

Thee. K.W. (1999), 'Export-oriented industrialisation and foreign direct investment in the ASEAN countries' (http://www.unu.edu/hq/academic/Pg_area4/Thee.html).

Thoburn, J.T. (2000), 'Could import protection drive manufacturing exports in Africa?', *Discussion Paper no. 85*, Graduate School of International Development, University of Nagoya, Japan, March.

Warr, P.G. (1983), 'The Jakarta export processing zone: benefits and costs', *Bulletin of Indonesian Economic Studies*, **20**, pp. 28–49.

Wellenius, B., A. Miller and C.J. Dahlman (eds) (1993), *Developing the Electronics Industry*, Washington, DC: World Bank Symposium.

World Bank (1994), *China: Foreign Trade Reform*, Washington, DC: World Bank.

6. Trade liberalisation and export diversification in Nepal

Kishor Sharma and Oliver Morrissey

1 INTRODUCTION

Nepal commenced trade liberalisation in the mid-1980s, intending to arrest the deteriorating macroeconomic performance brought about by the import substitution (IS) policy of the previous three decades. The liberalisation programme included substantial cuts in tariffs and non-tariff barriers (NTBs), devaluation of the Nepalese rupee, deregulation of marketing of primary products and liberalisation of investment policies, including foreign investment and banking sector reform. Given the country's landlocked position and open border with India, such that it was economically dependent on India, Nepal pursued only gradual liberalisation until after the Indian economy was substantially liberalised in the early 1990s. Consequently, the most important reforms were not implemented until 1992 and later.

The purpose of this chapter is to examine the impact of liberalisation on export growth and diversification in Nepal, one of the least developed countries. Being landlocked, the goods that Nepal wants to import or export must pass through India or be flown in by air (usually too costly). Although a road link with China exists, extensive trade contacts are inhibited by the high cost and seasonal nature of road transport through the Himalayas. There is no restriction on the movement of people along the 800 mile long open border between Nepal and India. Like many landlocked countries, Nepal also experiences high transport costs in its trade with overseas countries. Trade and transit facilities, including port facilities offered by India, play a significant role in making Nepal's industrial and export sector viable. Thus, the case of Nepal is particularly interesting.

The chapter is organised as follows. General issues and evidence relating to the impact of trade liberalisation are briefly outlined in Section 2. The nature of the trade policy regime and the extent of trade liberalisation in Nepal are discussed in Section 3. Section 4 documents the effects of liberalisation on export diversification and growth in Nepal, especially in manufacturing. The chapter concludes with some comments in Section 5, which compares the Nepalese experience to that of other low-income countries.

2 TRADE LIBERALISATION: SOME ISSUES AND EVIDENCE

Trade liberalisation refers essentially to the removal of restrictions, tariffs and NTBs on imports. By reducing protection, such reforms reduce discrimination against exports even in the absence of direct export promotion measures. The expected outcome is that economic growth, and especially exports, will be increased (Greenaway and Morrissey, 1994). The reduced bias against exports, following import liberalisation, may not be sufficient in itself to encourage investors. Consequently, investment incentives are often offered also. This can be very important to encourage a shift of resources into previously neglected activities, i.e. production (especially export) diversification.

The basic objective of trade reform is to remove the bias against exports and the anticipated beneficial effect is that exports will increase and, in turn, fuel economic growth. However, trade policy alone is not the only constraint on exports. For landlocked countries such as Nepal, transport costs will be high and are likely to be a major constraint on exports. For example, Milner *et al.* (2000) demonstrate that transport costs represent a high implicit tax on Ugandan exporters, often higher than the implicit tax associated with import protection (especially when the latter is reduced following liberalisation). As many infrastructure and institutional constraints exist, and are likely to be greater in low-income countries, one may not observe a quick export response to trade liberalisation.

There may also be costs associated with import liberalisation. The reduction of tariffs and removal of NTBs exposes domestic firms to increased competition from imports. If years of protection have rendered domestic firms inefficient, they will be unable to withstand such competition. However, Bennell (1998), in an African context finds that liberalisation does not appear to have had an adverse effect on the manufacturing sector in sub-Saharan African countries in general, although some countries experienced a decline in output. In this chapter we concentrate on the export response of Nepalese manufacturing enterprises, but can note that domestic production does not appear to have suffered unduly.

3   THE TRADE POLICY REGIME IN NEPAL

Prior to the 1950s, Nepal effectively had a free trade policy. Import substitution (IS) and trade protection were introduced in the economic plan of 1956. The IS policy was pursued to raise the standard of living through industrialisation, and included import restrictions, export regulations, industrial licensing and the management of large scale industries in the public sector. As the access to imported inputs and technologies was limited because of foreign exchange regulations and import licenses, there was a bias against exports. This contributed to a lacklustre export performance, a rise in imports, and huge deficits in the current account and government fiscal operations that persisted into the 1980s.[1] The other consequences of the IS policy were the black market in foreign currencies, overvaluation of exports and under-invoicing of imports. Clearly, the IS strategy promoted rent-seeking activities and discouraged exports.

To overcome the bias against exports, the government introduced several measures. The first was introduced in 1962 and was known as the Exporters Exchange Entitlement (EEE) scheme. The scheme allowed overseas exporters (to countries other than India) a bonus in the form of convertible currency that could be used to import a wide range of goods, including intermediate inputs and technologies. It was expected that the scheme would raise the export capability of the country and increase access to imports not available from India (or available only at a very high price). The scheme failed to achieve these objectives as it simply diverted Nepal's foreign trade from India to overseas countries.[2]

Consequentially, there was a tremendous increase in foreign exchange earnings during the period of the scheme (1962–78). However, it was not brought about by an increase in the export capability of the economy, as export orientation, measured as the export/GDP ratio, was fairly constant (between 5–6 per cent) during the period of the scheme. This indicates that the EEE scheme diverted Nepal's exports from India to overseas countries because of attractive export incentives.[3] The EEE scheme was replaced by the Dual Exchange Rate (DER) system in March 1978 to promote export diversification and growth. For this purpose two rates were fixed. The first rate was Rs. 11.90 per US$ and the second rate was Rs. 15.90 per US$. All receipts from exports to countries other than India were converted at the second rate, while imports of inputs, machinery and equipment were made available at the first rate. However, like the previous scheme, DER diverted exports from India to overseas countries instead of increasing the volume of exports.[4] Exports to India substantially declined while imports from India continued to rise. As a consequence, Nepal had a severe shortage of Indian rupees and had to sell convertible currencies to buy rupees.[5] This resulted in a huge financial

loss that forced the government to replace the DER with the Single Exchange
Rate (SER) system in September 1981.

The SER introduced export subsidises (between 10 and 20 per cent) to
promote Nepalese exports, especially to overseas markets. As these trade
diversification programmes under the IS policy relied heavily on direct incentive mechanisms (such as cash subsidies and bonuses) rather than indirect
mechanisms (such as liberalisation in factor and commodity markets) they
failed to create a strong export sector, leading to poor macroeconomic performance. By the mid-1980s export growth had stagnated, and trade and
government budget deficits had reached 12 per cent and 7 per cent of GDP
respectively. Against this background the government was forced to re-exam-
ine its policy environment, which gave rise to the liberalisation of 1985–86.
Table 6.1 summarises macroeconomic conditions during the pre- and post-
liberalisation periods.

Table 6.1   Macroeconomic indicators (% of Real GDP)

	1974/75	1976/77– 1986/87	1987/88– 1993/94
Real GDP growth	–	3.0	4.1
Exports	5.4	5.1	7.0
Imports	10.9	17.4	22.6
Trade deficit	5.6	12.3	14.8
Current account deficit	0.7	3.5	7.2
Budget deficit	1.3	6.9	7.2
International reserve equal to months of imports	7.0	3.8	6.5

Source: Computed from Sharma (1999)

The pace of liberalisation was slow initially, due mainly to Nepal's landlocked position and open border, implying dependence on India.[6] Nepal
embarked on a massive liberalisation programme only when India substantially liberalised its policy regime in the early 1990s. At the beginning,
attempts were made to relax quantitative restrictions (QRs) by replacing
import licenses with the auction system and placing several items under the
open general licence (OGL)/passbook system.[7] Tariffs, including sales tax,
excise duties and additional duties, were gradually reduced and dispersions in
tariff rates were narrowed, especially from the late 1980s. The bias against
exports was reduced through a real devaluation of the rupee and simplification of export procedures. Furthermore, a number of exportable items enjoyed

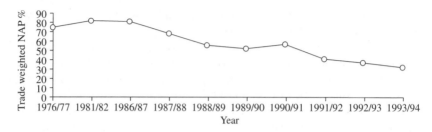

Note: Annual observations only available after 1986/87.

Source: Sharma (1999).

Figure 6.1   Trade-weighted nominal protection

preferential treatment under the generalised system of preferences (GSP) scheme. The trend in the trade-weighted nominal rate of protection (Figure 6.1) indicates a substantial fall in the level of protection from about 80 per cent by the mid-1980s to about 40 per cent by 1993/94.[8]

The major liberalisation reforms were implemented from 1991; all quota restrictions on imports were removed and tariffs were gradually reduced. The zero rated items are mostly agricultural, especially basic foods; the highest rates are levied on liquor and vehicles (which also attract high excise duties). The current range of tariffs is 0, 5, 10, 20, 30 and 80 per cent, although most imports are within the 10–20 per cent range (tariffs on imports from India are lower). A number of goods are tariff exempt, notably raw jute, threshing and husk machines, cold storage equipment for preserving agricultural goods (including fruit and fish), medical equipment for government health projects and books. The unweighted average tariff was reduced from 15.4 per cent in 1981/82, to 8.8 per cent in 1992/93 and 8.2 per cent in 1994/95; this had probably risen to about 10 per cent by 1998. Figure 6.1 has shown the reduction in the trade-weighted nominal rate of protection. Export subsidies, worth 10–30 per cent of free-on-board value, were suspended at the end of the 1980s as real devaluation and simplification of export procedures in the 1990s reduced the bias against exports.

The pattern of trade-weighted tariffs is reported in Table 6.2. The first point to note is that, at least in the mid-1990s, the principal export sectors (carpets and rugs, garments, jewellery and jute processing) attracted net taxes (the export tax was reduced in 1994 so the extent of negative protection on these sectors may now be less). This reflects the phasing out of subsidies mentioned above, and the disincentive effects appear to have been offset by non-fiscal support measures. Rates of nominal protection were very high on beverages and tobacco, quite high on manufactured goods and

Table 6.2   Trade-weighted NRPs, Nepal, 1990s (selected years)

	1989/90	1990/91	1992/93	1993/94
Dairy products	32.1	42.5	28.75	23.6
Canned fruits and vegetables	66.04	79.5	54.25	45.8
Vegetable fats	35.04	62.5	40.5	27.2
Grain mill products	19.6	20	15	15
Bakery products	29.4	25	25	40
Sugar	25.48	16	21	20
Confectionery	95.44	89.5	56.25	50.8
Food products	49.5	54.5	56.25	50.8
Animal feeds	12.5	5	5	5
Distilleries	189.4	178.5	155	144.4
Beer	140.4	178.5	155	144.4
Soft drinks	52.44	57.5	54.25	70.8
Cigarettes	135.5	153.5	130	129.4
Textiles	68	86.5	66.25	45.8
Knitting	−0.98	−1	−1	−3
Carpets and rugs	−0.98	−1	−1	−3
Jute processing	25.62	23.5	−1	−3
Garments	0	13	−1	−3
Leather	14.22	13	−1	−3
Footwear	49.5	86.5	51.25	45.8
Paper	49.5	54.5	37.5	37.2
Structural metal	39.7	66.5	41.25	40.8
Metal products	39.7	66.5	41.25	40.8
Radio and TV	125.7	143.5	95	64.4
Electric apparatus	102.3	133.5	63.25	45.8
Jewellery	−0.98	−1.0	−1.0	−3.0
Manufacturing average	51.65	55.87	36.21	31.52

Note: Figures relate to nominal rates of protection (NRPs). Manufacturing average is the weighted average using the share of each sector in manufacturing output. A negative value implies a net export tax (negative protection).

Source: Sharma (1999).

on most foodstuffs. The evidence suggests ample scope for trade liberalisation.

Investment policy has also been liberalised substantially. This, in particular, was expected to promote manufacturing. To facilitate foreign investment a 'one window' sanctioning procedure was introduced. Effective from early

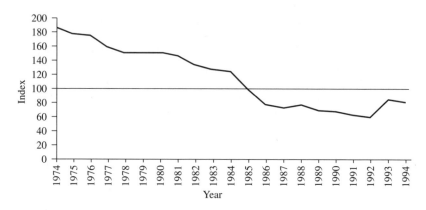

Source: Estimated from data in IMF (1993 and 1994).

Figure 6.2   REER index: 1974–94 (1985=100)

1996, foreign investment below US$300 000 did not need a license (with a few exceptions).[9] A large number of state-owned enterprises have been privatised or liquidated, foreign banks and finance companies are welcome, and commercial banks are given freedom to set their own interest rates. Since February 1993, the foreign exchange market has been liberalised for all current account transactions and exchange rates have been determined by market forces. The real effective exchange rate (REER) index[10] indicates a real devaluation of the Nepalese rupee from the mid-1980s, although there have been some fluctuations from year to year (Figure 6.2). These changes in policy environment might have some impact on export diversification and growth. These are examined below.

4   LIBERALISATION, TRADE DIVERSIFICATION AND GROWTH

The effects of liberalisation on export intensity are fairly clear. As trade liberalisation reduces the bias against exports, primarily through a real devaluation and greater access to imported inputs and technologies, one should expect a rise in export intensity following the liberalisation programme. However, there are no clear indications as to the effects of liberalisation on export diversification (i.e. diversification from exports of primary products to manufactured goods).[11] It is possible to argue that trade liberalisation, by attracting foreign investment and increasing access to imported inputs and technologies, encourages processing of manufactured goods for export. This may help in diversifying the export base from primary products to manufactured goods.

4.1   Liberalisation and Export Intensity

Growth in export intensity, defined as the export-output ratio, is influenced by a number of factors. An outward-oriented trade policy may be one of them. In the absence of supply-side rigidity, however, a liberal policy alone may not contribute to higher export intensity. As Linnemann *et al.* (1987) observe, a sufficient supply of labour at lower wages, adequate infrastructure and stimulating government policies are essential for a rise in export intensity.

Following the liberalisation programme from the mid-1980s, export intensity in Nepalese manufacturing rose. Our estimates presented in Figure 6.3 show that export intensity increased from less than five per cent in the early 1980s to about 20 per cent by 1993/94, with some variations from year to year. This substantial growth in export intensity could be attributed to a number of factors, namely removal of bias against exports, increased access to imported intermediate inputs, generous export incentives under the GSP scheme and exemption from income tax on export earnings. Furthermore, growth in foreign investment, especially in garments, which rose sharply in the post-reform period, may also have contributed to a rise in export intensity.

Note: Annual observations only available after 1886–87.

Source: Estimates based on data from CBS, *Census and Survey of Manufacturing Establishments*; TPC, *Nepal Overseas Trade Statistics* (various issues) and *Nepal Rastra Bank Database*.

Figure 6.3   Export intensity of manufacturing (1972/73–1993/94)

Export intensity of major manufacturing industries, measured at constant 1992/93 prices, is shown in Table 6.3. Within manufacturing, export intensity is high in the carpets and rugs, garments, jute products and leather subsectors. Liberalisation in trade and industrial policies since the mid-1980s further

Table 6.3 *Export intensity of major manufactures (1976/77–1993/94)*

	1976/77	1981/82	1986/87	1987/88	1988/89	1989/90	1990/91	1991/92	1993/94
Canned fruits	0.00	0.00	0.00	0.28	0.15	0.00	0.00	0.00	0.07
Vegetable fats	0.00	0.00	0.17	0.11	0.11	0.07	0.06	0.00	0.02
Grain products	0.03	0.03	0.11	0.00	0.00	0.00	0.00	0.00	0.00
Knitted products	0.00	0.02	0.11	0.00	0.00	0.01	0.00	0.04	0.00
Carpets and rugs	0.42	0.06	1.00	0.81	0.86	0.88	0.87	0.37	0.51
Jute products	0.00	0.64	0.57	0.73	0.50	0.07	0.91	0.54	0.63
Garments	0.00	0.00	0.51	0.96	0.95	0.66	0.99	0.82	0.95
Leather	0.00	0.00	0.06	0.79	0.83	0.66	0.95	0.64	0.72
Paper and paper products	0.02	0.68	0.01	0.03	0.04	0.00	0.01	0.05	0.13
Jewellery	0.00	0.00	0.00	0.00	0.00	0.36	0.57	0.87	0.76

Source: Estimates based on data from CBS, *Census and Survey of Manufacturing Establishments;* TPC, *Nepal Overseas Trade Statistics* (various issues) and *Nepal Rastra Bank Database.*

128

increased their export intensity. However, the carpet industry experienced a substantial fall in its export intensity from the early 1990s, mainly due to the boycott of Nepalese carpets in the European and American markets due to concerns about use of child labour. Export intensity in jewellery rose sharply from the early 1990s with the liberalisation of silver imports – the major intermediate input – and the simplification of export procedures. Exports of grain products have virtually disappeared since the mid-1980s because of high domestic demand and a fall in production. Export intensity has fluctuated widely in canned fruits, vegetable fats, knitted products, and paper and paper products.

4.2   Liberalisation and Export Diversification

Before Nepal embarked on the liberalisation programme in the mid-1980s, its exports were dominated by primary products. For example, these products contributed about 82 per cent of total export earnings while the share of manufactured exports was less than 18 per cent. Further, there were only a few manufactured goods in its export list. These included carpets and rugs, jute products, and paper and paper products. However, following liberalisation, new manufactured products (namely jewellery, ready-made garments, canned fruits and vegetable fats) have been added to the export list, and

Table 6.4   Composition of exports (average annual share)

	1974/75–1979/80	1980/81–1984/85	1985/86–1993/94
Jute goods	16.3	14.7	4.5
Raw jute	12.7	11.4	1.6
Hide/skin	8.4	11.7	6.7
Carpets and rugs	4.0	12.1	40.0
Handicrafts	2.9	2.6	1.2
Garments	nil	2.6	30.1
Pulses	5.6	4.2	5.2
Rice	26.0	11.0	neg
Timber	19.4	7.1	nil
Dried ginger	neg	2.3	neg
Silver jewellery	nil	nil	0.6
Other	4.7	20.3	10.1
Total	100.0	100.0	100.0

Sources: Ministry of Finance, *Economic Survey* (various issues) and TPC, *Nepal Overseas Trade Statistics* (various issues).

exports of carpets and rugs have grown rapidly (Table 6.4). The share of manufactured exports in total exports has been steadily increasing, reaching 36 per cent during the 1980/81–1985/86 period and 75 per cent during 1986/87–1993/94. Table 6.4 presents an overview of the composition of exports.

The higher shares of manufactured exports, especially in the last sub-period, followed the removal of the bias against manufactured exports brought about by the liberalisation programme. Linnemann *et al.* (1987) note that a rising share of manufacturing exports is not merely the inherent outcome of a normal process of growth and transformation. An increasing export share may also result from shifts in the types of industrialisation and trade strategies pursued. As shown in Table 6.4, in recent years carpets and garments have emerged as major export items, together contributing about 70 per cent of manufacturing export earnings. This is primarily due to GSP quotas (Sharma 1999). Initially, the US was the major market for garments, but quota restrictions since 1987 led to diversification to non-US markets, particularly to Canada. As a result, the US share of Nepalese exports of garments fell from 95 per cent in 1987 to 78 per cent by 1992 (in principle this is better as it is a case of export (market) diversification). Nepalese carpets are exported mainly to European markets, where its exports have suffered in recent times due to concern about the use of child labour.

With the introduction of trade liberalisation, silver ornaments have also been added to the export list although their share in total export earnings is still very low (Table 6.4). Exports of silver ornaments have become possible due to liberalisation of silver imports and the simplification of procedures for exports of silver jewelleries (previously restricted). Exports of jute goods, however, have fallen substantially in recent years due to a fall in international demand, as cheaper synthetic substitutes have become available. Its share in total export earnings has fallen to about five per cent in the post-reform period (1985/86–1993/94) as compared to about 15 per cent in the pre-reform period (1980/81–1984/85). Exports of handicrafts, items in which Nepal has traditional skills and which are produced mainly on a small scale, have also shown a declining trend.

There have also been some changes in the direction of Nepal's foreign trade (as shown in Table 6.5). Until the mid-1980s, India had been Nepal's major trading partner. However, trade diversification programmes that took place from the 1960s to the early 1980s changed the direction of foreign trade. For example, India's share in Nepal's foreign trade (exports as well as imports) fell from 97 per cent during 1956/57–1966/67 to 50 per cent by the mid-1980s. There has been a further decline in India's share following the liberalisation programme – by 1993/94 India had only a 30 per cent share in Nepal's foreign trade. Overseas countries other than India have begun to emerge as major trading partners in recent years. Their shares have increased

Table 6.5   Direction of Nepal's foreign trade (% of total trade, average annual share)

	1956/57–1966/67	1974/75–1979/80	1980/81–1984/85	1985/86–1993/94
India	97.2	62.8	50.3	30.5
Overseas	3.0	37.2	49.7	69.5
Total	100.0	100.0	100.0	100.0

Source: Calculated from Dahal (1987) and *Economic Survey*, 1997/98.

to 70 per cent during 1984/85–1993/94, from 50 per cent in 1980/81–1984/85.

4.3   Liberalisation and Output Diversification

Before Nepal embarked on trade liberalisation, manufacturing output was dominated by the IS industries (Table 6.5). This appears to be mainly due to a bias towards the home market that attracted resources away from export-oriented (EO) industries towards protected IS industries. As a consequence, by the mid-1980s, 87 per cent of manufacturing output was dominated by the IS industries, while the output share of EO industries was about 13 per cent.[12] However, with the liberalisation of the policy environment there has been a change in the incentive structure that appears to have encouraged increased production in EO industries. For example, by 1993/94 EO industries contributed 28 per cent to manufacturing output. Table 6.6 decomposes manufacturing output according to the nature of market orientation, and indicates the broad changes over time.

It must be noted, however, that despite an increase in the export intensity of manufactures, such exports finance only a small portion of the sector's import needs. For instance, during 1985/86–1993/94, manufactured exports financed only about 15 per cent of imports as compared with 11 per cent during 1979/80–1984/85. As repatriation of profits and royalty payments seem to have increased in recent years because of the growing involvement of foreign firms, especially in the garment, chemical and beverage industries, the sector has not been able to ease the pressure on the current account. However, this seems to be a normal phenomenon at the early stage of industrialisation:

> The net effect of manufacturing growth on the balance of payments is mixed. Rapid industrialisation tends to increase the demand for imported intermediates,

Table 6.6   Manufacturing output by market orientation (% share)

	1972/73	1976/77	1981/82	1986/87	1987/88	1988/89	1989/90	1990/91	1991/92	1993/94
IS Industries	96.26	99.40	93.78	87.10	86.04	82.48	80.11	75.10	66.90	71.70
EO Industries	3.74	0.60	6.22	12.89	13.96	17.52	19.89	24.90	33.10	28.30
Total	100.0	100.0	100.0	100.0	100.0	100.0	100.0	100.0	100.0	100.0

Source: Estimated from data obtained from Central Bureau of Statistics (CBS), various issues.

and manufactured exports are often concentrated in the sectors most dependent on imports. The net effect of manufacturing on the balance of payments is negative for much of the industrialisation process. Only in the latter stages, as an economy achieves import substitution in the 'harder' heavy manufacturing sectors, does the net contribution to the balance of trade of changes in manufacturing turn positive (Chenery *et al.*, 1986: 225).

In Nepal, the highly protective trade regimes lasted until the late 1980s but a degree of liberalisation was achieved in the 1990s, both absolutely and by South Asian standards. In 1989, protection in Nepal was roughly in the middle of the range for South Asian countries. All countries except Pakistan had liberalised significantly by 1997, but no comparable data are available for Nepal. However, there is evidence that Nepal had the lowest average tariff rate of any South Asian country in the early 1990s (Bandara and McGillivray, 1998), hence it appears that Nepal has progressed further.

The prospects for diversification and evolution of exports in Nepal vary according to whichever product is considered:

- Carpets (hand-made Tibetan-Nepalese woollen rugs) are an indigenous industry and the single most important export. Although the wool is imported, the labour and ownership is local and value added is adequate. However, exports are now mostly to Germany, hence quite vulnerable to shifts in demand in that market. Prospects for Nepalese carpet exports depend on their ability to diversify from dependence on the German market.
- Garment exports are mostly under quota to the US. The world market is highly competitive, and Nepal is especially concerned about competition from Bangladesh (and other low-income producers) under open trade once the Multi-Fibre Arrangement is abolished. Private producers feel that export quotas actually protect (guarantee) market share, which may fall under quota-free trade. The most realistic projection is that garment exports will contract, probably in both volume and value terms.
- Rules of origin may pose an additional problem for garments as there is typically only one stage of processing and local value added is low. There are government incentives for local fabric/textile production and such backward linkages would be beneficial; local textiles are, however, only sufficient for about ten per cent of demand. It is likely that textiles could be imported more cheaply from India (and potentially Pakistan). Nevertheless, the garment sector has fairly low linkages to the economy; the export earnings are somewhat offset by imported inputs; employment is important, but many skilled workers are Indian, and most of the firms are Indian owned. It is not clear that this sector is very beneficial to Nepal.

- Child labour is quite prevalent, especially in the garment industry, and could leave Nepal vulnerable to 'social dumping' actions. This is yet another reason to be concerned about prospects for garment exports.
- Currently, Nepal is a significant net food importer, although there are exports of lentils, mustard seeds, herbs and spices (mostly to India). The potential exists to expand agricultural output. A basic problem is poor infrastructure, especially transport, so that Nepalese markets are not integrated. Mountain areas could expand production of fruits and vegetables (high value added) if able to deliver to the valley markets; currently it is often easier for Kathmandhu to import from India. It is argued that Nepal could export to Tibet if there was a processing plant near the border. The prospects for agricultural trade depend on domestic agricultural policy. There is, however, potential for Nepal to expand domestic production if import prices rise.
- Leather goods, skins and handicrafts are relatively important exports, although volumes are low, and are unlikely to grow much (exports are likely to be related to the tourist industry).
- Nepal has a niche market in quality hand-made paper; accession to the World Trade Organisation (WTO) may help in protecting intellectual property rights (as Thailand and Philippines pass off their product as Nepalese). However, this market is too small for any effects to be noticeable on an economy-wide basis.

5   CONCLUSION

In this chapter we investigated the consequences of trade liberalisation on export diversification and growth in Nepal – a low-income landlocked country which has embarked on liberalisation since the mid-1980s. The liberalisation programme included substantial cuts in tariffs and non-tariff barriers, devaluation of the Nepalese rupee, liberalisation of investment policies, including foreign investment, and banking sector reform. However, due to Nepal's land-locked position and open border with India, it pursued a gradual rather than a massive liberalisation until the early 1990s.

Following the trade liberalisation programme, its reliance on exports of primary products declined, manufacturing export intensity rose and a few new manufactured goods (namely jewellery, garments, canned fruit and vegetable fats) have been added to the export list of the country. These provide some support for the view that trade liberalisation contributes to export diversification and growth. Further, there has been an increase in the share of export-oriented industries in manufacturing output that appears to be mainly due to a change in the incentive environment.

It must be mentioned, however, that the present structure is economically unhealthy. This is because export diversification and growth is primarily due to an increase in exports of garments and carpets that are determined by quotas. Further multilateral trade liberalisation under the auspices of the WTO may lead to an erosion of these quotas. Furthermore, the excessive reliance on a few items can lead to export instability. Thus, the present structure is vulnerable and does not fully represent the real comparative advantage of the country, with the exception of carpets. To reduce excessive reliance on exports of garments and carpets, it is desirable to offer production and export incentives to other potential exporters. The difficulty in this strategy is identifying viable export sectors and ensuring that the incentives do not become protective subsidies. The core problem is that exports are in a very narrow range of products. Whether garment exports do contract is conditional on the ability of Nepalese producers to increase efficiency in the face of a more competitive global market. Prospects for the other major export commodity, carpets, depend on demand conditions in overseas markets and the ability of Nepalese producers to diversify the markets they supply.

The most important potential source of benefit to Nepal lies in food exports, but this would require the implementation of policies to increase the efficiency and output of domestic agriculture. It is difficult to be optimistic in this regard. Although Nepal has a development plan for agriculture, allocations in the 1997/98 budget were inadequate and important policy decisions to promote agriculture had not been taken (World Bank, 1997: 24). Overall, the evidence shows that Nepal has not been adversely affected by trade liberalisation, and there has been an export supply response (albeit limited, in a narrow range of products and perhaps not sustainable). In this sense the experience of Nepal is comparable to Uganda (Milner *et al.,* 2000; Rudaheranwa, 1999), also a landlocked low-income country. Even for such constrained economies, trade liberalisation is in general beneficial. The evidence for Nepal is that a more liberalised trade regime, combined with investment incentives, offers the potential for an expansion of manufacturing exports.

NOTES

1. Exports stagnated at around five per cent of GDP while the current account deficit rose from less than one per cent of GDP up to the mid-1970s to about four per cent by the mid-1980s. International reserves fell to less than four months' worth of imports by the mid-1980s. Meanwhile the government's budget deficit rose from one per cent of GDP in the mid-1970s to about seven per cent by the mid-1980s. Manufactured exports were unable to meet even ten per cent of import requirements (Sharma, 1999).
2. In the 1960s over 95 per cent of Nepal's trade was with India, but this fell to 57 per cent by the mid-1970s. Nepalese exports were mainly primary products to India, creating

export instability, while it imported manufactured goods mainly from India. Heavy reliance on imports from India created shortages of essential manufactured goods, including cement and petroleum products (Dahal, 1987).

3. As a consequence, in some cases traders exported their products below cost and imported luxury goods with the bonus certificates obtained as these items attracted high premiums in the Indian market. The scheme also appeared to have encouraged re-exports of Indian goods. For example, during 1962–67 Nepalese exports of jute and jute goods were more than its domestic production, implying that there were either hidden imports of jute from India for re-export or over-invoicing of jute or both.

4. For example, during the period of the scheme (1978–81) the export-orientation of the economy was around seven per cent.

5. By the end of 1979/80 Nepal sold over Rs. 2000 million worth of convertible currencies to buy Indian rupees. The central bank purchased convertible currencies from exporters at a rate of Rs. 15.90 for one US dollar and sold such currency to India at the second rate of Rs. 11.90, thus making a loss of Rs. 4 per dollar transacted.

6. If trade and investment policies in Nepal were more liberal than in India, massive smuggling would drain Nepal's foreign exchange reserve.

7. Under the passbook system an annual import license was issued after which the importers were free to import the approved quantities throughout the year subject to monitoring by a passbook in order to verify that the earlier allocation had been utilised domestically.

8. According to the Indo-Nepal trade agreements, imports from India are subject to a lower level of restrictions. They attract basic tariffs only, while imports from the rest of the world are taxed using the basic plus additional tariff. Thus, using the trade share of India and the rest of the world, we obtain a single trade-weighted NRP.

9. Industries relating to environment, public health and national security need to obtain a license.

10. The REER index is calculated using the following formula:

$$REER = \Sigma_i \, (RER \; index)_i \, (W_i)$$

Where, *RER index* refers to the Nominal Exchange Rate adjusted for price changes at home and in the major trading partners and divided by the base year exchange rate. Wi refers to trade weights of major trading partners (weights sum to unity). Note that selection of currencies is based on the multilateral trade weights using 1985 trade figures. If trade weights have changed significantly, which is unlikely, this could affect our REER index. The following currencies are included in the REER estimates: Indian rupees, Japanese yen, US dollar, German mark, British pound and Singapore dollar.

11. Experience of African countries suggests that countries that rely heavily on exports of primary products are more vulnerable to external shocks than countries that export a range of manufactured goods.

12. Following Nishimizu and Robinson (1984) industries are classified as either export-oriented industries which export more than 10 per cent of total production, or import-substituting industries which import more than 10 per cent of total domestic supply (imports plus domestic production minus exports).

REFERENCES

Bandara, J. and M. McGillivray (1998), 'Trade Policy Reforms in South Asia', *The World Economy*, **21**, 881–96.

Bennell, P. (1998), 'Fighting for Survival: Manufacturing Industry and Adjustment in Sub-Saharan Africa', *Journal of International Development*, **10**, 621–37.

Central Bureau of Statistics (CBS), *Census and Annual Survey of Manufacturing Establishments*, various issues, Kathmandu, Nepal.

Chenery, H., S. Robinson and M. Syrquin (1986), *Industrialization and Growth: A Comparative Study*, New York: OUP.

Dahal, K. (1987), *Indo-Nepal Trade: Problems and Prospects*, Kathmandu: Ratna Pustak Bhandar.

Greenaway, D. and O. Morrissey (1994), 'Trade Liberalisation and Economic Growth in Developing Countries', in S.M. Murshed and K. Raffer (eds), *Trade Transfers and Development*, Cheltenham: Edward Elgar (pp. 210–32).

International Monetary Fund (IMF), *International Financial Statistics*, Washington DC, various issues.

Khan, S.R. (1999), *Do World Bank and IMF Policies Work?*, London: Macmillan.

Linnemann, H.P., V. Dijck and H. Verbruggens (1987), *Export-orientated Industrialisation in Developing Countries*, Singapore: Singapore University Press.

Milner, C., O. Morrissey and N. Rudaheranwa (2000), 'Policy and non-Policy Barriers to Trade and the Implicit Taxation of Exports in Uganda', *Journal of Development Studies*, 37(2), 67–90.

Ministry of Finance, *Economic Survey,* various issues, Kathmandu, Nepal.

Nepal Rastra Bank (NRB), *Quarterly Economic Bulletin*, various issues, Kathmandu, Nepal.

Nishimuzi, M. and S. Robinson (1984), 'Trade Policies and Productivity Change in Semi-industrialized Countries', *Journal of Development Economics*, 16, 137–48.

Rudaheranwa, N. (1999), *Transport Costs and Export Trade of Landlocked Countries: Evidence from Uganda*, unpublished PhD Thesis, University of Nottingham.

Sharma, K. (1995), 'Trade and Manufacturing in Nepal', *The Asian Economic Review*, 37, 58–86.

Sharma, K. (1999), *Trade Liberalisation and Manufacturing Performance in Developing Countries: New Evidence from Nepal*, New York: NOVA Science Publishers.

Sharma, K., S. Jayasuriya and E. Oczkowski (2000), Liberalisation and Productivity Growth: The Case of Manufacturing Industries in Nepal, *Oxford Development Studies*, 28, 205–22.

Trade Promotion Centre (TPC), *Nepal Overseas Trade Statistics*, various issues, Kathmandu, Nepal.

World Bank (1997), *Nepal 1997 Economic Update: The Challenge of Accelerating Economic Growth*, South Asia Region Report No. 17034-NEP, Washington, DC: The World Bank.

7. Liberalisation and the manufacturing sector: the Indian experience during the 1990s

T.G. Arun and Fred I. Nixson

1 INTRODUCTION

India's development experience since independence has been rooted in the presumption that industrialisation was a means to achieve rapid economic growth. The strategy was characterised by an inward orientation through import substitution by policies of extensive import licensing, high tariffs and a large public sector. Although many developing countries adapted their policies to take advantage of the growing opportunities for trade in the 1970s and 1980s, India persisted with its heavily protectionist policies and combined these with strong domestic regulation in an effort to influence the pattern of growth. Since 1991 however, successive Indian governments have been committed to policies of economic reform and liberalisation with greater openness to trade and foreign direct investment (FDI) and limited privatisation (usually referred to as disinvestment).

The objectives of this chapter are to consider the reforms in the industrial sector and in particular, the manufacturing sector. The structure of the chapter is as follows. After the introduction, Section 2 summarises the major industrial policies and their implications for development until 1991. In the third section, the industrial situation since 1991 is examined. Both the public sector and direct foreign investment have witnessed rapid and dramatic changes under the new policies, but even after a decade of reforms, the experiences of these two areas argue for a stronger commitment to reform on the part of policy makers, particularly at the regional level. Section 3.3 on industrial growth reveals that post-1991 growth rates are lower than in the 1980s, especially in the capital goods sector. The success of the new policies depends to a large extent on how firms position themselves in terms of strategies and choices in a more competitive environment. Drawing on various surveys, Section 4 shows how firms are moving strategically with respect to product differentiation and labour productivity. The liberalisation period also provides evidence of an increasing use of training, and more up-to-date organisational and managerial practices in the manufacturing sector in an attempt to improve competitiveness. Section 5 indicates in summary the progress that has been made so far but also highlights the problems that remain.

2   INDUSTRIAL POLICIES AND PERFORMANCE UP TO 1991

Having adopted a mixed economy where the public and private sectors coexisted but with the former dominating the core sectors of the economy, the Government of India (GOI) articulated its industrial policy through various Industrial Policy Resolutions (IPR). The IPR 1948 emphasised the importance to the economy of securing a continuous increase in production and its equitable distribution, and pointed out that the State must play a progressively more active role in the development of the industrial sector (GOI, 1948). The policy reserved industries such as arms and ammunition, atomic energy and railways for the public sector, particularly in the Central sector.[1] Coal, iron and steel, aircraft manufacturing, shipbuilding and minerals were reserved for production either by Central or State Government undertakings. The policy aimed to expand the public sector in those industries where the private sector would find it difficult or be unwilling to invest.

The IPR 1956 argued that:

> The adoption of the socialist pattern of society as the national objective, as well as the need for planned and rapid development, requires that all industries of basic and strategic importance, or in the nature of public utility services, should be in the public sector. Other industries, which are essential and require investment on a scale which only the state, in present circumstances, could provide, have also to be in the public sector. The state has, therefore, to assume direct responsibility for the future development of industries over a wide area (para. 6) (GOI, 1956).

The IPR 1973 identified high priority industries where investment from large industrial houses and foreign companies would be permitted (GOI, 1973). Under this policy, preference would be given to small and medium entrepreneurs over the large industrial houses and foreign companies in the setting up of new capacity. The IPR 1977 provided for a closer interaction between the agricultural and industrial sectors, accorded the highest priority to the generation and transmission of power, and identified industrial products which were capable of being produced in the small-scale sector (GOI, 1977). The IPR 1980 focused attention on the need for promoting competition in the domestic market, technological upgrading and modernisation (GOI, 1980). This policy laid the foundations for an increasingly competitive export

Table 7.1   Annual growth rates of industrial output

Year	Growth Rates
1951–56	7.3
1956–61	6.6
1961–66	9.0
1966–69	2.0
1969–74	4.7
1974–79	5.9
1979–80	−1.4
1980–85	5.9
1985–90	8.5

Source: Ahluwalia 1991, Table1.1, p. 11.

base and for encouraging foreign investment in high priority technology areas.

As mentioned above, these policies aimed to develop a self sufficient and competitive industrial sector to achieve rapid economic growth. But in reality, although India's pre-1991 planned approach to development had major achievements to its credit, it was clear that as compared to the performance of the economies of East and South East Asia and China, the overall growth record was poor. Table 7.1 indicates the increasingly weak growth performance of the industrial sector in the 1960s and 1970s, although the 1980s registered significant improvement, especially after 1985.

The debates on the causes of the fluctuations in industrial growth in India have not only considered the underlying causes of stagnation and acceleration but also the timing. Explanations for the fluctuations in growth rates have varied from demand-side factors such as the changes in the distribution of income, to supply-side factors such as the effects of changes in public investment, agricultural growth performance and industrial regulations. The increase in the growth rate in the 1980s is interpreted as a response to the relaxation of the policy-based constraints to growth (Gupta, 1993). During the 1980s there was a growing concern about the need for increasing competitiveness and thus the focus of policies was on sharpening the international competitiveness of Indian enterprises by exposing them to increased domestic and international competition (Arun, 1999). However, the improved growth performance of the 1980s was not sustainable because of growing macroeconomic imbalances (Ahluwalia, 1999).

Table 7.2 illustrates the process of industrial change that has accompanied economic growth. In India, as in other growing economies, the process of

Table 7.2   Sectoral composition of gross domestic product

Year	Agriculture	Mining and Manufacturing	Services
1950–51	55.8	15.2	29.0
1970–71	45.1	21.9	23.0
1987–88	30.5	29.9	39.5

Source: Chandok, 1990, Table 1.143a, p. 288, vol.1.

industrialisation has raised both the relative and the absolute importance of the manufacturing sector in the economy.

The other significant aspect of industrial development in India before 1991 was the strategic economic role given to the public sector, which here refers to all government activities including administration, utilities and commercial activities at both the Central and State levels. In the early years of independence, the activities of the public sector were restricted to a limited number of fields including irrigation, power, railways, ports, communications and some departmental undertakings. But increasingly, the areas of activity were extended across the economy and began to include non-infrastructure activities and non-core areas.[2] They included public investment in activities that were not at all strategic such as hotels and the manufacture of consumer goods such as scooters, soft drinks and bread.[3] However, the poor performance of the Public Sector Enterprises (PSEs), which was manifested in low or negative returns to public investment,[4] raised many concerns about the rationale of supporting these enterprises as an engine of growth. In short, by the late 1980s, their growth had become an end in itself, absorbing half of the total industrial investment regardless of the low returns obtained (Arun and Nixson, 1997).

It has been argued that policy-induced microeconomic rigidities had constrained firm choices during the pre-reform period, apart from protecting Indian enterprises from internal and external competition (Basant, 2000). For instance, the determination of plant capacity, product mix and location of the PSEs was based on non-economic factors which ignored market realities and which contributed to high levels of inefficiency. During this period, PSEs were prey to inappropriate locational, size and technology choices, and suffered from imposed marketing arrangements (Jalan, 1991), all of which were the outcome of political considerations and bureaucratic rent seeking, rather than being based on economic criteria.[5]

With respect to foreign investment, government policies played an important role in shaping investment patterns by affecting the relative configuration of ownership, internalisation and locational advantages of foreign investors

(Arun, 1999). Foreign Direct Investment (FDI) had always been channelled and controlled, and technical collaborations approved on an individual basis. The investment policies had been linked with technology policies such as selective licensing, which tended to increase the concentration of FDI in the manufacturing sector (Kumar, 1990).

One striking trend was the dramatic reduction of the FDI stock in the non-manufacturing sectors largely due to take-overs by Government of activities such as insurance (Kumar, 1990). New inflows were directed to the manufacturing sector. As a result, the manufacturing sector doubled its share in the stock of FDI, from 40.5 per cent in 1964 to 86.9 per cent in 1980 (Kumar, 1995). Within the manufacturing sector, new inflows were directed to technology intensive sectors such as machinery and machine tools, electrical goods and chemical and allied products. These three broad sectors accounted for nearly 58 per cent of total FDI in manufacturing in 1980 compared to 41 per cent in 1964 (Kumar, 1995). This rise in the importance of technology-intensive products in the FDI stock was at the expense of traditional consumer goods industries such as food, beverages and textile products. The share of metal products and chemicals declined during this period. Consumer goods industries appeared to have a lower concentration of foreign shares, because of entry regulations that discouraged FDI in industries where local capabilities were available. In the 1980s, in certain branches such as chemicals and allied products, and metal and metal products, the foreign shares declined because of increasing public sector participation (Kumar, 1990).

The regulation of private foreign capital was accompanied by restrictions which sought to minimise the total cost of technology acquisitions, and to unbundle them from foreign equity participation (Athreye and Kapur, 1999). Restrictive legislation such as the Foreign Exchange Regulation Act (FERA) also sought to regulate the use of scarce foreign exchange resources, which limited the freedom of foreign investors[6] (Arun, 1999). The manufacturing sector was prioritised into three different categories in relation to technology imports: (1) if the indigenous technological capability was sufficient, technology imports were not permitted; (2) if it was a simple or stable technology, licensing was the preferred mode of technology acquisition, and (3) if the technology was sophisticated and unlikely to be available through licensing, then foreign equity participation was permitted. These policies allowed existing foreign firms to operate technologies that were internationally obsolete, but nevertheless superior to those used by domestic firms (Athreye and Kapur, 1999). The indigenous availability criterion which stipulated that any good which could be supplied by a domestic producer could not be imported led to complete insulation of domestic production from international competitive pressures (Lal, 1999). Although these protective policies had helped India to build a manufacturing base, they diverted resources from technological activity and burdened the economy with a high degree of technological obsolescence that affected the competitiveness of industries as well as having an adverse effect on economic growth.

The inward-oriented policies that protected Indian firms from competition, both domestic and foreign, resulted in a concentrated market structure. The average concentration ratio for all 38 leading sectors was 70.2 in 1976 and 68.4 in 1983 (Kaplinsky, 1997). High concentration meant rather high prices being charged and also little or no incentive to effect technological improvements. In fact in the pre-reform policy environment, the Indian industrial sector was characterised as one in which even the normal strategic rivalry of oligopoly was constrained or frozen (Marjit and Singh, 1993). Also, during the period 1959–60 to 1985–86, which was primarily an import substituting regime, total factor productivity growth (TFPG) in the Indian manufacturing sector declined at an average rate of 0.4 per cent per year, indicating the relative inefficiency of factor use and the lack of technological dynamism (Ahluwalia, 1991). Lal (1980) produced evidence of the declining social profitability of industrial investment during the import substituting period. In short, factors such as the lack of technological dynamism, absence of competition and protected markets drastically restricted the development of a competitive industrial sector in India.

3   THE INDUSTRIAL SECTOR SINCE 1991

Since 1991, the Government of India (GOI) has introduced a series of economic reforms, including policies of liberalisation, deregulation, disinvestment and privatisation, and changed policies towards FDI. The broad thrust of the new policies is a move away from centralised allocation of resources in some key sectors by the government to allocation by market forces. The reforms are intended to redress the balance between the public and private sectors and to improve productivity and competitiveness. This in turn will help the country to translate its investment into high and sustainable growth rates of output and employment (World Bank, 1994).

The IPR 1991 was intended to bring market discipline and public accountability to the performance of PSEs by broadening the base of their management and ownership patterns (GOI, 1991). This shift in attitude was interpreted as a belated realisation by government of the poor performance of PSEs and reflected the need for the development of a dynamic private sector and the move towards market-oriented policies (Arun and Nixson, 1997). The thrust of the new policy was to inject competition in order to induce greater industrial efficiency by delicensing industries and by liberalising policies related to the public sector and FDI. The new policies turned around from the 'selective' approach to an all-out effort to woo foreign investment with an aim to exploit 'attendant advantages of technology transfer, marketing expertise, introduction of modern management techniques in the country and export promotion' (GOI, 1991).

3.1   Public Sector Reforms

Private participation in economic development has emerged as an alternative to the state-oriented development strategy in the reform period. However, the GOI preferred to use the terms 'disinvestment' and 'public sector reforms' to privatisation. The disinvestment of GOI holdings in the equity of selected PSEs is an important step towards wider private sector participation in economic development. But ownership change may not deliver increased efficiency and consumer benefits if industrial restructuring and subsequent regulation fail to create competitive pressures (Vickers and Yarrow, 1988). This is very much the case for India, where improving industrial performance has a lower priority than revenue generation (Arun and Nixson, 2000). Even though the disinvestment programme was conceived of as part of the broader process of structural adjustment, the Indian experience indicates that limited disinvestment with the retention of majority public control has served a fiscal rather than a structural adjustment objective. Owing to the rigidity of exit laws, retrenchment and downsizing are not at present practical in India, even with majority private control, and this puts a further restriction on industrial restructuring (see Arun and Nixson (2000) for a detailed discussion of the disinvestment of PSEs in India).

The changes in industrial licensing and controls are considered an important part of new policies. The policy abolished industrial licensing for all industries, except for those specified, irrespective of levels of investment.[7] The policy also envisaged abolishing sectoral monopolies in any field of manufacturing, except for strategic or military considerations, while opening up all manufacturing activities to competition. The process of domestic deregulation, which had begun in the 1980s, was further strengthened through dispensing with industrial licensing requirements for most industries and providing larger scope for the private sector through de-reserving many areas that were earlier reserved for the public sector.[8]

With respect to the reform of PSEs, Memoranda of Understanding[9] have been extended to all PSEs except for the ones which were to be referred to the Board for Industrial and Financial Reconstruction (BIFR). The main goal of the Memoranda of Understanding is to reduce the quantity of control and increase the quality of accountability by specifying measurable goals for the PSE and giving greater operational autonomy to it to pursue those goals.

The Sick Industrial Companies (Special Provisions) Act (SICA) (which was amended in 1993) defines a sick industrial company as one (being a company registered for not less than five years) which has at the end of any financial year accumulated losses equal to or exceeding its entire net worth (GOI, 1996). This Act also made provision for the establishment of the Board for Industrial and Financial Reconstruction (BIFR) to act as an agency for implementing the various provisions through the jurisdiction and powers as vested in the Board under the SICA Act. On receipt of a reference for a company, the BIFR will determine whether the enterprise has become a sick industrial company. Since the amendment of the SICA Act in 1993, BIFR had received references for 225 Central and State PSEs up to the end of November 1998 (GOI, 1999). Rehabilitation schemes were sanctioned for 21 Central PSEs and 29 State PSEs. It was recommended that 10 Central PSEs and 19 State PSEs be wound up. However both the PSE reforms and disinvestment policies require a much stronger commitment on the part of policy makers regarding the need to make PSEs more autonomous, competitive and commercially-oriented business organisations.

3.2 Foreign Direct Investment

Foreign investment and technology collaboration were welcomed in the new policy era as contributing to the acquisition of more advanced technology, increased exports and a broader production base (Arun, 1999). The new policies relaxed or abolished the restrictions on private and foreign investment in key sectors of the economy. Many areas of economic activity formerly reserved for the public sector (petroleum exploration, refining and retailing, for example) have been opened up to the private sector, while restrictions on the expansion of the large private industrial houses have been removed. The new policies accept the argument that a continuous relationship between the suppliers and users of technology becomes difficult when the approval process includes unnecessary governmental interference (GOI, 1997). As compared to the pre-reform period, a distinctive feature of the liberalisation phase is the simplification of procedures towards FDI approvals.

Data on approved foreign investment flows reflect the growing confidence of foreign investors in the liberalisation policy. The approvals, however, have been slow in materialising into actual inflows. The real inflow as a per cent of approvals was only 29.7 per cent during 1991–99 (Table 7.3). But the ratio of actual inflows in a year as a percentage of approved amounts in the same year fluctuates widely, depending upon the time lag and investment spread-out in industrial projects. Other than this, a number of reasons have been advanced to explain the slow response of foreign investment actually to materialise after its approval. The possible political reasons range from the stock scam[10] (1993) to the Ayodhya incident (1992) and bomb blasts in Bombay (1993). These incidents, along with other factors such as the inability of the collab-

Table 7.3   FDI approvals and actuals 1991–99 (Rs. billions)

Year	Approvals	Actuals	Actual as % of approvals
1991	5.3	3.5	66.1
1992	38.9	6.8	17.5
1993	88.6	17.9	20.2
1994	141.9	32.9	23.2
1995	320.7	68.2	21.3
1996	361.5	103.9	28.7
1997	548.9	164.3	29.9
1998	308.1	133.3	43.2
1999*	78.5	31.7	40.4
Total	1892.4	562.4	29.7

Note: * up to 1999 February only.

Source: *IIC Bulletins* various dates; *SIA Newsletter*, April 1999.

orators to fulfil their commitments, raw material difficulties, delays in promised policy changes in specific sectors and finally the inability of the Government to loosen bureaucratic rigidities, have resulted in a slow rate of FDI inflows (Arun, 1999).

Interestingly, even though both financial and technical collaborations have maintained the increasing trend of the 1980s in the post-1991 liberalisation period, the rate of growth of financial approvals has been higher than the rate of growth of all approvals (financial and technical collaborations). There is thus an increasing trend towards financial collaboration (Table 7.4) during the period 1991–99 compared to the increase in the total number of collaborations. The increasing share of financial collaborations indicates a changing balance between licensing and FDI in favour of the latter, indicating, *ceteris paribus*, that liberalisation tends to tilt the balance away from less-packaged forms of technology transfer (licensing agreements) to highly packaged forms (FDI).

The number of financial collaborations outnumbered technical collaborations in industries like fuels, including power, telecommunications, services and food processing (Arun, 1999). In chemicals, drugs and pharmaceuticals, and in the metallurgical subsector, technical collaborations outnumbered financial collaborations.

Table 7.5 shows the top ten industries with respect to FDI inflows, indicating the concentration of FDI in a few sectors, particularly infrastructure. It emerges that the sectors that were previously reserved for the public sector

Table 7.4   The pattern of foreign collaboration approvals 1991–99

Year	Total collaborations	Financial collaborations	FC as % of TC
1991	950	289	30.4
1992	1520	692	45.5
1993	1476	785	53.2
1994	1854	1062	57.3
1995	2337	1355	58.0
1996	2303	1559	67.7
1997	2325	1665	71.6
1998	1786	1191	66.7
1999*	322	269	83.5
Total	11367	6444	56.7

Note: Up to 1999 February only.

Source: *IIC Bulletin*, various dates; *SIA Newsletter*, April 1999.

Table 7.5   Industries receiving FDI approvals 1991–99

Industry	Total amount of FDI approved (Rs. billions)	Percentage of total FDI approvals
Fuels (including power)	607.83	32.14
Telecommunications	340.64	18.01
Transportation	128.97	6.82
Service sector	117.90	6.23
Chemicals	113.35	5.99
Metallurgy	111.67	5.90
Electrical equipment	96.88	5.12
Food processing	84.10	4.45
Hotels and tourism	35.14	1.86
Misc. industries	26.42	1.40

Source: *SIA Newsletter*, April 1999.

have attracted the largest amount of FDI. The fuel industry (power and oil
refining) had the largest share with 32 per cent of total approvals. Fuels and
telecommunications together accounted for approximately 50 per cent of the
total FDI approvals. The service sector had also increased its share consider-

ably during the 1991–99 period. Increased investment in infrastructure is expected to create new and improved facilities, leading to an overall improvement in competitiveness.

The ratio of actual to approved FDI is higher in China, Indonesia, Korea, the Philippines and Thailand, which rely heavily on FDI and are pulling ahead of India in terms of economic growth, income levels and productivity (Bajpai and Sachs, 2000). It is important to investigate why India cannot even match these countries in attracting FDI, given India's locational advantages with respect to the rule of law, democracy, and the English language. But even after a decade of reforms, India's FDI policies are quite restrictive as compared to its competitors. For instance, *The Global Competitiveness Report* (World Economic Forum, 1999) ranked India 57th with regard to cross-border ventures and 59th in terms of openness (out of 59 countries).

In a survey of manufacturing firms, it emerged that poor co-ordination among various government agencies resulted in delays in the clearing of projects (Arun, 1999). The multiple levels of clearances and the involvement of several departments in a single project have contributed to delays in project implementation. Arun (1999) also found that the time gap between filing an application for collaboration approval and the final clearance was very long and that there was inadequate understanding and implementation of policies at the regional/state levels.

State governments are less committed to the reform process due to their limited freedom in making decisions and the lack of effective competition among states (Arun, 1999). The examples of Brazil, China and Russia show the need and importance of regional governments taking the lead in pushing reforms and prompting further actions by the central government (Bajpai and Sachs, 2000). State governments try to ensure that investors get speedy clearances for land use, as well as adequate supplies of electricity, water and access to other facilities. In India, six states[11] out of 26 accounted for over half of total FDI approved (Arun, 1999). Since private investment is highly mobile across states, it is natural that FDI is attracted to states which have better infrastructure and governance, and an investor-friendly bureaucracy. The successful states have introduced a number of specific measures in a consistent sequence to promote investor confidence and to attract large amounts of investment. To achieve the ambitious target of $10 billion in actual FDI inflows per year set by the GOI (Bajpai and Sachs, 2000), it is essential to design, develop and implement policies at the national level, which encourage more competition between various states. Porter (1994) observed that micro-level reforms at the state level are also essential to develop the competitive industrial climate in India, which eventually helps to attract higher levels of FDI (*The Economic Times*, 27 September 1994). There is also a fear that inter-state disparities in growth and development will increase as a result of liberalisation.

3.3 Industrial Growth

Data on industrial growth rates in India between 1991–92 and 1998–99 show an average growth rate of 5.78 per cent in the industrial sector as a whole and 6.88 per cent for the manufacturing sector. The industrial growth rate peaked at 12.8 per cent in 1995–96 and then fell to 4 per cent in 1998–99 (Table 7.6). The average growth rate for 1991–2000 was only 5.8 per cent, which is not very encouraging considering that India had registered an average annual industrial growth rate of 8 per cent during the 1980s.

Table 7.6   Annual growth rates in major sectors of industry (per cent)

Period (Weights)	Mining (10.47) (11.46)*	Manufacturing (79.36) (77.11)*	Electricity (10.17) (11.43)*	General (100) (100)*
1991–92	0.6	–0.8	8.5	0.6
1992–93	0.5	2.2	5.0	2.3
1993–94	3.5	6.1	7.4	6.0
1994–95	7.6	8.5	8.5	8.4
1995–96	9.6	13.8	8.1	12.8
1996–97	–2.0	6.7	4.0	5.6
1997–98	5.9	6.6	6.6	6.6
1998–99	–1.7	4.3	6.5	4.0
1999–00**	0.0	6.7	7.7	6.2

Note: Growth rates from 1994–95 are as per the IIP base: 1993–94 = 100, and those for earlier years are for IIP base: 1980–81 = 100.
 * Relates to weights for IIP base: 1980–81 = 100.
** Relates to April to December.

Source: GOI (1999); GOI (2000).

Table 7.7 indicates the high growth rates of the intermediate goods sector (9.2 per cent) compared with the consumer goods sector (7.1 per cent). During the period 1980–81 to 1988–89, the annual growth rates of the intermediate and durable consumer goods sector were 5.8 per cent and 12.4 per cent respectively (Kaplinsky, 1997). The significant characteristic of industrial growth since the 1980s has been the expansion of the consumer goods sector, which indicates the extent to which industrial growth has been fuelled by an expansion of middle-income purchasing power (Kaplinsky, 1997). Kaplinsky (1997, p. 685), further argues that 'during the 1990s, not only has the expansion of middle-income demand been sustained, but the openness to

Table 7.7   Growth rate of industrial production (Base 1993–94=100)

Year Weight	Basic goods 35.5	Capital goods 9.7	Intermediate goods 26.4	Consumer goods 28.4	Industrial sector 100
1994–95	8.9	5.7	5.3	11.8	8.4
1995–96	10.7	4.1	19.1	12.3	12.8
1996–97	3.1	9.3	8.1	5.2	5.6
1997–98	6.5	5.3	8.1	5.7	6.6
1998–99	1.4	12.7	5.9	2.4	4.0
1999–00*	5.1	6.6	8.7	4.9	6.2
Average	6.0	7.3	9.2	7.1	7.3

Note: * Relates to April to December.

Source: GOI (2000).

imports and to international taste-patterns has for the first time forced manu-facturers to "win over" consumers rather than to produce poor quality standardised products in a supply-constrained market'.

During the period 1994–95 to 1998–99, the capital goods sector grew at an average annual growth rate of 7.42 per cent. This was below the average annual rate of growth of the industrial sector as a whole over that period and was lower than the rate of growth of the capital goods sector during the 1980s. The development of the capital goods sector is important for the industrialisation process as a whole through its beneficial impact on produc-tivity and innovation in user industries. Rosenberg (1963, p. 223) pointed out the importance of the capital goods sector in that countries that do not have a local capital goods sector tend to lack the 'technological base of skills, knowledge, facilities and organisation upon which technical progress so largely depends'. Although the lower growth rate of the capital goods sector in the liberalisation period could be a cause for concern, it may nevertheless repre-sent a predictable reallocation of resources between and within sectors resulting from the greater openness of the economy. The performance of the industrial sector as a whole however, could be said to be less than satisfactory.

4   FIRM-LEVEL STRATEGIES UNDER LIBERALISATION

Industrialisation is a process of acquiring technological capability in the course of continuing technological change (Pack and Westphal, 1986). Lall

(1987) has argued that the main agent for technological activity is the individual firm, which learns to use new technologies, adapt them, improve upon them and create new knowledge. This approach to industrial development, based on micro-level processes of capability building, indicates the importance of tacit elements in technology transfer, which the buyer needs to develop through new skills, techniques and organisational improvements.

A survey of 190 non-equity alliances,[12] both domestic and foreign, during the period 1995–97 shows that a significant proportion of alliances (two-thirds) was designed to access critical complementary assets such as marketing (Table 7.8). In another survey of 50 joint ventures in the manufacturing sector, Arun (1999) also found that foreign inputs in marketing (38 per cent of the sample) and advertising (40 per cent of the sample) were high, which demonstrates their importance in stimulating demand in a deregulated economy.[13] This is different from the findings in the regulated period, which showed a lesser importance for marketing and advertising (an indicator of product differentiation) in the FDI package (Lall and Mohammad, 1983). The reason cited for this was the less advantageous nature of sophisticated marketing and advertising techniques in a country that was characterised by low income levels and huge differences in consumption patterns, tastes and culture.

Table 7.8 Distribution of alliances by objectives, 1995–97 (percentage of total alliances)

Technology development	4.8
Technology licensing	19.6
Manufacturing	17.5
Plant and division setting	4.8
Distribution	4.2
Marketing	38.1
Marketing and manufacturing	5.3
Input sourcing	2.1
Financial support	2.1
Consultancy services	2.1

Source: Basant, 2000.

The other significant point is the increasing role of product differentiation since 1991. Although the total selling expenses as a proportion of sales for the Indian corporate sector increased in the early 1990s, it has declined since 1994–95. The rise in such expenses was essentially due to increases in the expenditure on advertising and marketing (Table 7.9). The product level analysis shows that advertising expenditures have increased significantly in

1

52 Economic policy and manufacturing performance

Table 7.9   Some aspects of non-price competition

| | Selling expenses (percentages) | | | | |
Year	Advertising/ sales	Marketing/ sales	Distribution/ sales	Total/ sales	Number of firms
1991–92	0.41	3.34	2.50	6.25	4031
1992–93	0.46	3.80	2.64	6.89	4577
1993–94	0.56	4.14	2.70	7.40	5682
1994–95	0.55	3.31	2.19	6.06	7332
1995–96	0.59	3.02	2.17	5.78	8373
1996–97	0.58	3.49	2.17	6.24	8022

Source: Centre for Monitoring Indian Economy (CMIE) Database cited in Basant, 2000.

all the sectors, at a pace much faster than marketing and distribution expenses. Rapid growth in advertising expenditures in industries like iron and steel, petroleum products and non-metallic mineral products signifies the emergence of product differentiation strategies in sectors which were hitherto known for their homogeneous products (Basant, 2000). Basant further argues that lower investment in complementary assets other than advertising can result in a decline in the relative competitiveness of Indian industries.

Chandra and Sastry (1998) argue that Indian firms are giving highest priority to shop floor improvement programmes in the manufacturing sector, such as on-time delivery and design changes (Table 7.10). All these aim to increase the reliability and durability of manufacturing products. However, Chandra and Sastry (1998) also noted that though the mean improvement scores for factors such as worker productivity and customer returns were the highest, the variance was also high, which implies that not all the firms performed well during the period.

Training is an important issue that affects most levels of employees, from single manufacturing operatives through supervisors to technically advanced professionals and top-level managers. Enos (1992) concluded that training is essential for the optimum utilisation of new technologies, resulting in enhanced productivity and competitiveness. Lillard and Tan (1986) and Mincer (1990) found empirical support for the relationship between training and technological change. Chandra and Sastry (1998) cited the importance of training as a factor in increasing productivity. They found that 10 per cent of the sample firms had increased their spending on training during the period 1995–97.

In a survey of a sample of manufacturing enterprises carried out in 1996–1997, Arun (1999) also found that training activities contributed towards

Table 7.10   Improvements in manufacturing 1995–97

Category of improvement	Percentage improvements during 1995–97
Worker productivity	37.5
Customer return rates	37.2
Profitability	26.9
First year yield	23.4
Customer's perception of quality	21.7
On-time delivery	18.9
Manufacturing to design changes	13.7
Manufacturing cycle time	13.7
Speed of new product development	13.5
Delivery lead time	13.5
Finished goods inventory	13.3
Market share	11.9
Changes over times	11.0
Procurement lead time	10.5
Raw materials inventory	8.9
Work-in-process inventory	8.2
Raw material defect rates	7.4
On-time completion of new production projects	7.2
Average unit production cost	5.9

Source: Chandra and Sastry, 1998.

creating quality consciousness and also helped workers to develop positive work behaviour. Twelve per cent of the sample firms had increased their spending on training and 10 per cent of firms had increased expenditure on training overseas.

In a few cases, subjective factors other than employee capability, specialisation and efficiency influenced selection for training, which in part negated the purpose of training. Similarly, the practice of identifying training needs prior to designing training programmes was virtually absent in the firms. However, 12 per cent of the sample firms had increased their spending on training in 1996–97.

We noted above the increasing importance of shop floor improvement programmes in the manufacturing sector. Although it is difficult to measure the relative importance of organisational and managerial practices in explaining the competitive position of firms due to the intuitive nature of these practices, they are increasingly recognised as factors central to the competitiveness of firms (Doz and Prahalad, 1984). In many cases shared norms and expectations have been shown to shape employee orientations towards work and determine the extent to which individuals direct their behaviour toward achieving goals defined by the organisation (Schein, 1996).

Arun (1999) also found that increasingly in the reform period in many firms, job descriptions and rules about hiring, remuneration, and promotion clearly communicated performance expectations by indicating what the employee needed to do in order to be retained or promoted. In many firms the norms for commitment, efficiency, effectiveness and responsiveness were communicated at the same time that new employees were being taught about the specific requirements of the jobs for which they had been hired. It was also noted that the adoption of these organisational and managerial practices helped the firms to increase the levels of awareness and the commitment of workers towards the organisation.

5   CONCLUSIONS

Before 1991 the regulatory framework was used extensively to encourage the growth of the public sector and to control flows of capital and technology into India. This strategy came under increasing strain in the 1980s, and in 1991 the government of India (GOI) introduced a package of reform measures including liberalisation, deregulation and disinvestment aimed at the opening up and restructuring of the Indian economy.

In this chapter we have considered the reform process as it has affected PSEs, FDI and the industrial sector. The basic argument is that the reform process has tended to be somewhat incomplete and erratic. With respect to PSEs, for example, disinvestment coupled with the maintenance of significant public ownership and control has led to a partial transfer of productive assets from the public to the private sector, but improved competitiveness and increased productivity have not been given the highest priority.

With respect to FDI, although the investment regime has been changed radically, problems remain. India has a low ratio of actual to approved FDI, indicating that foreign companies still appear to experience problems investing in India. There is some evidence of a shift away from non-equity relationships (licensing of technology) towards FDI, which has implications for technology transfer and the development of domestic technological capabilities. The concentration of FDI in a relatively limited number of sectors is also notable. Overall, India still retains a relatively low ranking as far as global competitiveness is concerned.

In the industrial sector, there has been a decline in the rate of growth in the 1990s as compared to the 1980s. There is evidence of structural change within the sector, with a shift towards intermediate and consumer goods subsectors, away from capital goods. This is an indication that industrial growth has been shaped by the wants of an expanded middle-income purchasing power along with the associated phenomena of greater product differentiation and advertising. The slower rate of growth of the capital goods sector may well limit India's ability to expand further its indigenous technological capabilities.

The limited firm-level evidence presented in this chapter tends to suggest that Indian enterprises are increasingly using foreign collaborations to improve their marketing and advertising capabilities and develop their product differentiation strategies. Quality improvement and better training, organisational and managerial practices are also being accorded a higher priority by the enterprises surveyed.

Clearly the success or failure of the new policy regime depends to a large extent on the extent to which enterprises are able to position themselves competitively. The limited evidence available tends to suggest that there is a higher level of awareness among Indian firms of the opportunities to increase competitiveness that the new policy regime has opened up. But firm choices and their growth prospects appear to be constrained by the formulation and implementation of policy at both Central and State levels. The GOI needs to promote greater transparency in policy formulation and implementation and better governance at both central and state levels, with the aim of increasing the absorptive capacity of the economy, improving the investment climate and positioning the economy so that it can take advantage of the opportunities opened up by the 1991 reforms.

NOTES

1. The Central sector includes departmental undertakings such as Posts and Telecommunications and Railways and the non-departmental enterprises of Government corporations. Public sector enterprises include departmental and non-departmental enterprises. Departmental enterprises form part of the Government financial system but have separate accounts for income and expenditure. Non-departmental enterprises are legally separate from the Government and maintain separate accounts for their financial transactions.
2. In the 1956 Industrial Policy Resolution, 17 industries were exclusively reserved for the public sector. But this did not preclude the expansion of the existing private units, or the possibility of the state securing the co-operation of private enterprise in the establishment of new units when the national interest so required. These core industries were classified as Schedule A industries – (1) arms and ammunition (2) atomic energy (3) iron and steel (4) heavy castings and forging of iron and steel (5) heavy plant and machinery required for iron and steel production (6) heavy electrical plant (7) coal and lignite (8) mineral oils (9) mining of iron ore, manganese ore, etc. (10) mining and processing of copper, lead, zinc, etc. (11) minerals specified in the schedule for atomic energy (12) aircraft (13) air transport (14) railway transport (15) shipbuilding (16) telephones and telephone cables and (17) generation and distribution of electricity (GOI, 1997).

3. The number of Central PSEs increased from five in 1951 to 243 in 1996. During this period total investment in these enterprises increased from Rs. 290 million to Rs. 1786.3 billion in current prices.
4. The return on PSEs was around 2.0 to 4.5 per cent between 1980–81 and 1992–93 (Arun and Nixson, 1997).
5. The Industrial Policy Resolution (IPR) of 1991 (GOI, 1997) cited factors like poor project management, overmanning, lack of continuous technological upgrading, inadequate attention to R&D and human resource development as preventing the enterprises from increasing their productivity and competitiveness.
6. The Foreign Exchange Regulation Act (FERA) of 1973 required all non-banking foreign branches and companies incorporated under the Indian Companies Act with more than 40 per cent foreign equity participation to obtain the permission of the Reserve Bank of India to continue their business in the country. This policy also required those all-foreign branches that had up to 40 per cent equity to transfer all their business to Indian companies.
7. Until 1991, industrial licensing was mainly governed by the Industries (Development and Regulation) Act, 1951. To implement the new policy, Notification No. 477 (E) dated 25 July 1991 was issued under the I (D &R) Act 1951. Under this notification, industrial undertakings have been exempted from the operation of sections 10, 11, 11(a) and 13 of the I (D&R) Act 1951 subject to fulfilment of certain conditions. Section 10 refers to the requirement of registration of existing industrial units. Section 11 refers to the requirement of licensing of new industrial undertakings. Section 11(a) deals with licences for the production of new articles. Section 13 refers to the requirement of licensing for effecting substantial expansion.
8. The reforms also reduced the list of industries reserved for the public sector from seventeen to six with the intention of increasing the flow of resources to priority sectors and enhancing the competitiveness of the public sector. These industries are (1) arms and ammunition and allied items of defence equipment, defence aircraft and warships (2) atomic energy (3) coal and lignite (4) mineral oils (5) minerals specified for atomic energy and (6) railway transport (GOI, 1997).
9. The Memoranda of Understanding (MOU) attempt to bring a proper balance between accountability and autonomy, and emphasise the fulfilment of the negotiated and agreed objectives rather than interfering in the day-to-day affairs of the PSEs.
10. This was a financial scandal involving a Bombay Stock Exchange trader, who swindled billions of rupees' worth of shares with the help of nationalised banks, government officials and politicians (Arun, 1999).
11. These states are Delhi, Maharashtra, Karnataka, Tamil Nadu, Madhya Pradesh and West Bengal (Arun, 1999).
12. In this survey, the information was compiled from the Centre for Monitoring Indian Economy (CMIE) publications based on a total of 190 non-equity alliances for the period 1995–97 (Basant, 2000).
13. In this survey, the sample was confined mainly to those firms in the manufacturing sector which were established between 1980 and 1985, with a minimum 25 per cent and maximum of less than 100 per cent foreign equity. The main intention of selecting companies established in the 1980s was that by 1991, when the liberalisation process really started, the firms might have gained the necessary experience to decide on the future of their collaborations. Out of 50 firms, 34 belonged to the medium size category (100–499 employees) and 16 firms to the large size category (500+) (Arun, 1999).

REFERENCES

Ahluwalia, I.J. (1991), *Productivity and Growth in Indian Manufacturing*, New Delhi: Oxford University Press.

Ahluwalia, I.J. (1999), 'The Indian Economy: Looking Ahead' in *Contemporary India* (ed.) Pai Panandiker and Ashis Nandy, New Delhi: Tata McGraw-Hill.

Arun, T.G. (1999), *Economic Reform in India since 1991 with Particular Reference to Direct Foreign Investment and Privatisation*, PhD thesis, University of Manchester.

Arun, T.G. and F.I. Nixson (1997), 'Privatisation and Foreign Participation: The Indian Experience', *Journal of Asia Pacific Economy*, **2**(2), pp. 201–24.

Arun, T.G. and F.I. Nixson (2000), 'The Disinvestment of Public Sector Enterprises: The Indian Experience', *Oxford Development Studies*, **28**(1), pp. 19–32.

Athreye, S. and S. Kapur (1999), *Private Foreign Investment in India: Pain or Panacea?, Discussion Paper 17*, Birkbeck College, University of London.

Bajpai, N. and J.D. Sachs (2000), *Foreign Direct Investment in India: Issues and Problems*, Development Discussion Paper No. 759, Harvard Institute for International Development, Harvard University.

Basant, R. (2000), 'Corporate Response to Economic Reforms', *Economic and Political Weekly*, 4 March, pp. 813–22.

Chandok, H.L. and the Policy Group (1990), *India Database: The Economy, Annual Time Series Data* Vols I and II, New Delhi: Living Media India Ltd.

Chandra, P. and T. Sastry (1998), 'Competitiveness of Indian Manufacturing: Findings of the 1997 Manufacturing Futures Survey', *Vikalpa*, **23**(3), pp. 25–36.

Doz, Y. and C.K. Prahlad (1984), 'Patterns of Strategic Control in Multinational Corporations', *Journal of International Business Studies*, **15**(2), pp. 55–72.

Enos, J. (1992), *The Creation of Technological Capabilities in Developing Countries*, London: Pinter.

GOI (1948), *Industrial Policy Resolution*, New Delhi: Ministry of Industry.

GOI (1956), *Industrial Policy Resolution*, New Delhi: Ministry of Industry.

GOI (1973), *Industrial Policy Resolution*, New Delhi: Ministry of Industry.

GOI (1977), *Industrial Policy Resolution*, New Delhi: Ministry of Industry.

GOI (1980), *Industrial Policy Resolution*, New Delhi: Ministry of Industry.

GOI (1991), *Industrial Policy Resolution*, New Delhi: Ministry of Industry.

GOI (1996), *Public Enterprises Survey 1995–96*, Volumes 1–3, New Delhi: Ministry of Industry, Department of Public Enterprises.

GOI (1997), *Handbook of Industrial Policy and Statistics*, New Delhi: Ministry of Industry.

GOI (1999), *Economic Survey 1999–2000*, New Delhi: Ministry of Finance.

GOI (2000), *Economic Survey 2000–01*, New Delhi: Ministry of Finance.

Gupta, S.P. (1993), *Liberalisation: Its Impact on the Indian Economy*, New Delhi: Macmillan.

IIC (1991–1998), *Bulletin on Direct Foreign Investment*, various years, New Delhi: Indian Investment Centre.

Jalan, B. (1991), *India's Economic Crisis*, New Delhi: Oxford University Press.

Kaplinsky, R. (1997), India's Industrial Development: An Interpretative Survey, *World Development*, **25**(5) pp. 681–94.

Kumar, N. (1990), *Multinational Enterprises in India: Industrial Distribution, Characteristics and Performance*, London: Routledge.

Kumar, N. (1995), 'Industrialisation, Liberalisation and Two Way Flows of Foreign Direct Investments: Case of India', *Economic and Political Weekly*, **30**(50), pp. 3228–37.

Lal, D. (1980), *Prices for Planning*, London: Heinemann Educational Books.

Lal, D. (1999), *Unfinished Business: India in the World Economy*, New Delhi: Oxford University Press.

Lall, S. (1987), *Learning to Industrialise*, Basingstoke: Macmillan Press.

Lall, S. and S. Mohammed (1983), 'Foreign Ownership and Export Performance in the Large Corporate Sector of India', *Journal of Development Economics*, **13**, pp. 143–57.

Lillard, L. and H. Tan (1986), *Private Sector Training: Who Gets It and Why*, The Rand Corporation.

Marjit, S. and N. Singh (1993), *Technology and Indian Industry*, University of California at Santa Cruz, mimeo, Santa Cruz.

Mincer, J. (1990), *Labour Market Effects of Human Capital and of its Adjustment to Technological Change*, New York: Department of Economics, Columbia University.

Mookherjee, D. (1995), *Indian Industry: Policies and Performance*, New Delhi: Oxford University Press.

Pack, H. and L.E. Westphal (1986), 'Industrial Strategy and Technological Change: Theory versus Reality', *Journal of Development Economics*, **22**, pp. 87–128.

Porter (1994), *The Economic Times*, 27 September 1994.

Rosenberg, N. (1963), 'Capital Goods, Technology and Economic Growth', *Oxford Economic Papers*, **15**(3), pp. 217–27.

Schein, L. (1996), *Strategic Pragmatism: The Culture of Singapore's Economic Development Board*, Singapore: Tappan Company.

Secretariat of Industrial Approval (1999), *News Letter*, New Delhi: Ministry of Industry.

Vickers, J. and G. Yarrow (1988), *Privatisation: An Economic Analysis*, London: MIT Press.

World Bank (1994), *India: Recent Economic Development and Prospects*, Country Report, Washington, DC: World Bank.

World Economic Forum (1999), *Global Competitiveness Report*, Geneva: World Economic Forum.

8. Small enterprise development in Cambodia: the role of credit

Ian Livingstone

1 INTRODUCTION

Cambodia is a country still undergoing reconstruction. Most economic activity is informal, and national-level economic policies have little relevance to the mass of the population. Manufacturing activity is predominantly small-scale. This does not mean, however, that policy is irrelevant. Government policies are important in stimulating a vibrant small-scale sector, but perhaps there is a prior stage before such policies can have an impact. This prior stage is enterprise start-up, and the single most important policy issue in this regard is access to credit. In practice, at the micro level, most credit initiatives are by the private sector, specifically non-governmental organisations (NGOs), rather than government. It is this very early, core policy on which we focus in this chapter.

Section 2 briefly reviews some statistical evidence regarding the nature and importance of small enterprises in Cambodia, to set the scene. Section 3 then discusses the constraints under which they operate. Some indications of the entrepreneurial capacities of rural Cambodians are suggested, based on the range of activities for which loans have been secured in two different regions of Cambodia. A number of exceptionally successful (so far) micro-credit programmes for small enterprise have been developed in the country by NGOs. These are described in Section 4. Section 5 identifies a major current issue. Should these programmes continue to focus, as in the past, on micro-enterprises and poverty among poor households attempting to diversify their sources of income or, as they appear to be doing increasingly, direct their efforts to developing more substantial enterprises with more potential for growth. Related to this, consideration is also given, secondly, to the question whether the focus should remain, as now, on rural enterprise, on grounds of equity and poverty alleviation, or be expanded to incorporate assistance to urban small and medium enterprise.

2   THE NEED TO RAISE INCOMES AND CREATE EMPLOYMENT

According to the 1996 Socio-Economic Survey of Cambodia (SESC, 1996), 78 per cent of the labour force of some five million persons were engaged as a primary occupation in the Agriculture, Forestry and Fishery sector, only 4.7 per cent in industry and 17.1 per cent in services and trade. At the same time, however, one in four persons had a secondary occupation, often a household enterprise. In line with this, almost 90 per cent were working on their own account or as unpaid family workers, and just 10 per cent as employees (including 3.5 per cent as full professionals or in the Armed Forces). Deducting the 78 per cent in the Agriculture, Forestry and Fishery sector from the 90 per cent operating on their own account leaves a significant 12 per cent operating on their own account outside the primary sectors, that is, in micro and small enterprises in manufacturing, trade and services.

There is only limited open unemployment, in rural or urban areas, due to the absence of any social security provision. An immediate employment problem relates to the prospective demobilisation of some 55 000 redundant soldiers; and to 27 000 refugees due to return from Thailand, the latter hopefully to be reabsorbed in rural areas. To this must be added further substantial retrenchment from the Civil Service, as part of the reforms aimed at raising levels of pay and increasing efficiency. There is also evidence of an embryonic youth employment problem: the latest available labour force survey for Phnom Penh, for the second quarter of 1998, shows unemployment rates of over 5 per cent among males in the age groups 20–29 and as high as 6.0 per cent among females aged 15–19. In the same survey, the overall unemployment rate is not especially high, at 2.1 per cent (1.7 per cent among males and 2.5 per cent among females).

Future unemployment is likely to manifest itself in Phnom Penh, as a result of job seekers drifting to the capital city, which accounts for a dominant share of the urban population in Cambodia. However, given the high current rates of rural-urban migration, these rates may increase significantly in the future. Already the share of urban population in the total for Cambodia is estimated to have increased from 15.5 per cent in 1993/4 to 16.7 per cent in 1996. This implies an increase of 13.5 per cent in the absolute size of the urban population in that relatively short time, and thus an annual rate of increase of 5.2 per cent. This rate would produce a further increase over the next five years of half a million people.

In fact, the likely rate of rural-urban migration will be still higher, due to two related observable phenomena in rural Cambodia. The first is that agricultural mechanisation is proceeding apace in many parts, displacing and reducing the demand for labour. Secondly, this opportunity for more mechanised agriculture serves as an incentive also for unethical or forced expulsion under threat of small farmers from their own holdings, in what is widely described as land grabbing. In the north-west of Cambodia this has led to an even less desirable form of migration, the increased search by Cambodians for employment outside the country, in Thailand.

There is a further problem of disguised unemployment in rural areas. As evidence of this, a recent survey in Phnom Penh (Sophal *et al.*, 1998) revealed that 89 per cent of cyclo drivers interviewed and 80 per cent of porters were based residentially in rural areas, coming into the capital intermittently in search of work. This indicates both a need and an opportunity for the development of non-farm employment.

Although open unemployment remains limited, as in other developing countries the fundamental problem translates itself into one of low incomes and outright poverty through being engaged, often overworked, in low income, low return activities such as one-crop rice production. The problem thus becomes in large part one of rural development in order to raise incomes above the (1998) per capita level of just $255, one of the lowest in the region. This calls for the urgent raising of both farm and non-farm income in the rural areas as well as the provision of urban employment.

Given the low incomes secured from crop production by most farm households, it has already been necessary for rural households to diversify income sources, as revealed by the 1993–94 Socio-Economic Survey of Cambodia (SESC, 1993–94) (Table 8.1). This suggested that 44 per cent of monetary and non-monetary income of households in Cambodia came from business, broadly defined (adding the 36.8 per cent and 7.7 per cent in the upper half of the table) – 49 per cent in the case of Phnom Penh but even in rural areas as much as 41 per cent. In both cases the values for agriculture are probably substantial underestimates, it should be said, viewed against labour force survey figures for 1998. The SESC found that one-third of rural workers had secondary occupations, compared with 8.5 per cent in Phnom Penh and 16.5 per cent in other urban areas. Here the low level of salaries in the public sector of $20–30 per month has led public servants of all categories to take up small enterprises in order to secure a livelihood.

In discussing small and micro-enterprise, we may distinguish between household-based enterprises and independent small enterprises, both of which fall into the category of what has been described as the 'informal sector'. A large proportion of group loans through NGO agencies probably goes, apart from household farm production, to other household-based activities. A feature of Cambodia, however, is that in urban areas also, small-scale enterprises are often household-based, with residences and enterprises existing cheek-by-jowl, unzoned and intermingled.[1]

Table 8.1   Sources of household income: Phnom Penh, other urban and rural areas, 1993/4

Source of income	Phnom Penh	Other urban	Rural	Cambodia
Monetary	63.2	61.4	69.5	67.4
Wages	14.2	13.7	6.6	9.2
Business	40.2	38.9	33.6	36.8
Agriculture	1.2	5.8	27.2	18.1
Other	7.6	3.0	2.1	3.3
Non-monetary	36.8	38.6	30.5	32.6
Own household	26.5	23.5	6.3	12.7
Business	9.0	9.3	7.2	7.7
Agriculture	0.6	5.1	16.3	11.4
Other	0.7	0.7	0.7	0.8
Monetary and Non-monetary				
Business	49.2	48.2	40.8	44.5
Agriculture	1.8	10.9	43.9	29.5
Total	100.0	100.0	100.0	100.0
Riel per household per month	535 542	264 350	130 849	
Number of households	121 134	124 012	947 747	

Note: All figures are percentages unless indicated otherwise.

Source: SES Cambodia, 1993/4, all rounds, reproduced in SEDP.

The 1996 SESC gives (the only) good information on this aspect, being based on a stratified sample of 9000 households in 750 villages and spanning both rural and urban areas. This showed that across all areas 11 per cent of households, one in nine, operated a business from their household premises, and 20 per cent, one in five, in Phnom Penh. Extrapolated to the national level this gave more than 185 000 households engaged in the six most common activities, retailing accounting for more than half, with textiles and wearing apparel (tailoring) also important (see Table 8.2).

Data on registered industrial establishments are collected by the Industrial Statistics Division of the Ministry of Industry, Mines and Energy (MIME). We can refer to establishments employing 1–9 persons as micro-enterprises (including 1–2 as self-employed) and 10–49 persons as small enterprises.[2] There are a vast number of establishments in the former category, as can be seen in Table 8.3. The total number in 1998 in both categories, 24 663, compares with 28 554 recorded in 1997 and 25 620 in 1996, an apparent

Table 8.2   Most common household-based enterprises in Cambodia, 1996

Activity	No. of enterprises 1000s	% of enterprises
Retailing	98.6	53.2
Textiles manufacture	37.9	20.5
Weaving apparel manufacture	21.2	11.4
Wood and wood products	13.9	7.5
Grain milling	6.8	3.7
Sugar making	6.8	3.7
Total	185.2	100

Source: SESC (1996).

Table 8.3   Number of small and micro industrial establishments by industry, 1998

	No. of establishments (by employment)			
Industry	< 10	10–49	< 50	50+
Mining and quarrying	35	74	109	28
Manufacturing	23 588	510	24 098	218
Food, beverages and tobacco	18 419	171	18 590	33
Textiles, wearing apparel	291	19	310	130
Wood, wood products	847	48	895	22
Paper and paper products	15	11	26	2
Chemicals, rubber and plastic products	25	30	55	10
Non-metallic mineral products	624	187	811	15
Basic metals	–	4	4	1
Fabricated metal	1 334	37	1 371	5
Other manufactured	2 033	2	2 035	0
Electricity, gas and water	438	19	457	6
Total	24 061	603	24 664	252

Source: MIME (1998).

decline which reflects clearly enough the effects of the regional crisis and reduced aggregate demand. The figure of 24 663 for small and micro industrial establishments in 1998 compares with 252 establishments employing 50 persons or more. The vast majority of manufacturing/industrial establishments in Cambodia thus fall in the micro/small category. Of course, one large garment factory, which may employ 800 persons or more in Cambodia's rapidly expanding export sector, will employ as many people as 160 average sized micro establishments.

Table 8.4   Distribution of small manufacturing industrial establishments in Cambodia, 1998, by province (10–49 persons in size)

Province	Food	Wood	Non-metal	Metals	Other	Total No.	%
Phnom Penh	50	10	48	33	60	201	39.4
Kandal	18	4	51	1	4	78	15.3
Sub-total	*68*	*14*	*99*	*34*	*64*	*279*	*54.7*
Kratie	17	13	15	–	–	45	8.8
Kampong-Cham	19	2	15	–	1	37	7.3
Battambang	14	–	15	2	1	32	6.3
Siem Reap	8	–	15	1	–	24	4.7
Other	45	19	28	–	1	93	18.2
Total	171	48	187	37	67	510	100

Notes: Foods includes beverages, Wood includes wood products, 'non-metal' is non-metallic mineral products, 'metals' is fabricated metal products, and 'other' is other manufactures.

Source: SESC (1996).

Table 8.3 brings out the overwhelming importance, in terms of number of establishments, of the Food, Beverages and Tobacco industry, accounting for more than three-quarters of the total number of industrial establishments. It should be observed that, while micro-enterprises are much more widely distributed across the country, partly in line with population, the 'small industry' category is less so (Table 8.4). These are much more concentrated in Phnom Penh and the surrounding Kandal Province, together accounting for 55 per cent of establishments. Together with just four other provinces (Kratie, Kampong Cham, Battambang, and Siem Reap) they account for 82 per cent of the total.

3 CONSTRAINTS ON SME DEVELOPMENT IN CAMBODIA

A number of major constraints on small and micro enterprise (SME) development in Cambodia may be listed: (i) low incomes and purchasing power; (ii) poor national and local roads; (iii) competition from imports and poor product quality; (iv) lack of good information on domestic and foreign markets, and on domestic and foreign sources of technology and equipment; (v) shortage of working capital and low household propensities to save; (vi) high cost and limited availability of power; (vii) high 'informal' road taxes; (viii) low levels of education and technical skills.

A basic constraint on the development of all kinds of enterprise in Cambodia, including SMEs, is the level of purchasing power, determining demand and the size of the market. This stems from the low per capita income of (in 1998) only $255, including a large percentage of non-monetary income. About 87 per cent of arable land in Cambodia is under rice, a good part of it single-cropped, yielding little more than subsistence. With incomes so low, right across the country, the pattern of demand is biased towards goods that are affordable by the poor, that is, towards 'informal sector' micro-enterprise production. The limitations of the domestic market reduce the scope for large scale factory production – though it has been possible, as already noted, to expand very rapidly the number of garment factories, directed towards the international market. This has reduced the possibilities for 'backward or forward linkages' between large and small enterprise in Cambodia, which can be quite important in other developing countries, including neighbouring Thailand, where subcontracting to small enterprise has been a feature. Though uninvestigated, linkages could be quite significant among and between the small enterprises themselves, however.

A second major constraint is the state of the national road network and of rural access roads. The main east and west highways across the country (Highways 5 and 6) are still under construction, with some sections still awaiting donor funding. It takes as much as 14 hours to drive from Phnom Penh to Battambang, the second largest town, which is in the northwest; this trip would take no more than 5–6 hours with a good tarmac road. The northeast of the country has still to be developed, and populated, due to lack of communications. As a result, Cambodia has been said to possess a 'fragmented economy', with the northwest region developing market links with Thailand, and the northeast with Vietnam. There are, therefore, sub-markets within Cambodia, rather than an integrated national market that can offer economies of scale in production. The poor condition of rural access roads fragments the market further, limiting the scope for specialisation and local trade.

The state of the roads, national and local, increases the cost of materials and the price payable by consumers and, where this cannot be increased, the profitability and viability of enterprises. In contrast, where good roads have been introduced the impact has been immediate. Following the construction of Highway 3 to Sihanoukville, for example, there has been a dramatic increase in agricultural and non-agricultural activity, with substantial expansion of settled population. Again, a survey of rural road traffic carried out in Siem Reap Province by the ILO in 1998 showed that, following rehabilitation, road users almost doubled the number of trips made, with even more than this in the vicinity of several remote towns. Transporters also reported a doubling in the volume of goods transported. Among villages, bicycle transport frequencies increased by 89 per cent. The average reduction in reported travel time was 44 per cent, with a decrease in charges for all transport means of 38 per cent. In addition, 60 per cent of road users travelled to the district centre or further, compared with 40 per cent of users on non-rehabilitated roads, implying both increased access for buying and selling goods and increased access to health and other facilities only available at the district centre. These changes were associated with the decrease in travel time required and a reduction in transport charges for most road users of at least 20–30 per cent, in respect of both goods and passengers. Road rehabilitation was also found to have boosted motor cycle ownership significantly (and also, presumably, the number of motor cycle repair shops), possibly by as much as a quarter. Further, records at five market centres located outside Siem Reap showed a six-fold increase in the total number of market stands, reflecting a sharp increase in the number of vendors, and implying a corresponding increase in trade volume, based no doubt on increased farm and non-farm enterprise production (ILO, 1998). Road transport is thus of critical importance to SME development, directly, but also indirectly by making possible increases in agricultural production and incomes and thus increases in rural purchasing power for the purchase of SME products.

Another significant obstacle to the development of SME production, however, is strong competition from imported consumer and other goods, which enter through 'porous borders' from neighbouring countries, especially Thailand. These countries, being able to take advantage of economies of scale to produce and sell very cheaply, are adept at producing the types of cheap consumer goods that are in general demand in Cambodia, competing directly with domestic SMEs. Most wholesale and retail enterprises in Cambodia are largely re-selling products imported from Thailand, Vietnam and China, with some proportion from Phnom Penh. While SMEs in different parts of Cambodia are able to obtain some natural protection, due to transport costs, this will diminish as transport facilities improve.

The poor quality of domestic products is a further handicap in competing with foreign imports, which are of better quality as well as being cheaper. Following the years of relative isolation, there is a total lack of information both regarding international market requirements, for both agricultural and non-agricultural exports, and in respect of available technologies and equipment which could be used in agro-processing and other small-scale industries. There is, moreover, no one for an entrepreneur to go to in order to secure any such information.

The strong and clearly unsatisfied demand for NGO loans is indicative of an acute shortage of working capital among SMEs: working capital, because the limited loan period, mostly 12 months, restricts the value of such credit for longer term investments. Moreover, NGO credit to a great extent replaces the loans previously secured from moneylenders at high interest rates. These rates, up to 30 per cent per month, equivalent to 360 per cent per annum, preclude the use of such credit over periods longer than a few months. This accounts also for the high proportions of NGO credit employed in trading and in seasonal agriculture. One effect of working capital shortage among SMEs is a reduced capacity to produce goods locally to compete with imported goods.

The commercial banking system itself hardly extends into the rural areas in Cambodia, while the moneylender market is highly imperfect. Amongst a small group of entrepreneurs interviewed in Prey Veng, local market rates experienced varied from 10, 15, 20 and 30 per cent per month in different villages, access of borrowers being limited to the villages in which they were personally known to the lender.

This problem is exacerbated by the low level of savings in rural Cambodia. The proposed Asian Development Bank (ADB) rural credit programme identifies this as a major problem nationally and plans to incorporate a savings element into the rural credit programme. The fundamental cause of the low level of savings is evidently the low level of incomes, but in addition the absence of banking facilities in rural areas will have had a negative effect on the development of the savings habit. This will clearly retard and reduce the growth and development of SMEs.

A major handicap for both large and small industrial enterprise in Cambodia is the high cost of power. Electricity generation and distribution was recently observed as being mainly still in the 'technological dark ages'.[3] As a result of the erratic public power supply in Phnom Penh, factories have tended to generate their own electricity, which is still cheaper and more reliable than the public source. SMEs are at a significant disadvantage here, however, because of the economies of scale in electricity generation, and shortage of capital for investment in generators. Significantly, small-scale electric power supply is a common industry in rural and urban Cambodia (see Appendix Tables 8.A1 and 8.A2).

MIME has now produced a Power Sector Strategy 1999–2016 document as a draft plan for the sector. This proposes to develop a combination of (i) base load thermal generation at Sihanoukville, based on imported oil; (ii) only peak load generation in the provincial towns and cities; and (iii) new hydropower development based first on the smaller, easily accessible sites such as Kirirom, Prek Thuo and Kamchay and then through a number of mid-size hydro projects. These outputs will be integrated into a National Transmission System, which will also permit reduced dependence on imported oil and transmission of such oil. The incorporation of provincial towns will also facilitate the development of SMEs. However, the plan is also to develop rural electrification, on a limited scale. Recognising that capital investment in rural electrification has a very low rate of return, which will limit private participation, a proposal exists to base development on rural electrification co-operatives in the rural areas, benefiting from soft loans.

A further handicap is the existence of unofficial taxes, levies collected along the roads in rural Cambodia by military personnel. An example given (Ueda, 1995) is of a refreshment and ice manufacturer in Battambang who in 1995 regularly paid between $320 and $800 per trip to transport 20 000 empty bottles from the Thai border. Such taxes are still in evidence and have a particular impact on micro-enterprises and on farmers and small traders whose goods and materials are transported within the provinces.

The civil strife of the past several decades, and the poor quality of education on offer, have left a legacy of an uneducated or poorly educated and unskilled workforce, particularly in the countryside. This means not only a substantial training backlog, but special problems now in the delivery of technical or business training.

4   RURAL ENTREPRENEURSHIP IN CAMBODIA

In order to have a better idea of what entrepreneurial activities are actually going on in rural Cambodia, an analysis was carried out in two separate provinces of loans granted for different activities by ACLEDA, the main credit NGO. In Kampong Cham Province (all four districts) 1416 loans made to individual clients during the full year 1998 were examined. In Battambang Province (where the rate of loan issue has been slower) 1128 loans were made over the entire period 1994 to February 1999 (after which such data ceased to be collected).

It should be stressed that the data does not represent any very accurate sampling of rural activity; indeed, the sectoral distributions in the two provinces differ significantly (Table 8.5), reflecting differences in ACLEDA lending policy. Actual distributions are shown in official statistics as quoted earlier.

Table 8.5   Sectoral distribution of ACLEDA loans in two provinces

Sector	Kampong Cham (1998) (%)	Battambang (1994–99) (%)
Farm/fish production	22.8	15.2
Agro-processing	11.8	6.7
Manufacturing	7.6	24.0
Repair	1.4	5.0
Selling	37.4	38.1
General services	19.0	10.9
Total	100	100

Source: Derived from ACLEDA loan applications.

The purpose is to provide some disaggregated figures in order to see in detail something of the range of rural activities being carried on (including those in the two provincial towns, which are rural centres). The data, given in Tables 8.A1 and 8.A2, cover only loans made to individual clients, not group loans, since the objective of the credit component was to focus on small enterprises with more development potential.

What is significant is the impressive diversity of activities for which loans have been sought (and it is not suggested that these are the only ones that have potential). There are indications here of specialisation in particular lines that show commercial promise: for example, in farm production, mushroom growing, seed production and small tree growing. In manufacturing there is considerable diversity, including concrete pipes, water jars, trailers, wooden shutters, stoves, ploughshares, mattresses, motorcycle saddles, ladders, threshing and firewood-cutting machinery. In services there is also a wide range, including karaoke, a minibus service, house renting, purchase and sale, language and music schools, and a library.

The lists are sufficiently impressive to contradict the view often expressed by observers in developing countries, including Cambodia, that 'enterprises tend to choose the same line of business, thus creating competition in small markets [suggesting that] the abilities of SMEs to identify viable … business opportunities are lacking' (ILO 1997: 21). In fact, this tendency may reflect the limited opportunities open locally, for instance in the face of competition in alternative lines from imports, and free entry into limited local activities among a large number of similarly capable persons.

5 CREDIT FOR SMALL ENTERPRISE: POLICY ISSUES

The expansion of micro-enterprise credit by NGOs in Cambodia has been a major success story. Despite its main focus on the rural poor and a very high rate of expansion, repayment rates approaching 100 per cent and thus a high degree of sustainability of revolving funds have been achieved and maintained. ACLEDA, initiated in 1993 with ILO support, has been the dominant vehicle, but as many as 80 NGOs are now involved in the extension of microcredit to some degree. The bulk of credit being disbursed is through groups of five to ten persons, generally women, in some cases using a village bank model in which the village as a whole serves as guarantor.

At an early stage, in February 1995, the Cambodian government established the Credit Committee for Rural Development (CCRD) with the purpose of improving the co-ordination of policy among the disparate NGOs and of establishing in due course a Rural Development Bank (RDB). The latter now exists, in embryonic form. The main objectives of the RDB in rural credit were stated in 1997 to be to 'foster the development of rural credit ... achieve high efficiency of rural credit activities ... and maintain sustainability of rural credit activities' (CCRD, 1997). It is envisaged that the RDB would act largely as a 'wholesaler' of credit, which would be distributed through an expanded NGO system based especially on legalised micro-finance institutions (MFIs).

According to the 1996 Socio-economic Survey of Cambodia (SESC) an estimated 704 000 rural households, about 40 per cent of the total, took loans during the two years 1994 and 1995. Of this, one per cent came from banks and another 10 per cent (since increased) from NGOs and other such agencies. This implies enormous scope for the substitution of cheaper NGO credit for existing sources of loans. Different estimates have been made of the total and the unsatisfied demand for credit among rural households, a recent one by the Asian Development Bank (ADB) putting these at US$69 million and $37–40 million respectively. The demand for rural credit in Cambodia is thus extremely large. NGOs interviewed by its mission were of the unanimous view that a large unsatisfied demand exists.

It should be noted that not all borrowing is intended for investment, by any means. A study of three provinces by Murshid (1998), dividing rural households into six income strata ranging from the 'rich' and 'well off' to the 'very poor', showed great differences between strata in the uses to which credit was put. In the case of the 'very poor', 70 per cent of borrowing from all sources was for family rice consumption and 20 per cent for health treatment, both representing borrowing for the relief of distress. Among the 'well off', only 11 per cent of loans were for rice consumption and 9 per cent for health treatment, leaving 80 per cent for other purposes, including more directly productive ones. This offers something of a dilemma for NGOs aiming particularly at rural poverty alleviation but also wishing to promote more positive rural development.

5.1 Absorptive Capacity of the NGO-MFI System

Credit lines have been available to NGOs in Cambodia from a number of international sources, notably UNDP-ILO and the EU. With the restructuring of the sector under the umbrella of the RDB and a proposed conversion of some of the leading credit NGOs into MFIs, a major injection of funds by the ADB, which could be as much as $26 million, is anticipated. This has encouraged several NGOs to put forward extremely ambitious expansion programmes, particularly since most are starting from relatively small bases.

At the moment the sector is dominated by ACLEDA (Table 8.6). ACLEDA accounts for 70 per cent of lending by the 25 main NGOs involved in credit operations, the next four together accounting for only a further 20 per cent and the remaining 20 just 10 per cent between them. GRET (Ennatien Moulethan Tchonnebat) anticipates a new injection of external funding of some $3.5 million and plans a more than five-fold increase in loan disbursements over the period 1998–2004, implying annual rates of increase of 25–27 per cent. Cambodia Community Building (CCB) proposes to increase the value of loans outstanding from $818 000 in 1994 to $5 425 000 in 1999, a seven-fold increase over five years, implying annual rates of increase of 40 per cent or more. Catholic Relief Services (CRS) is more cautious, given the need to expand only as fast as more trained credit agents can be produced, and aims first to consolidate its activities. A particular element here is that CRS has operated as a 'wholesaler' through other NGOs so that only two of its eight credit outlets are its own branches. In order to establish itself as an MFI it will need to expand its own credit structures. Taking the five prospective MFIs together, there appears to be some danger that existing structures become 'flooded' with new credit at the expense of their existing high efficiencies.

5.2 Group Loans Versus Individual Small Enterprise Loans

Apart from poverty alleviation, an objective of micro-credit should be the expansion of small enterprises. Substantial portions of many NGO programmes in Cambodia are for group credit, these almost entirely to women grouped into units of five to ten, each woman receiving a relatively small loan. As shown in Table 8.6, in December 1998, 23 out of 25 leading credit NGOs had average loan sizes below $50 and 16 had average loan sizes below $30. Where these are used for income-generating purposes (the loans are poten-

Table 8.6   Credit provision by the 25 largest NGO credit providers, as at 31 December 1998

Name of organisation	Loans [1] KR m.	%	Borrowers [2] No.	%	Average loan KR	$
1. ACLEDA *	37 385	70	62 215	31	600 900	159
2. GRET *	4 687	9	39 824	20	117 693	31
3. CRS*	2 598	5	19 618	10	132 429	35
4. CCB*	1 885	4	12 404	6	151 967	40
5. Seilaniti	1 816	3	10 435	5	174 030	46
6. Hattha Kaksekar*	1 323	2	2 926	1	452 153	119
7. Action Nord Sud	850	2	8 062	4	105 433	28
8. WVI-C	1 065	2	17 285	9	61 614	16
9. Adhoc	357	1	2 979	1	119 839	32
10. Samarky	224	0.4	1 822	0.9	122 942	32
11. CHC	187	0.4	1 873	0.9	99 840	26
12. LWS	174	0.3	1 753	0.9	99 258	26
13. CWDA	125	0.2	1 290	0.6	96 899	26
14. MCC	103	0.2	1 405	0.7	73 310	19
15. Camfed	97	0.2	1 192	0.6	81 376	21
16. Concern	93	0.2	3 400	1.7	27 353	7
17. Arunreah	91	0.2	785	0.4	115 924	31
18. Samarkithor	81	0.2	897	0.4	90 301	24
19. CIDSE	73	0.1	3 299	1.6	22 128	6
20. Help the Widows	69	0.1	663	0.3	104 072	27
21. Padeck	41	0.1	6 517	3.2	6 291	2
22. KRDA	36	0.1	628	0.3	57 325	15
23. SDR	17	0.0	274	0.1	62 044	16
24. WOSO	3	0.0	185	0.1	16 216	4
25. Cadet	2	0.0	435	0.2	4 598	1
Total	53 382 $14.08m	100	202 166	100	264 050	70

Note: All agencies are NGOs; those designated * expressed interest in becoming a licensed microfinance institution (MFI) or bank. For a list of acronyms, please refer to page 177. [1] Generally excludes loan loss provision. [2] In some cases the numbers refer to members rather than borrowers.

Source: Compiled from data supplied by NBC Supervision Office of Decentralized Banking System.

tially fungible) they are often used to improve existing farm production rather than to establish new non-farm enterprises.

An example of a poverty alleviation programme with a strong focus on group credit and very small loans is that of Cambodia Community Building (CCB) which, as its name suggests, aims to target communities, in terms of impact, rather than individual enterprises. CCB provides lending through 'village banks' with an average of above 11 clients, through smaller 'solidarity groups' with four to eight clients, and to individuals. At the end of March 1999, it was supplying 680 banks and 330 groups, and 224 individual clients (Table 8.7). Banks and groups together accounted for about 82 per cent of loans outstanding, although the 1.6 per cent of individual clients were able to secure 18 per cent of the total.

Table 8.7   Distribution of loans by Cambodia Community Building, March, 1999

	Community banks	Solidarity groups	Individuals	Total
No. of units	680	330	–	–
No. of clients	12 199	1 649	224	14 072
% of clients	86.7	11.7	1.6	100
Loans outstanding ($)	426 435	211 257	141 695	779 386
(%)	54.7	27.1	18.2	100
Mean size of loan ($)	66	227	894	–

Source: Cambodia Community Building Business Plan, Years 2000–2004, CCB/World Relief, April, 1999.

Similarly, GRET/EMT currently has only 100 small business clients among a total of 40 000 clients, these accounting for only 1.4 per cent of loans outstanding at the end of 1998, about $100 000 out of $7 256 000. Although it plans to retain poverty alleviation through group lending as its primary focus, and sees its move towards MFI status as a means to sustainability, its programme for individual loans implies a 35-fold increase to 2004, with annual rates of increase initially of 100 per cent. Mean loan size for individual clients at the end of 1998 was $167, much lower than for CCB, which averaged $894. CRS currently only provides credit through (women's) groups and proposes to maintain this policy.

ACLEDA, however, now dominating the rural credit market, has modified its policy progressively over time, with increasing importance being given to the small/medium enterprise component. At the end of 1998 this accounted

Table 8.8   ACLEDA: Loans outstanding and disbursed, December 1998

| Period and type | Loans outstanding | | Value of loans | | Mean value |
	No.	%	$	%	$
End-Dec, 1998:					
Group loans*	54 679	(87.9)	3 635 200	(35.2)	66
Small loans	7 362	(11.8)	5 590 254	(54.2)	759
Medium loans	174	(0.3)	1 093 145	(10.6)	6 282
Total	62 215	(100)	10 318 599	(100)	166
Disbursed, Dec 98:					
Group loans*	6 299	(88.1)	678 040	(34.8)	108
Small loans	809	(11.3)	962 820	(49.4)	1 190
Medium loans	38	(0.5)	308 500	(15.8)	8 118
Total	7 146	(100)	1 949 360	(100)	273
Full year 1998:					
Group loans*	90 309	(92.8)	9 022 169	(49.4)	100
Small/medium	6 957	(7.2)	9 250 288	(50.6)	1 330
Total	97 266	(100)	18 272 457	(100)	188

Note: * Group loans converted at $1=KR3,500.

Source: ACLEDA data.

for 12 per cent of loans but 65 per cent of loans outstanding, with similar percentages for loans disbursed in the month of December (but only 7 per cent and 51 per cent, respectively, for the full year). The sub-component of medium enterprises, with only 0.5 per cent of the total number of borrowers, secured nearly 16 per cent of loans disbursed in December. The mean sizes of loans disbursed in December were respectively $108, $1194 and $8118 for group, small and individual loans. (Table 8.8).

There is clearly a major issue as to what the appropriate balance of loan disbursement should be nationally between group loans and small enterprises. In ACLEDA's case, with the average loan sizes cited, one small enterprise loan could fund 11 group loans, and one medium enterprise loan could fund 75. There is thus a trade-off between a poverty alleviation focus associated with group loans and a rural growth focus associated with individual loans to small enterprises, although the latter will also contribute to poverty alleviation to the extent that paid employment is generated.

In fact, most of the ACLEDA small enterprises are very small indeed, employing three to five persons (ACLEDA, 1998) and, if internationally accepted definitions of micro-enterprise (one to nine persons engaged) were used, would easily fall into this category. The 1993 Survey of Industrial Establishments shows that in manufacturing the average number of workers in the one to nine category was 4.5. There does not appear to be any clear policy on this or the other issues discussed above among the key actors in SME development in Cambodia – the NGO Forum, the Credit Committee for Rural Development (CCRD) or the Small Industry Unit in the Ministry.

5.3   Allocation of NGO Credit Among Activities

Referring back to the ACLEDA data in Tables 8.A1 and 8.A2, in line with the importance of trade as indicated in official data, the share of selling activities in both provinces is substantial, here 37–38 per cent of value. Outside this sector, however, very different sector allocations have been made in the two provinces: much less to farm production and to general services in Battambang and much more to manufacturing, compared with the other province. This seems unlikely to be explained only by differences in local resource bases, or differences in the time periods selected, but rather to differences in the policies pursued, deliberate or otherwise. What this implies is not that one or the other policy has been the correct one, but rather that each might have been able to expand further in specific directions had the effort been made, farm credit, for instance, in Battambang and loans to manufacturing in Kampong Cham. Lending by ACLEDA is largely passive, responding to loan applications which emerge, rather than proactive. The respective gaps also imply a substantial potential increase in total volume of supportable activity.

Specific mention may be made of truck transport, which accounted for 12 per cent of loan value in Kampong Cham and hardly any in Battambang: development of the trucking industry could be important in improving farm-gate prices and widening local markets. This is a further example of a rural industry that could with benefit be promoted.

5.4   Using NGO Programmes for Agricultural Credit

Referring again to the ACLEDA data in Tables 8.A1 and 8.A2, a significant portion of lending is for farm/fish production, i.e. is agricultural credit (group lending is not included here, which will be very much more agricultural). In Kampong Cham, 23 per cent of loan value was for farm and fish production, including 16 per cent for crop production, especially for commercial bananas and soya beans. This suggests that, assuming that the same very satisfactory repayment rates were secured by ACLEDA for this component, NGO lending to small-scale farm businesses could be an effective medium for the distribution of agricultural credit. It could also substitute for more common government programmes and government-sponsored agricultural development banks, which have often had poor records. Agricultural development banks generally support larger farms, while commercial banks may not reach the farm sector at all.

5.5   Providing Credit to Urban Small Enterprises

Evidently, the small enterprise sector in Phnom Penh is many times more vibrant than that in provincial towns and rural areas, and for that reason may be considered to be in less need of assistance. NGOs may be concerned that assistance to SMEs in Phnom Penh might only contribute to further rural-urban migration. Whatever the reason, the pattern of lending favours rural areas and agriculture-based businesses. In April 1999, about 10 per cent of ACLEDA loans were distributed in Phnom Penh, in the case of both group and individual loans. Other credit NGOs have concentrated largely on provincial areas away from the capital, in line with their poverty alleviation focus.

It may be asked, however, whether the overwhelming concentration on rural areas is justified on economic grounds and perhaps also in terms of the poverty-alleviation objective. Urban-based enterprises in Phnom Penh, particularly, may have much greater potential for enterprise development, for much needed import substitution and for employment creation, contributing to the absorption of vocational school leavers; they may possibly serve as a training ground, with skill acquisition in informal sector apprenticeships and on-the-job. Current lending patterns do not seem to recognise adequately this potential.

5.6   The Provision of Training for Small Enterprises

A final issue is how far lending programmes should be accompanied by training and, more generally, whether training is of much benefit in the case of small informal enterprises. ACLEDA, having considered this important initially, have now reduced this to minimal assistance in making loan applications. Group members are in much less need of training of any kind and less interested in receiving it. This is related partly to the small size of loans and their short-term nature, which do not allow much, if any, enterprise development. With a significant proportion of loans used in farm production, what may be more relevant in, for example, pig or poultry raising, are measures for disease control. In the absence of an effective national extension system, local donor or NGO programmes incorporating these have had a positive impact.

Training, both technical and business, would appear to be more appropriately directed towards the larger end of the SME category, where opportunities for enterprise development offer themselves in areas such as construction, brick and tile manufacture and tourism. Training in support of enterprise development is also likely to be much more fruitful in the urban environment, where indeed informal apprenticeship systems appear in Phnom Penh to be quite strong and productive, as evidenced by the willingness of recruits to pay significant fees.

6   CONCLUSION

We can now return to the question set at the start. Should these programmes continue to focus on micro-enterprises among poor households attempting to diversify their sources of income? While this is desirable from a poverty-alleviation perspective, it is not the optimal strategy to promote growth of enterprise. This may well, however, be an appropriate activity for NGOs. Should, on the other hand, credit be directed towards more substantial enterprises with more potential for growth? This is essential if Cambodia is to develop an SME sector, predominantly urban-based, capable of absorbing and employing the increasing population. The answer would seem to be that both dimensions need to be pursued, though in what proportions by which institutions is still unclear. It is incumbent on the Government to develop a credit policy to promote SME development as the cornerstone of a vibrant manufacturing sector.

LIST OF ACRONYMS

ACLEDA	Association of Cambodian Local Economic Development Agencies
CCB	Cambodia Community Building
CHC	Cambodian Health Committee
CIDSE	Cooperation Internationale pour le Developpement et la Solidarite (Belgium)
CRS	Catholic Relief Services
CWDA	Cambodian Women's Development Association
GRET	Groupe de Recherche et d'Echanges Technologique
KRDA	Khmer Rural Development Association
LWS	Lutheran World Service (Switzerland)
MCC	Mennonite Central Committee (USA)
SDR	Social Development in Rural Areas
WOSO	Women's Service Organisation
WVI-C	World Vision International – Cambodia

APPENDIX

Table 8.A1   Activities receiving ACLEDA loans, 1998, Kampong Cham
Province

	No. of loans	Value ($)	Mean value ($)
A. FARM/FISH PRODUCTION			
Crop production and sale	240	318 500 (15.8%)	1 327
(esp. soya, bananas, vegetables)			
Mushroom growing	3	5 500	1 833
Palm sugar production/sale	5	9 500	1 900
Rubber-tree processing	7	10 500	1 500
Flower production/sale	3	2 200	733
Fishing/fish raising	21	16 200	771
Fish selling	58	63 500	1 078
Cow-raising/sale	1	1 000	1 000
Pig raising/sale	9	11 900	1 322
Poultry/egg production	9	8 700	967
Duck raising/sale	7	9 200	1 314
Milk production/sale	1	3 000	3 000
SUBTOTAL	364	459 700 (22.8%)	1 263
B. AGRO-PROCESSING			
Rice milling	31	41 300	1 332
Wood processing	2	6 000	3 000
Charcoal production	3	2 100	700
Tobacco drying/sale	31	84 100	2 713
Silk weaving	10	4 800	480
Raw leather	2	8 000	4 000
Noodle manufacture	15	22 700	1 513
Fish sauce	1	1 500	1 500
Cake making/bakery	11	12 300	1 118
Cheese production/sale	2	2 000	1 000
Ice-cream/ice making	7	8 200	1 171
Desert sale	1	400	400
Beverages	23	43 100	1 874
Wine making	2	1 300	650
SUB TOTAL	141	237 800 (11.8%)	1 687

Table 8.A1   (continued)

	No. of loans	Value ($)	Mean value ($)
C. OTHER MANUFACTURING			
Carpentry/furniture-making	27	49 900	1 848
Lathe work	2	3 800	1 900
Ladder manufacture	2	1 000	500
Brick and tile production	6	10 000	1 667
Drainage pipe production	2	4 000	2 000
Pot production	19	18 800	989
Goldsmithing	9	13 100	1 456
Metal working	4	10 500	2 625
Welding/blacksmithing	5	5 400	1 080
Tailoring/embroidery	15	14 050	937
Basket making	1	400	400
Buddha carving	2	3 000	1 500
Power supply	6	15 500	2 583
Machine making	3	4 500	1 500
(threshing, firewood cutting)			
SUB TOTAL	103	153 950 (7.6%)	1 495
D. TRADE/RETAILING			
Rice/cereal sales	153	266 500 (13.2%)	1 742
Paddy buying and selling	6	7 000	1 167
Vegetable/fruit selling	22	14 250	648
Coffee selling	2	2 000	1 000
Wood selling	17	38 700	2 276
Firewood/fuel selling	11	13 200	1 200
Dealing in cows	8	13 500	1 688
Dealing in cow bones	2	4 000	2 000
Sale of hides	1	1 000	1 000
Slaughter/sale of meat	39	55 600	1 426
Retail sales n.e.s.	74	123 800	1 673
Groceries	114	118 300	1 038
Jewellery	21	44 700	2 129
Medicinal product sales	34	46 900	1 379
Water selling	1	300	300
Scrap dealing	3	2 000	667
Gas station	2	4 000	2 000
SUB TOTAL	584	755 750 (37.4%)	1 294

Table 8.A1   (continued)

	No. of loans	Value ($)	Mean value ($)
E. REPAIR SERVICES			
Engine/machinery repair	3	5 000	1 667
Motorcar repair	6	8 500	1 417
Bicycle repair	5	2 200	440
Battery charging	10	7 500	750
Car air pumping	1	300	300
TV/radio repair	3	5 100	1 700
Tap repair (plumbing)	1	500	500
SUB TOTAL	29	29 100 (1.4%)	1 003
F. GENERAL SERVICES			
Tractor hire	6	7 000	1 167
Rice threshing service	1	400	400
Truck transport	111	236 200 (11.7%)	2 128
Boat transport	5	16 500	3 300
Minibus service	1	4 000	4 000
Push cart transport	8	4 850	606
Taxi business	4	3 900	975
Motorbike taxi	2	500	250
Car wash	1	1 300	1 300
Electrician	2	11 000	5 500
Restaurant	11	22 100	2009
Cooked rice/chicken	11	8 400	764
Roasted meat	2	2 000	1 000
Photography	9	13 000	1 444
Photocopy	1	3 000	3 000
Guest house	4	8 000	2 000
Karaoke	4	8 800	2 200
Snooker	2	400	200
Wedding supplies	4	19 000	4 750
Clinic	1	400	400
Dentist	1	4 000	4 000
House renting	2	1 500	750
Purchase/sale of houses	2	6 500	3 250
SUB TOTAL	195	382 750 (19.0%)	1 963
GRAND TOTAL	1 416	2 019 050 (100%)	1 426

Table 8.A2   Activities receiving ACLEDA loans, 1994–1999 (February),
            Battambang Province

	No. of loans	Value ($)	Mean value ($)
A. FARM/FISH PRODUCTION			
Agricultural production	12	26 800	2 233
Tractor purchases	39	112 900	2 895
Mushroom growing	5	750	150
Mushroom seed production	1	1 500	1 500
Small tree production/sale	1	700	700
Egg hatcheries/chicken raising	37	25 796	697
Duck raising	54	15 150	281
Pig raising	18	22 500	1 250
SUB TOTAL	167	206 096 (15.2%)	1 234
B. AGRO-PROCESSING			
Sawmilling	1	2 000	2 000
Fish processing	39	32 800	841
Slaughter/butchery	10	8 600	860
Rice milling	15	34 600	2 307
Rice powder grinding	3	3 100	1 033
Soya bean mill	1	3 500	3 500
Soya sauce/pickle	6	5 700	950
SUB TOTAL	75	90 300 (6.7%)	1 204
C. MANUFACTURING			
Stone crushing	1	2 000	2 000
Concrete pipe production	27	26 100	967
Ceramics	1	600	600
Water jar manufacture	4	1 900	475
Brick production	5	13 500	2 700
Salt grinding	1	500	500
Carpentry	15	14 200	947
Furniture making	2	3 000	1 500
Rattan furniture	3	2 300	767
Trailer manufacture	1	3 000	3 000
Handcraft production	2	1 500	750
Wooden shutters	1	1 800	1 800
Incense sticks	1	800	800
Mechanical workshop	1	15 000	15 000

Table 8.A2   (continued)

	No. of loans	Value ($)	Mean value ($)
Welding	3	2 900	967
Tinsmithing	7	7 900	1 129
Stove manufacture	2	2 700	1 350
Ploughshares	3	5 200	1 733
Wine making equipment	1	2 000	2 000
Key making	4	840	210
Electrician	1	2 500	2 500
Power supply	34	31 100	915
Gem cutting	8	13 000	1 625
Goldsmithing	19	27 600	1 453
Fishing nets	1	2 000	2 000
Tailoring	34	27 200	800
Weaving	6	2 900	483
Knitting	1	300	300
Mattress production	3	4 750	1 583
Sandal making	1	4 000	4 000
Motorbicycle saddles	2	4 000	2 000
Candle making	1	4 000	4 000
Noodle manufacture	20	32 384	1 619
Cake production/bakery	32	22 000	1 532
Ice cream, ice production	14	36 250	2 589
Wine making	3	3 500	2 783
SUB TOTAL	265	325 224 (24.0%)	1 227
D. REPAIR			
Machine repair	6	8 000	1 333
Motorbicycle repair	20	18 400	920
Motor vehicle repair	12	14 550	1 213
Bicycle repair	14	3 700	264
Tyre repair	2	1 200	600
Boat repair	1	300	300
Water pump repair	2	350	175
Sewing machine repair	2	3 000	1 500
Watch repair	6	4 800	800
Radio/TV repair	18	13 050	725
SUB TOTAL	83	67 350 (5.0%)	811

Table 8.A2   (continued)

	No. of loans	Value ($)	Mean value ($)
E. SELLING			
Fish selling	7	4 500	643
Rice selling	69	78 423	1 137
Vegetable and fruit selling	13	11 100	854
Vegetable seed selling	1	500	500
Tobacco selling	5	4 500	900
Building materials	20	36 300	1 815
Wood, including bamboo	14	15 100	1 079
Firewood/fuel	18	17 903	995
Groceries	130	140 760	1 083
Retailers	107	125 730	1 175
Pharmacies (medical supplies)	10	23 300	2 330
Leather sales	6	24 500	4 083
Stationery shops	6	8 600	1 433
Bookstore	1	800	800
Furniture shop	2	1 800	900
Handicraft shop	1	300	300
Water distribution	14	19 200	1 372
Petrol station	1	3 000	3 000
SUB TOTAL	425	516 316 (38.1%)	1 215
F. GENERAL SERVICES			
Land transport	3	4 750	1 583
Boat transport	3	1 500	500
Battery charging	11	11 300	1 027
Car wash	6	5 000	833
Photocopying	4	9 000	2 250
Printing	2	5 500	2 750
Photography	1	4 000	4 000
Hairdressing/beauticians	24	22 200	925
Laundry	1	200	200
Restaurant	18	28 850	1 603
Cooked food selling	8	5 100	638
Videos	10	10 900	1 090
Karaoke	8	7 200	900
Wedding hire	1	4 000	4 000
Computer service	2	3 500	1 750

Table 8.A2   (continued)

	No. of loans	Value ($)	Mean value ($)
Interphone	1	4 000	4 000
Language school	5	15 000	3 000
Music school	1	1 000	1 000
Library	1	2 500	2 500
Dental clinic	3	2 600	867
SUB TOTAL	113	148 100 (10.9%)	1 311
GRAND TOTAL	1 128	1 353 386 (100%)	1 200

NOTES

1. This is in fact quite common in Asia and is also observable, if less dominantly, in Bangkok.
2. Credit NGOs in Cambodia use different definitions in their operations, as will become apparent.
3. Article in *Phnom Penh Post*, March 5–18, 1999.

REFERENCES

ACLEDA (1998), *Impact Survey Report*, Phnom Penh, June.
CCRD (1997), *Policy and Strategy of the Royal Government of the Kingdom of Cambodia on Rural Credit,* Credit Committee for Rural Development.
ILO (1997), *Small Enterprise Development in Cambodia, Situation Review*, ILO, Bangkok.
ILO (1998), *Report of the Labour-Based Infrastructure Project*, ILO, Bangkok.
MIME (1998), *Activity Report of the Industry, Mines and Electricity Sector and Plans for 1999*, Ministry of Industry, Mines and Energy.
Murshid, K.A.S. (1998), *Food Security in a Transitional Economy – the Case of Cambodia*, CDRI-UNRISD, Phnom Penh and Geneva.
SESC (1993–94), *Socio-Economic Survey of Cambodia, 1993–94*, National Institute of Statistics, Phnom Penh.
SESC (1996), *Socio-Economic Survey of Cambodia, 1996*, National Institute of Statistics, Phnom Penh.
Sophal, C., T. Savora and S. Savannarith (1998), 'Impact of the Regional Economic Crisis', *Cambodian Development Review*, **2**, 2, June.
Ueda, T. (1995), *Opportunities and Constraints in the Informal Sector in Cambodia*, mimeo, ILO: East Asia Multidisciplinary Advisory Team (EASMAT), Bangkok.

9. Economic policy and the changing structure of small-scale manufacturing in Quito, Ecuador, 1975–95

Alan Middleton*

1 CONTEXT: THE ECONOMY OF ECUADOR SINCE THE 1970s

The changing position of Ecuador in the international economic system has had a profound effect on its development trajectory. The dramatic changes in international oil prices in 1972, at a time when Ecuador's production was coming on stream, produced considerable structural change in the national economy. For most of the post-war period, Ecuador has been the world's largest banana producer and in the early 1970s it became the smallest member of the Organisation of Petroleum Exporting Countries (OPEC). This heralded the beginning of a period of rapid economic growth. However, by the late 1970s the economy was in decline, and 1982 saw the beginning of a period of severe economic adjustment. The aim of this chapter is to examine the performance of small-scale enterprises in Quito during these two periods – the boom in the mid-1970s and adjustment in the 1980s. The study is based on successive fieldwork visits undertaken by the author (see the Appendix for details) which reveal dramatic changes in the structure and fortunes of small-scale enterprises. We begin with an overview of the performance of the economy.

Between 1972 and 1973, GDP grew by 25.3 per cent and for the rest of the decade it grew by an annual average rate of 6 per cent (Banco Central, 1980). Growth after 1972 was not due to oil production alone. Other sectors of the economy were also stimulated by the oil bonanza and, excluding oil, the economy grew at a rate of 10.4 per cent per annum between 1972 and 1976. Manufacturing grew at an average rate of 14 per cent between 1970 and 1975 (Salgado, 1987) and in 1975 alone, the year in which the first piece of

* *Acknowledgement*: The research for this chapter was funded by the Economic and Social Research Council in 1975, 1982 and 1995. The author also wishes to acknowledge the technical assistance of Robert Kelly in the production of the data.

fieldwork for the project reported here was carried out, it grew by 19 per cent. However, as a result of the inflow of foreign exchange and the demand pressure that resulted, inflation reached 23 per cent in 1974.

The new oil revenues also increased Ecuador's attractiveness to an international finance system that was awash with petro-dollars. From 1976, foreign debt began to increase dramatically and by 1979 debt servicing accounted for 65 per cent of export earnings (Salgado, 1987). Imports also increased rapidly between 1970 and 1979 (22 per cent per annum), partly due to government efforts to reduce the cost of imports of capital and intermediate goods to stimulate industrialisation. However, while industry was increasingly dependent on imported inputs, these years also saw the beginning of the export of manufactured goods, and the overall growth of exports, at 30 per cent per annum, was higher than that of imports (Salgado, 1987).

The impact of this growth on employment structure was that over 59 000 jobs were created in industry between the census years of 1974 and 1982; agricultural employment fell in absolute as well as relative terms; and those working in services increased from 36 per cent to 50 per cent of the economically active population. In the urban areas there was a rapid growth in employment in the formal sector of the economy and an expansion of middle class employment, but income distribution worsened and there is some evidence that the conditions of the poorest did not improve in absolute terms (Salgado, 1987).

Between 1979 and 1982, the year of the second survey of petty producers, the increasing foreign debt and resultant financial pressures led to a large drop in international reserves and a flight of capital. In 1981 and 1982, more than 70 per cent of export earnings had to go on debt servicing, amounting to almost half of GDP in the latter year (Salgado, 1987). The impact on public sector finances was such that the government was forced to boost current revenues through increases in gasoline prices and a range of taxes, including those on commercial transactions. As a result of these pressures, GDP began to fall in 1981 and there was a drop in investment in the same year. The situation deteriorated further in 1982 and the worsening of the balance of payments problem led to devaluation of the *sucre* and a series of measures to discourage imports. GDP went into decline in 1982. It registered a decline of 2.8 per cent in 1983 and in the same year imports fell by 35 per cent.

The year 1982 was a watershed for Ecuador. It saw the beginning of adjustment policies, with an increase in interest rates, the creation of two official markets for exchange rates, and devaluation. It was around this time that a remarkable growth in the influence of the IMF and the World Bank began, aiming to encourage governments to 'avoid large macro-economic imbalances; pursue market-friendly policies; [and] take maximum advantage of opportunities in foreign trade and for foreign investment' (Killick, 1996:

212). In order to achieve policy change, 'conditionality' became increasingly important and the governments of developing countries were set preconditions and performance criteria relating to structural adjustment before they could access loans.

Ecuador was drawn into this system relatively early, with considerable adverse effects on key sectors of the national economy between 1982 and 1995. Furthermore, without wishing to attribute a relation of cause and effect between the fluctuations of the national economy and the fortunes of petty enterprises, an investigation of artisanal production in Quito does provide us with some insights into this relationship. The analysis suggests that the very sector of the economy that should have benefited from the introduction of neo-liberal measures has, in fact, suffered disproportionately. However, as we shall see, the experience of petty producers has not been uniform across the sector.

When a follow-up study of small-scale manufacturers was carried out in 1982, these measures had not yet had an impact. Consumer spending was still high and the informal sector was still under the influence of the years of growth. The period 1975–82 presents a relatively self-contained period in the history of Ecuador's economy and, as we shall see, the surveys which were carried out in each of these years provide us with an insight into the impact of economic growth on the fortunes of small-scale manufacturers.

Since the neo-liberal adjustment measures were introduced in 1982, one government after another has pursued a similar strategy, to a greater or lesser degree (Acosta, 1996). Policies initially revolved around a series of mini-devaluations, higher interest rates and control of public expenditure. Public sector pay rises were suspended, as were public sector expenditures on some goods. Fuel prices were raised, new import controls were introduced and tariffs were increased. A change of government in September 1984 gave a new emphasis to the neo-liberal direction of government policy. The control of inflation became a priority and freeing up the exchange system and the management of interest rates became the main tools of economic policy. Interest rates were further increased, devaluation became the main means of tackling the balance of payments problem and protection of domestic production was reduced. The control of consumer prices ceased, taxes on commercial transactions were increased, new indirect taxes were introduced, other indirect taxes were increased, and fuel prices were raised again. Industrial output contracted for three years in succession between 1983 and 1985, non-oil exports fell to below 1979 levels (with a sharp decline in the export of industrial goods), and there was a sharp drop in the import of capital goods. The state budget deficit increased by 58 per cent between 1984 and 1985. By 1986, real wages were only 78 per cent of their 1980 level and unemployment and underemployment had increased significantly (Salgado, 1987).

An earthquake in 1987 gave a new impetus to the downward spiral. A fractured oil pipeline caused exports of oil to be suspended, which, along with deteriorating oil prices, led to the value of oil exports falling by 39 per cent in that year. GDP fell by 6 per cent in 1987 (Banco Central, 1995). This was the second time in four years that the country experienced severe negative growth. However, manufacturing, which had grown at an average annual rate of 10 per cent between 1975 and the end of 1981, declined at a rate of –0.64 per cent per year in the period 1982–86, and grew by 1.7 per cent in 1987 and 2 per cent in 1988.

The austerity continued with the new government that took power in 1988. The government took a more gradual approach to the control of inflation and dealing with a massive external debt and a record fiscal deficit, but subsidies for basic needs were removed and the prices of petrol and electricity were raised substantially. Although real minimum wages also increased, this ultimate measure did not help those in the informal sector who had to confront higher input and subsistence costs. There was a return to mini-devaluations and a greater control of imports (Thoumi and Grindle, 1992). In 1989, manufacturing output fell by 5 per cent, and there was no growth in 1990. In the early 1990s, there was an annual average growth rate for manufacturing of around 3 per cent. In contrast to the optimism and growth of the 1970s, throughout the period between 1982 and 1994 the average annual growth in manufacturing industry was a meagre 0.78 per cent. At the same time, a growing urban labour force was swelling the numbers in the informal sector.

In the period between 1980 and 1992, there was a growing informalisation of the urban labour force across Latin America (ILO, 1995). In Ecuador, this trend has been taking place since at least 1974 (Pita, 1992). Although the economically active population grew by 112 per cent between 1974 and 1990, the number of self-employed in Quito, which may be taken as a proxy for the informal sector, grew by 179 per cent (calculated from Census data). Manufacturing employment increased in absolute terms throughout the period, but as a proportion of the total labour force, its importance declined considerably between 1982 and 1990.

This context is important for understanding the processes of change within petty production between 1975 and 1982 and between 1982 and 1995. Throughout the 20 year period, Ecuadorian 'artisans' also benefited from an 'enabling environment', in the sense that various laws and statutes offered to defend them, promote them, exempt them from certain taxes and exclude them from the need to comply with labour laws (Lawson, 1995). We might reasonably expect that this combination of enabling policies and structural adjustment would have had a positive impact on the fortunes of these small-scale producers. Before we look at what did happen, however, it is necessary to set the theoretical context within which debates about small-scale manufacturers in the 'informal sector' have evolved. We will then go on to explain a little about the methodology used in this research.

2 SMALL-SCALE MANUFACTURING: THE THEORETICAL BACKGROUND

In the development debates of the 1960s and the 1970s, neo-classical economics and orthodox Marxism were agreed about one thing – that small-scale production would disappear with the evolution of capitalism in Latin America. With a growing interest in the 'informal sector' and 'marginality' in the 1970s, however, alternative views began to emerge. It is more than 25 years since Anibal Quijano argued that, rather than disappearing, small-scale production was being expanded and modified by its new mode of articulation in the overall economic structure (Quijano, 1974: 403). Similarly, while in the developed countries 'petty' production is residual and tends to disappear, in peripheral economies 'it seems to be the conservation aspect which predominates' (Le Brun and Gerry, 1975: 9). Contrary to previous thinking, based on the experience of nineteenth Century Britain, the experience of developing countries in the late twentieth Century was leading economists to the conclusion that small-scale producers in the informal sector would grow in number.

If these activities were being expanded, as Quijano and others suggested, there was no evidence to suggest how this was taking place. It was not known, for example if all small-scale production activities were being expanded; or if some types of activities were expanding and others declining, with the net result being a growth in the number of enterprises. If they were being modified, in what sense? Was the structure of the sector changing, were the internal structures of the enterprises being modified, and/or were their external relations with other enterprises undergoing change? If one or more of these, what precisely was happening in this process of change? Non-capitalist forms of production could disappear, in the sense that they would be 'restructured (partly dissolved) and thus subordinated to the predominant capitalist relationships (and so conserved)' (Bettleheim, 1972: 279).

These theoretical issues were not addressed empirically. Policy makers were left with a broad unsubstantiated consensus that small-scale economic activities were unlikely to decline in importance in the way that they had done in the developed countries and that the dynamics of change could not be explained. However, the question of the conservation or dissolution of small-scale production in developing countries is of central importance for the elaboration of policies for the elimination of urban poverty and the promotion of economic growth. The lack of evidence and subsequent policy vacuum also left the door open for neo-liberal economists and political scientists to return to, and develop, the traditional neo-classical interpretations of the future of small-scale producers, characterising them as *micro-empresarios* who could be the golden future of capitalism in Latin America (de Soto, 1986).

Given this perspective, the fundamental question for neo-liberal economists with respect to small-scale producers was 'why are they not growing into capitalist enterprises?' According to this frame of reference, small-scale producers in the informal sector should have been developing into large-scale formal enterprises and, if this is not happening, the key issue logically becomes 'what are the barriers to their growth?' The legalistic interpretation of the process of change, or the lack of it, assumed that small-scale producers are part of a restricted sector of the economy which could be the engine of growth if government restrictions were removed (de Soto, 1986; see Middleton, 1991 and Bromley, 1990). Part of the solution was thought to lie in the application of neo-liberal adjustment policies which free up markets and reduce the role of the state in the economy. That is, precisely the policies introduced in Ecuador in 1982 were those thought to be required to provide the growth and development of small-scale producers.

There are a number of underlying assumptions in the neo-liberal view of small-scale producers which are questionable, three of which we shall address. These are that the sector is homogeneous, that all sectors of the sub-economy have potential for growth and that adjustment policies will benefit small-scale non-capitalist enterprises. An earlier chapter argued that it is not helpful to analyse the activities of the informal sector as though they were a homogeneous mass and that the identification of some level of disaggregation is necessary if we are to develop meaningful policies for small-scale economic activities (Middleton, 1981). Discussion of the disaggregated activities can be made more difficult by different meanings being attached to the categories used to define processes of change. When we discuss conservation and dissolution, for example, we may be referring to changes in the total numbers of firms on the one hand, or growth and decline within firms on the other. These two types of changes may be taking place simultaneously.

In this chapter we are only concerned with the numbers of small firms. We are interested in what happens to their numbers as the economy develops or declines, how different types of activity are affected by economic change in the national economy, and how this national context affects the local structure of small-scale manufacturing production. The historico-structural framework used in this research differentiates between different 'forms' of production on the basis of social relations of production and distribution (Middleton, 1989: 141):

1 Capitalist Forms of Production

a. *Relations of production:* the owners of the means of production are not directly involved in the process of production. Only wage labour is employed.
b. *Relations of distribution:* production is for the free market.

2 Non-capitalist Forms of Production

a. *Relations of production:* the owners of the means of production are also directly involved in the process of production. Wage labour may or may not be employed, but the nuclear and extended family is an important source of labour.
b. *Relations of distribution:*
    i.   Artisan production, for individuals who order the goods to be made;
    ii.   Open market production, non-client-oriented and for the free market;
    iii. Enterprise-oriented production.

This type of theoretical framework is no longer fashionable. Its structuralist assumptions have been swamped by the neo-liberal paradigm and the methods associated with it can be dismissed as irrelevant in a post-modern and post-capitalist discourse about globalisation. The concept of the informal sector, with its loose and flexible definition, is much less demanding intellectually, glossing over the complexities of the relationships between the multitude of elements that are its constituent parts. In this study, the informal sector is retained as a useful generic concept that encompasses a variety of non-capitalist forms of production and distribution. It is, however, a concept of little analytical value, given the heterogeneity of the types of activity to which it generally refers (for a discussion see Middleton, 1989). In this chapter, the small-scale, non-capitalist manufacturers in Quito will be referred to as artisans (which the vast majority of them are) or petty producers in the informal sector. There is a size limit for non-capitalist producers. As enterprises grow the owner is forced to dedicate his time to administration alone and becomes a petty capitalist. We confine attention to firms with up to seven persons working in them.

The heterogeneity found within non-capitalist economic activity can be structured on a number of levels. We can distinguish between the legal and illegal, in the criminal sense; there are those who are mobile (unstable), such as street vendors, and those who operate from a fixed location (stable); and some are involved in distribution and others in production. Within petty production, activity can be expressed in terms of the standard United Nations classification of small producers which was in use in 1975 (such as tailors, dressmakers, etc.; shoemakers, leather-workers, etc.; furniture-makers, etc.; metal workers, mechanics, etc.; sign-writers, painters, etc.; jewellers, watch repairers, etc.; printers, photographers, etc.). On the other hand, these activities can be regrouped and presented in terms of those who mainly produce means of production, those who produce means of subsistence, and the producers of luxury goods. Producers of subsistence goods (or the means of subsistence, MoS) are those who produce basic needs (goods consumed directly), and would include, for example, tailors and dressmakers, shoemakers and furniture makers. Producers of the means of production (MoP) are those whose products and/or sporadic labour re-enter the production process, and includes mechanical and electrical engineers, printers, and painters and sign-writers. Those producing luxury goods (which do not re-enter the process of production) would include, for example, jewellers.

The evidence shows how the experience of these groups differs in periods of growth and decline. Research carried out in 1982 showed that in the period of economic growth and in the context of a growing city, the overall number of petty producers within the central and southern areas of Quito remained relatively constant (Middleton, 1989). It also showed, however, that this relative stability was the result of differential growth patterns for different types of activity. That is, some activities grew in number, while others declined. This was consistent with Middleton (1981), which anticipated that as the market for subsistence goods increases, labour-saving capital investment results in increased competition between petty manufacturers and capitalist producers. Thus, rather than growth in petty production to meet the growing market, there was a decline. Large-scale investment from above displaced small-scale producers of subsistence goods. On the other hand, the numbers of producers of capital goods whose labour could re-enter the production process increased.

These changes were taking place in the context of the rapid growth of the Ecuadorian economy between 1975 and 1982. In this chapter we take the earlier analysis a stage further. Recent research has been undertaken to find out what has happened in the period 1982–95, when the Ecuadorian economy was subjected to neo-liberal adjustment policies in an attempt to deal with the growing debt problem (details on the fieldwork method are provided in the Appendix). In this period the economy went through intermittent natural crises, experienced two separate years of decline of GDP, and had generally much slower growth rates overall.

3   INFORMALISATION OF THE LABOUR FORCE AND GROWTH AND DECLINE OF PETTY PRODUCERS

Between 1975 and 1982, the period of rapid growth in the Ecuadorian economy, the total number of workshops in the study area showed a slight increase of three per cent (Table 9.1). In the second period, between 1982 and 1995, characterised by government support for micro-enterprises but also slow growth in the economy with periods of decline and stagnation, the number of enterprises declined by 25 per cent. This produced an overall decline in the number of small producers of 23 per cent in the 20 year period.

Table 9.1   Growth and decline in the number of workshops in each area

	1975		1982		1995		Percentage change		
	No.	%	No.	%	No.	%	1975–82	1982–95	1975–95
Peri-Centre	1 031	44.7	980	41.2	598	33.5	–4.9	–39.0	–42.0
South	899	39.0	917	38.5	870	48.7	2.0	–5.1	–3.2
Historic Centre	378	16.3	483	20.3	318	17.8	27.8	–34.2	–15.9
Total	2 308	100.0	2 380	100.0	1 786	100.0			

Table 9.1 also shows that the change over the period has not been uniform over the three geographical areas of the study. In the first period, a small decline in the peri-central area (5 per cent), which had been the heart of artisan activity in the city, was offset by a small increase in the south (2 per cent) and a large percentage increase in the Historic Centre of the city (28 per cent). In the second period, the picture is quite different. There was a decline across all three areas but there was also a change in the way that the decline was spatially distributed. Between 1982 and 1995, the peri-centre continued to be the area of greatest decline (–39 per cent), but this was closely followed by the Historic Centre (–34 per cent). From a period of artisanal growth in the years immediately after the oil boom, the importance of this area as a centre of production deteriorated rapidly as production was replaced by commerce and new commercial centres were created in other parts of the city. Compared to the peri-centre and the Historic Centre, the decline in the South was slight (–5 per cent).

The overall decline of 23 per cent for the 20 year period, therefore, is made up of distinct patterns of growth and decline in different periods and in different geographical areas of the city. Clearly, the question of conservation and dissolution is more complex than neo-classical and neo-Marxist theory would lead us to believe. If we now look at the changes that are taking place in the different types of activity, this complexity becomes more explicit.

4   THE CHANGING STRUCTURE OF PRODUCTION

Changes in the numbers of petty enterprises between 1975 and 1995 are broken down by activity in Table 9.2. The table also aggregates the activities of the different artisanal activities into producers of the means of subsistence (MoS), producers of the means of production (MoP), jewellers and others. Over the 20 years, a number of patterns can be identified:

- An overall decline in the number of producers of the MoS over the two study periods. This is true for all categories of activity within the producers of the MoS (tailors, shoemakers and carpenters) and over both the period of economic growth and the era of structural adjustment and national economic stagnation. The number of petty producers of basic articles of consumption halved in the 20 year period. The biggest fall in numbers, however, was between 1982 and 1995.
- A steady decline in the relative importance of producers of the MoS in petty production in Quito.
- Correspondingly, there has been a steady increase in the relative importance of the producers of the MoP, which also show a small increase in absolute numbers between 1975 and 1995.
- However, this overall increase is the result of a rapid expansion of these petty producers in the first period of growth and a decline in the period of crisis.
- The number of jewellers increased in the first period but declined in the second.
- The number in the category of 'others' increased in both periods.
- The average annual rate of change was different in both periods. A small annual rate of growth (0.44 per cent) in the first period was replaced by an annual rate of decline of 2.2 per cent in the second.
- The annual rate of decline of the producers of the means of subsistence deteriorated further in the second period.
- An annual rate of growth of 3.4 per cent for the producers who found a niche with the expansion of capitalism in the country was reversed. There was an annual rate of decline of 1.3 per cent in the long period of crisis and structural adjustment.

Taking the two periods in turn, the numbers of traditional producers of the means of subsistence in Quito decreased by 16 per cent between 1975 and

Table 9.2 The changing structure of production in Quito by activity 1975–95 (in all three areas)

Activity	1975		1982		1995		% Change 1975–82	% Change 1982–95	% Change 1975–95	Average annual change 1975–82	1982–95
	No.	%	No.	%	No.	%					
Tailors	594	25.74	501	21.05	293	16.41	-15.66	-41.50	-50.67	-2.40	-4.04
Shoemakers	504	21.84	427	17.94	235	13.16	-15.28	-45.00	-53.37	-2.34	-4.49
Carpenters	272	11.79	218	9.16	153	8.57	-19.85	-29.80	-43.75	-3.11	-2.69
Total MoS	1 370	59.36	1 146	48.15	681	38.13	-16.35	-40.60	-50.29	-2.52	-3.93
Mechanics	341	14.77	377	15.84	316	17.69	10.56	-16.20	-7.33	1.44	-1.35
Painters	90	3.90	131	5.50	93	5.21	45.56	-29.00	3.33	5.51	-2.60
Printers	79	3.42	137	5.76	132	7.39	73.42	-3.60	67.09	8.18	-0.28
Total MoP	510	22.10	645	27.10	541	30.29	26.47	-16.10	6.08	3.41	-1.34
Jewellers	136	5.89	201	8.45	133	7.45	47.79	-33.80	-2.21	5.74	-3.12
Others	292	12.65	388	16.30	431	24.13	32.88	11.10	47.60	4.14	0.81
Total	2 308	100.00	2 380	100.00	1 786	100.00	3.12	-24.90	22.62	0.44	-2.18

1982, while the more modern activities which produce the means of production or which provide labour for the formal sector increased by 26 per cent.
The numbers of tailors, shoemakers and carpenters all declined, whilst mechanics, painters and printers increased. The number of producers of luxury
goods, including jewellers, increased even more rapidly than the producers of
MoP (Table 9.2).

In this period of rapid economic growth, therefore, complicated structural changes had been taking place within petty manufacturing. A slight
change in the overall numbers masks a deeper dynamic, and despite the fact
that the population of the areas under study and of Quito as a whole
increased during the 1970s, the number of petty producers satisfying the
demand for basic needs declined. The increased demand for subsistence
goods was being met by a growth in capitalist production and the number of
traditional producers declined. During this period, however, an increased
demand for inputs from the growing capitalist manufacturers stimulated
certain types of small-scale production, such that these activities increased
and small-scale producers of the means of production grew from 21 per
cent to 27 per cent of all petty producers. The category of printers includes
photographers, but if these are removed the growth rate for printers alone is
87 per cent. An important question for the 1995 fieldwork was whether
these trends would be maintained over a period of stagnation and intermittent crises.

Over the following period, 1982–95, the number of enterprises in all
branches of activity declined, with the exception of 'others'. The traditional
producers of clothes and shoes declined at an even faster annual rate than
previously and all the producers of the means of production also declined in
numbers, compared to increases in the first period. Only carpenters declined
at a slower rate than before. Mechanical workshops, which had grown by 11
per cent in the first period and whose skills could be adapted to meet the
increasing demand for repairs of goods produced by the capitalist sector,
declined by 16 per cent between 1982 and 1995. For painters and sign-
writers, the change was even more dramatic. Growth of 46 per cent collapsed
into a decline of 29 per cent, as modern technology and the introduction of
new materials squeezed the traditional craftsmen. Only in printing was anything like the same number of workshops maintained, although there was
also a small decline in this subsector as well. Jewellers, who had shown an
increase of almost 7 per cent per annum in the first period, declined by 2.6
per cent per annum between 1982 and 1995, resulting in fewer jewellers in
1995 than in 1975. From interviews with jewellers, there is no doubt that this
is related to a rise in crime, causing the public to buy less jewellery than
before, and by the elasticity of this type of demand (luxury goods are the first
to be sacrificed by consumers in times of crisis).

There is little doubt that throughout the period of adjustment since 1982, the artisans of Quito have suffered considerably and they now play a lesser role in the urban economy. For reasons which we will not develop here, even those producers whose goods and labour could be absorbed by a growing capitalism or whose skills could be converted into repair activities relevant for extending the life of goods produced by the capitalist sector, started to go into decline.

Some types of activity, however, did expand in number. Within the category of 'others' the rise is almost wholly accounted for by the increase in the number of bakers and beauty salons over the period (300 per cent and 160 per cent respectively). Modern forms of production and distribution of bread and other flour products have not yet penetrated working class barrios in the city. The reasons for this may be complex, but at least part of the explanation may lie with the fact that many of these barrios are relatively inaccessible or expensive to reach by delivery trucks on a daily basis. Furthermore, the people who inhabit them increasingly earn their income on a daily basis and only buy enough to sustain themselves and their families from day to day. The growth in beauty salons in Quito is also considerable. Traditional hairdressers, on the other hand, declined by 39 per cent. Taken together, hairdressers and beauty salons, who are considered to be artisans in Ecuadorian law but would be counted as service sector workers in a developed economy, increased by 49 per cent.

Despite the decline that has taken place in almost all activities between 1982 and 1995, the structure of production has continued to change in the same way as before. That is, as a proportion of all petty activities, the producers of subsistence goods have continued to become relatively less important than the producers of the means of production. Between 1975 and 1995, the proportion of producers of subsistence goods fell from 59 per cent of all petty producers to 38 per cent, and the proportion of MoP producers increased from 22 per cent to 30 per cent. Even though there has been a downward spiral for all these activities in the second period, the growing relative importance of MoP producers remains a feature of the changing structure.

The change in the number of enterprises between 1975 and 1995 is the result of a combination of factors. Some of the petty producers have survived over the 20 year period. Others have disappeared and new ones have been created. It is the sum of these three factors – survival, disappearance and openings – which produce the figures for 1982 and 1995. Table 9.3 shows the number of enterprises in each type of activity in 1975, 1982 and 1995; the numbers that disappeared between 1975 and 1982 and between 1975 and 1995; the number that were new in 1982 and 1995; and the replacement rates for those that had disappeared.

Table 9.3 *Disappearance and replacement rates: 1975–82 and 1975–95: all three areas*

Activity	Total in 1975		Situation in 1982				Situation in 1995			
			No longer exist		New in 1982	Repl. rate	No longer exist		New in 1982	Repl. rate
	No.	%	No.	%	No.	%o.	No.	%	No.	%
Tailors	594	25.74	403	67.85	310	76.92	531	89.39	230	43.31
Shoemakers	504	21.84	288	57.14	211	73.26	422	83.73	153	36.26
Carpenters	272	11.79	187	68.75	130	69.52	235	86.40	116	49.36
Total MoS	1 370	59.36	878	64.09	651	74.15	1 188	86.72	499	42.00
Mechanics	341	14.77	216	63.34	262	121.30	302	88.56	277	91.72
Painters	90	3.90	50	55.56	91	182.00	70	77.78	73	104.29
Printers	79	3.42	46	58.23	104	226.09	64	81.01	117	182.81
Total MoP	510	22.10	312	61.18	457	146.47	436	85.49	467	107.11
Jewellers	136	5.89	60	44.12	125	208.33	103	75.74	100	97.09
Others	292	12.65	183	62.87	279	152.46	252	86.30	391	155.16
Total	2 308	100.00	1 433	62.09	1 512	105.51	1 979	85.75	1 457	73.62

The 1982 survey showed that the changes in the structure of petty production were the result of the fact that new firms were failing to reappear in the production of the means of subsistence. Overall closure rates were only slightly higher than those for the producers of the MoP (64 per cent against 61 per cent), while the replacement rates were quite different. The replacement rates for MoS firms were around half of the rates for MoP firms. The replacement rates for tailors, shoemakers and carpenters were reasonably consistent, such that between 70 per cent and 77 per cent of the firms that disappeared were being replaced. In contrast, there was a wide variation in the rates for mechanical workshops, painters and printers, producing an average replacement rate of 146 per cent. However the overall range was such that while only 70 per cent of carpenters were being replaced, the replacement rate for printers during this period of economic growth was 226 per cent.

By 1995, between 80 per cent and 90 per cent of all activities except painters and jewellers had disappeared, with little difference between the MoS and MoP groups (87 per cent and 85 per cent respectively). Eighty-nine per cent of tailors who existed in 1975 had disappeared by 1995 and the percentage of mechanics and carpenters who had gone was almost as high. There were, however, still major differences in the replacement rates between the two groups. The mechanical and metal workshops, which had increased in number between 1975 and 1982 but showed an even greater decline in the second period, were the only MoP activities not showing a 100 per cent replacement rate by 1995. Only 42 per cent of the MoS group had been replaced, against 107 per cent of the producers of the means of production. Within the former, the position of shoemakers had deteriorated most, while that of carpenters was not deteriorating as quickly. In the second period, the deteriorating position of jewellers meant that a replacement rate of 208 per cent in 1982 had been reduced to 97 per cent by 1995.

The variations in the replacement rates for different types of activities therefore explain the mechanisms of conservation and dissolution and how the changing structure of petty production is created. The consistency in the rates of disappearance across the activities is perhaps surprising, but it can be noted that the lowest survival rates for firms are for painters and sign-writers, who also have one of the highest replacement rates. There are therefore high rates of dissolution at the level of the firm and, because of high replacement rates, high rates of conservation as an activity. This would suggest that there is no direct link between firm failure rates and the conservation or dissolution of a particular sector of activity. However, it is important to understand what lies behind firms disappearing, for disappearance can be the result of either closure or movement to a new location.

5   REASONS FOR CLOSURE AND MOVING

In both 1982 and 1995, we tried to find out what had happened to the original petty producers who were no longer in existence. We conducted a survey in both years with a short questionnaire that asked the new occupiers of the property and neighbours for information about what had happened. We obtained information on 309 cases in 1982 and 270 in 1995. Since the information gathered in 1995 may have required a considerable feat of memory on the part of respondents, we should note that the 1982 responses are likely to be more reliable. Although there was a remarkable consistency in the resident population and every effort was made to seek out older residents, after 20 years in some cases, it was much more difficult to obtain reliable information about the original petty producers. However, since the responses were not inconsistent with what was found in 1982 and what might have been expected over a longer period of time, they are included here.

In 1982, we discovered that 68 per cent of those who had disappeared had not gone out of business, but had relocated to other premises. Only 29 per cent had closed down completely and 2 per cent were in the same location but had changed their activity. In 1995, we were told that 52 per cent had closed down completely and 48 per cent had moved. The difference between the two years, particularly the high rate of closures by 1995, may reflect the circumstances of the national economy, but the ageing ownership of the workshops will also have been a factor. We also discovered that some of those who had been reported as moved by 1982 had closed between 1975 and 1995. There is also no doubt that some of those who had moved will have moved on again.

When we asked why the businesses had closed in 1982 there was a wide variety of personal and other reasons but no clear pattern of what the owners were doing at that time. When we asked the same question in 1995, it was not surprising that the most frequent reason given for closure was the death of the owner (44 per cent). When we asked why enterprises had moved, we might have expected a reasonable proportion to have done so because their business had expanded. If many of them had grown in size and had moved to bigger and better premises, this would be consistent with the development model proposed by de Soto (1986) and others. In fact, very few of them had experienced growth. From the valid responses in 1982, only 13 per cent had moved because of business growth or because the workshop was too small. In 1995, we were told that only 9 per cent had moved for these reasons.

In both years, by far the most reasons for people leaving their business locations were not related to the internal dynamics of the firms or their relationship to the market. They were property-related. The main reasons relocations took place were because the owner of the property demanded the return of the workshop (34 per cent and 33 per cent in 1982 and 1995 respectively) or because the artisan moved home (24 per cent and 28 per cent respectively). There were no reported cases of businesses closing or moving because of government bureaucracy, regulations or red tape. The most important single reason for instability was to be found in the economic interests of another part of the private sector.

6 CONCLUSIONS

There is no doubt that certain sectors of the population have gained from neo-liberal adjustment policies and that the prolonged crisis has not affected everyone equally. Nevertheless, there is no evidence that it has done anything but harm to petty manufacturers, that segment of the economy that neo-liberals hold up as *micro-empresarios* and the future of capitalism. The growth of the financial sector, the strengthening of sectors associated with importing certain consumer goods and the development of new types of agro-exportation have led to a new pattern of accumulation in Ecuador. In the course of these changes, manufacturing has stagnated and small-scale producers of almost all types have declined. In the period of economic boom between 1975 and 1982, small-scale manufacturers of subsistence goods were squeezed by the capitalist producers of basic consumption goods. On the other hand, the producers of production goods were able to take advantage of the space that was created by capitalist expansion and the built-in obsolescence of the goods they produce.

These changes were not uniform geographically across the city: there were distinct patterns of growth and decline for small-scale non-capitalist manufacturers in different periods and in different areas of the city. The changes in the overall numbers also masked complicated structural dynamics, as the direction of conservation and dissolution was changing at different levels (firm, subsector of activity and small-scale production as a whole) in different periods. The traditional producers of basic consumer goods appear to be in terminal decline. Producers whose goods and labour can re-enter the production process are at the mercy of the changes in national economic circumstances. In the Ecuadorian case, they grew as the economy grew and declined as the country became subject to structural adjustment, stagnation and crisis.

Ecuador's development stalled with the debt crisis, traditional petty manufacturers continued to decline and the producers of the means of production went into reverse. The rate at which firms were disappearing was high and reasonably constant across all MoS and MoP activities. The big difference between the different types of activity was the rate at which replacements were taking place. The reasons for the disappearance of the petty manufacturers was mainly movement to other places in the 1970s, but the main reason for this was not the State but the interests of other parts of the private sector.

APPENDIX: THE FIELDWORK

The first survey of petty manufacturing was carried out in Quito in 1975 after discussions with colleagues in the Junta Nacional de Planificacion who were familiar with the economic structure of the city. It was decided to carry out the research in three areas of Quito which were adjacent to each other and which had slightly different economic characteristics but which had been identified as the main areas of petty manufacturing and trading in the city at that time (Middleton, 1979: Appendix 1). One of these locations was the main area of artisan production in the city, stretching from La Libertad, down through San Roque along the northern edge of the Panecillo, as far as the Cumanda bus station and La Recoleta. The proliferation of small enterprises of all types was judged to be representative of the 'peri-centre' of the city as a whole.

The second area ran from the Recoleta southwards along Avenida Maldonado and eastwards up the *cordillero* to take in the barrios of Chaguarquingo, Ferroviaria Bajo and Ferroviaria Alta. This area, which also included some lower middle class housing, is considered to be typical of the south of the city.

The third area was the old commercial centre of barrio Gonzales Suarez, now referred to as the *Centro Historico*. This was the centre of formal and informal trading activities in 1975.

Over a period of two months, all the establishments in the three areas employing up to seven persons, including the owner, were mapped. These maps provided the starting point for the re-mapping of the three areas in 1982 and 1995. In 1975, all petty enterprises were recorded, including small shops, bars, restaurants and other services. In 1982 and 1995, only those activities which were considered to be artisanal activities within Ecuadorian law were counted. The mapping exercise was followed by a series of surveys and interviews.

It should be noted that the research focused only on one part of the city. We therefore have to be modest about what we claim for the results. The city has been growing and it is possible that increased demand will perhaps have caused a change in the total number of petty producers right across the city that the field research did not pick up. However, the results offer an insight into the processes of change that are taking place.

REFERENCES

Acosta, A. (1996), 'Apuntes para una economia politica del ajuste neoliberal', *Ecuador Debate*, **37**, 49–65.

Banco Central (1980), *Memoria 1980*, Quito, Banco Central del Ecuador.

Banco Central (1995), *Boletín Anuario 1995*, Quito: Banco Central del Ecuador.

Bettleheim, C. (1972), 'Theoretical comments' in Emanuel, A., *Unequal Exchange*, New York: Monthly Review Press.

Bromley, R. (1990), 'A new path to development? The significance and impact of Hernando de Soto's ideas on underdevelopment, production and reproduction', *Economic Geography*, **66**, 328–48.

De Soto, H. (1986), *El Otro Sendero*, Lima: Editorial El Barranco.

ILO (1995), *World Employment Report*, Geneva: ILO.

Killick, T. (1996), 'Principals, agents and the limitations of BWI conditionality', *The World Economy*, **19**, 211–29.

Lawson, V. (1995), 'Beyond the firm: restructuring gender divisions of labor in Quito's garment industry under austerity', *Environment and Planning D: Society and Space*, **13**, 415–44.

Le Brun, O. and C. Gerry (1975), 'Petty producers and capitalism', *Review of African Political Economy*, **3**, 20–32.

Middleton, A. (1979), *Poverty, Production and Power: The Case of Petty Manufacturing in Ecuador*, D.Phil. Thesis, Brighton: University of Sussex.

Middleton, A. (1981), 'Petty manufacturing, capitalist enterprises and the process of accumulation in Ecuador', *Development and Change*, **12**, 505–24.

Middleton, A. (1989), 'The changing structure of petty production in Ecuador', *World Development*, **17**, 139–55.

Middleton, A. (1991), 'El sector informal y el neo-liberalismo en la Region Andina', in Middleton, A., *La Dinamica del Sector Informal Urbano en el Ecuador*, Quito: CIRE.

Pita, E. (1992), *Informalidad Urbana: Dinamica y Perspectivas en el Ecuador*, Quito: CONADE.

Quijano, A. (1974), 'The marginal pole of the economy and the marginalised labour force', *Economy and Society*, **3**, 393–428.

Salgado, G. (1987), 'Ecuador: crisis and adjustment policies. Their effect on Agriculture', *CEPAL Review*, **33**, 129–45.

Thoumi, F. and M. Grindle (1992), *La Politica de la Economia del Ajuste: La Actual Experiencia Ecuatoriana*, Quito: FLACSO.

10. Small-scale industry in the Gaza Strip

Muhammed Migdad, Hossein Jalilian and John Weiss

1 INTRODUCTION

This chapter discusses the current situation of the small-scale industrial sector in the Gaza Strip (with the West Bank, one of the two Occupied Territories of Palestine) a small land area of around 360 sq. km occupied by Israel since the 1967 war and now part of the New Palestinian Entity (NPE). Gaza is one of the most densely populated areas of the world (total population is estimated at more than one million) and is subject to a lack of natural resources, particularly water. Unemployment is a very serious problem with a high level of external migration of those with qualifications and skills and a heavy dependence on Israel for employment. Currently around 40 per cent of the population with jobs work in Israel (World Bank, 1993–96). Industry in the Gaza Strip is largely small-scale and has suffered severely from the political instability of the region with the major disruption to economic life of the Intifada period and the more recent border closures imposed by Israeli governments.

The chapter commences by giving a brief background to the economy of Gaza and the problems facing industry there. It then discusses the results of a survey of firms conducted in 1996–97 by one of the authors, covering a sample of 150 firms, which is approximately 30 per cent of all formally registered firms with five or more workers. To our knowledge this is the most detailed study to date on industry in the Gaza Strip. In the tradition of cost-benefit calculations it attempts to provide precise efficiency indicators for the sampled firms. Calculations such as these are relatively rare in the literature on small enterprises, with a few notable exceptions, such as Little *et al.* (1987) and Liedholm and Mead (1999). A third section considers explanations for these results using both regression and logistic analysis. Finally, a concluding section comments on the implications of the findings.

2   THE ECONOMY OF GAZA AND THE INDUSTRIAL SECTOR

The small domestic market, large refugee community and lack of natural resources, combined with the political turmoil of the region, has meant declining income since the mid-1980s. GNP exceeds GDP significantly due to the importance of workers' remittances, but GNP per capita in constant US dollars fell by nearly one-third during 1987–92.[1] The economy of Gaza is dominated by services, with industry taking no more than 12 per cent of GDP (ICBS various). The vast majority of industrial enterprises in Gaza are small, with the majority employing less than 20 workers and only nine employing more than 50 workers.[2] There is a well-established empirical pattern for the share of small, handicraft and artisan industry as a proportion of total industrial activity to be high at low income per capita levels and then to decline with growth (Anderson, 1982); this seems not to have applied in Gaza, where the small-scale sector remains the dominant mode of industrial activity, even at income per capita of over $1000. In terms of industrial classifications, the majority of firms are found in clothing, wood products, metal products, glass and building materials and food and beverages (see Table 10.1). Industry is heavily dependent on imported raw materials, with only slightly more than 20 per cent by value coming from Gaza itself or the West Bank (Okasha and Abo Zarifa, 1992: 84).

Obstacles to industrial development in Gaza are well known. Infrastructure is poor, while local raw materials are scarce. There is a shortage of profes-

Table 10.1   Classification of industry in the survey

Type of industry	Number
Clothing	45
Food, beverages and tobacco	14
Textiles	8
Leather products	2
Wood products	8
Paper and printing	4
Plastic and chemical products	8
Building materials	5
Metallic, maintenance and electrical products	6
Other traditional products	5
Total	105

Source: Migdad, 1999.

sional and skilled workers and a lack of institutions to play an effective financial intermediary role. In addition, there are obvious political problems due to the current status of the NPE. The relations between the Occupied Territories of Gaza and the West Bank with Israel have been described as a one-sided customs union. Israeli goods enter Gaza and the West Bank without restriction whilst labour and certain types of goods flow in the other direction. However industry in the Territories has operated under various official and unofficial restrictions.[3] Licensing controls for exports and imports and the use of permits for building, it has been argued, have blocked local development in Gaza (Roy, 1994). There have been various allegations of dumping of Israeli goods in the Territories, particularly spoiled foodstuffs (Ministry of Information, 1997). Taxation is higher in the Territories than in Israel due to the imposition of additional taxes (Shaded, 1989; Baxendale, 1989). Since the establishment of the NPE, direct taxation is now set by the Palestinian National Authority, although trade taxes remain under the control of the Israeli government.

However, in line with the principle that industry should be encouraged which is complementary to rather than competitive with Israeli firms, there has been a significant growth in subcontracting activity, chiefly in clothing. Palestinian firms have been provided with cloth for sewing by Israeli firms and are paid by the piece for the sewn materials. Subcontracting also exists in areas such as carpets, furniture manufacture, shoes and construction materials. However clothing, which now provides roughly one-third of all industrial firms in Gaza (ICBS, various), is far the most significant area for subcontracting, with roughly 80 per cent of clothing firms working as subcontractors. Subcontracting allows local firms access to the Israeli domestic market and minimises their working capital requirements. On the other hand, it allows Israeli firms to tap the low labour costs of Palestinian workers without their physical movement across the border into Israel. A World Bank study on the Occupied Territories pointed to the higher profitability, more modern equipment and relatively rapid growth of subcontracting Palestinian firms compared with those that do not have this relationship with Israeli firms (World Bank, 1993). Arguably the importance of subcontracting stems from the fact that Israeli firms dealing with Palestinian suppliers do not face the type of restrictions, both official and unofficial, that independent Palestinian firms wishing to trade with the rest of the world are faced with.

In the short term, it is clear that subcontracting is the most dynamic branch of industry in the Gaza Strip and the results of our survey reinforce this point; however doubts remain concerning the longer-term implications of this pattern of industrial development. We return to these points below.

3   THE INDUSTRIAL SURVEY

Our survey is based on a random sample of 150 firms. These were selected from firms listed with the Palestinian Bureau of Statistics (PBS) for the 1994 industrial census, with some amendments up to 1996.[4] This list covers 969 firms, of which those employing five persons or more number 523 and these comprise the population from which our sample is drawn. The population characteristics were constrained on the grounds that very small firms are more likely to be unstable, with start-ups and closures related to general macroeconomic and political conditions rather than to the underlying efficiency of the firms themselves. In addition, quantitative data is less likely to be available for the smallest firms

From the population of 523 firms a sample of 150 firms was selected and organised into three industrial groups – Clothing, Food (and related activities including beverages) and Others (including furniture, carpets, and metal products) – on the basis of the data provided by the firms themselves. The survey was conducted in 1996–97. The response rate was relatively high, in part due to the care taken to revisit firms. Out of a sample of 150 firms, 105 which were still working provided data. Of these, 14, whilst still working at the time of the survey, employed less than five workers. Thirty-seven firms out of 150 had closed in the period between 1994 and the date of the survey and eight refused to respond.

By size all firms covered can be considered small. The average employment size of the firms was 14 workers; only four firms have more than 50 workers and none have more than 60 workers. Approximately 40 per cent of firms are subcontractors, principally in clothing. Regarding the general situation, nearly 80 per cent of firms reported falling profits over the three years prior to the survey and only half of those responding felt things would improve significantly under the NPE. Only 53 per cent of responding firms had grown in employment terms since the start of their operations and the remainder had contracted. Over 70 per cent of the firms classified themselves as self-financed rather than relying on external sources such as banks or non-family investors.

Table 10.2 summarises some basic data on the firms covered in the study. Migdad (1999) reports these results in detail. Here we focus on the main performance indicators normally applied in studies of small enterprise development – growth of employment, cost per job and two alternative profit ratios.

3.1   Employment and Firm Closures

No official data are available at the industrial sector level with which to compare the survey results, although there is an estimate of growth in industrial

Table 10.2   Performance of industry in Gaza 1996–97

Indicator	GE (%)	CJC (JD)	PR (%)	PM (%)
Type of firm				
Clothing	8*	2 467*	28*	17
Food	–2	26 251	18	22
Others	–1.5	22 867	11	9*
Subcontractor	6*	2 077*	27*	17
Local	1	13 946	15	13
Size (no. of employees)				
5–9	–2*	10 110	15	12
10 and above	6	8 910	24	17
All firms	3	9 464	20	14

Notes: GE is growth of employment from start of life of the firm until the end of 1996. CJC is cost per job derived as total assets as reported in the survey divided by full time equivalent workers. JD is Jordanian Dinar. PR is profit ratio derived as operating profits before tax divided by total assets. PM is profit margin derived as operating profits before tax divided by total sales revenue. All figures are averages and * indicates a significant difference in means between the different categories by a *t* test.

Source: Field survey as analysed in Migdad (1999).

employment of 10 per cent over the three year period 1989–92 (ICBS, various). The survey implies an annual employment growth in the sample firms of 3 per cent. This is average annual growth over the period from the start of operation (which obviously varies between firms) and the end of 1996. However this relatively respectable growth is very unevenly distributed, being negative on average in food and 'other' firms but averaging 8 per cent annually in the clothing group. Similarly, given the concentration of subcontracting in the clothing sector, employment growth averages over 6 per cent amongst subcontracting firms and less than 1 per cent amongst non-subcontracting firms. These averages apply only to firms that have remained in operation; given the overall closure rate of 25 per cent over the two-year period 1994–96, total industrial employment must have grown considerably less than these figures imply. In terms of size comparison, micro firms in the sample (those with fewer than 10 workers) suffered a decline in employment compared with 6 per cent average growth amongst small firms (those with 10 workers or more).

Closure rates amongst small firms are notoriously high in all economies and 25 per cent over a two-year period may not be exceptional. Liedholm and Mead (1999) report an average annual closure rate of 12 per cent from a series of studies of small firms in a number of economies, principally in sub-

Saharan Africa. It is noteworthy that for our sample the closure rate is considerably lower in clothing firms (16 per cent) compared with food (31 per cent) and others (32 per cent). The implication is that, at present, subcontracting has provided a more stable source of earnings and employment than activities less closely linked with Israeli firms.

3.2 Cost per Job

Collection of data on total assets of firms is of course subject to considerable difficulties. The figures reported here are owners' own estimates of the replacement value of their total assets, fixed plus current, in 1996. Numbers of workers employed are full-time equivalents derived by adjusting part-time employment by months worked per year. The ratio of total asset value to number of full-time jobs gives cost per job (CJC). Table 10.2 reveals that the clothing sector has by far the lowest CJC at little more than 25 per cent of the average cost for all firms.[5] This is likely to be due to the low investment requirements associated with subcontracting, whereby Palestinian firms are saved heavy initial commitments particularly in relation to working capital. This interpretation is supported by the much lower cost per job in subcontracting as compared with local firms. A final point of note on CJC relates to firm size. Although the difference is not statistically significant, cost per job created is higher in the micro firms than in the small firms. This supports other research that has suggested that very small firms are often more capital-intensive than slightly larger small firms.[6]

3.3 Profitability

Here we measure profitability by two ratios – operating profits before tax to total assets (PR), with assets valued as above, and operating profits before tax to total sales revenue (PM). We include information on the second ratio due to the greater uncertainty attached to asset data. Overall the PR, at an average return of 20 per cent, appears surprisingly high given the difficulties associated with operating in Gaza. It should be remembered that this is an average for surviving firms (presumably the most profitable), not for all firms. Furthermore, given the uncertainty attached to operations, firms would be expected to add a high risk premium to their target rate of return. The PR is considerably higher in clothing and subcontracting firms than in other activities, due in part to their lower capital requirements noted above. Average profits in the 'other' group are only 11 per cent, however, and indicate the lower profitability of existing enterprises outside the clothing and food groups.

The comparison between micro and small firms reveals the latter to have higher returns. This is consistent with the cost per job data presented above and with some evidence from other countries (Wagner and Korka, 1995).[7] However the differences in both PR and PM between the two size categories are not significant.

A similar pattern emerges when profitability is measured by PM rather than PR, although PM is conceptually a weaker measure of profitability since, *ceteris paribus*, firms with a higher capital to value-added ratio will require a higher profits to value-added ratio to generate a given PR. We find this in our results with the PM ratio being lower for the clothing group compared with the food group, presumably due to the lower capital intensity of the former.

4   DISCUSSION OF RESULTS

To test our initial intuitive explanations for these survey results we undertook regression and logit analyses. Our procedure is to identify a set of explanatory variables that would be expected to explain firm performance *a priori*; these are based on individual firm characteristics (such as age of firm, sources of finance, or educational background of the owner), sector characteristics (such as trends in demand and the nature of technology involved) and variables reflecting the general political and macroeconomic situation. A number of potential explanatory variables are identified and these are combined in a correlation matrix, so that significantly correlated independent variables can be omitted (see Migdad, 1999). Table 10.3 reports the main regression equations relating to the three performance indicators, growth of employment (GE), cost per job (CJC) and profit ratio (PR).

The explanatory variables used in Table 10.3 can be explained as follows. Age of firm (in years) will be significant where infant industry effects and/or learning by doing are important. This implies that age should be positively correlated with profits and employment growth. Its impact on investment cost per job is ambiguous, as the latter refers to technical characteristics of operations, rather than efficiency *per se*. A dummy variable for the use of bookkeeping procedures can be seen as a proxy for good management practice and hence is expected to be positively associated with both profits and employment growth. Variables for both profitability and investment (growth of total assets) are used to explain employment growth, with the expected relationship being positive.

Two alternative measures of size (one based on assets and the other on employment) are used to establish whether within the sample a scale effect can be detected. Economies of scale suggest that size will be positively correlated with profitability and employment, whilst negatively correlated with cost per job. A dummy variable for self-finance is applied to test whether

Table 10.3   Regression results for performance indicators (all firms)

Dependent variable	GE	CJC	PR
Constant	–0.13***	–9 897*	0.24***
Age of firm	–	4 239**	–0.004*
Bookkeeping	–	–	0.13***
Profit ratio	0.10**	–	–
Growth assets	0.28***	–	–
Size (by number of workers)	0.001*	–	–
Size (by total assets)	–	0.05***	–
Self finance	0.12***	–	–
Average wage	–	37.56**	–
Local firm	–	10 460***	–
Imported technology	–	3 992*	–
Clothing	–	–	0.08**
Raw material problem	–	–	–0.12***
Single owner	–	–	–0.12***
Adjusted R^2	0.70	0.58	0.51
F statistic	56**	27***	21***
Number of observations	103	101	99

Notes: ***, ** and * indicate significance at 1%, 5% and 10% levels respectively. A number of dummies are used: bookkeeping (1 if firm uses bookkeeping and 0 otherwise); self-finance (1 if firm is financed by the owner and 0 otherwise); local firm (1 if the firm produces for the local markets); imported technology (1 if the firm uses imported technology); clothing (1 if the firm is in a clothing group); raw material (1 if the firm faces problems in getting raw materials); single owner (1 if the firm is owned by only one person).

firms are at a disadvantage if they have to rely on external sources for funds (access to credit is usually listed as one of the major obstacles facing small firms in Gaza as elsewhere). Hence the expectation is that the sign on this dummy will be negative for profits and employment and probably positive for cost per job, if interest charges to external lenders raise investment costs significantly. A measure of average wages is included in the cost per job equation to test whether the capital intensity of the technology used responds to wage levels. If it does, the expected sign will be positive between the wage variable and investment cost per worker.

Dummy variables are also included for firms that serve the local, as opposed to the export market, and for firms that use imported, as opposed to local technology. The normal expectation is that export-oriented small firms will be more efficient than locally-oriented firms, as will firms that use foreign as opposed to local technology. Hence the expectation is that the local dummy will be negatively correlated with employment growth and profits and that the imported technology dummy will be positively related to both of these dependent variables. On the issue of technology and investment cost per job, the expectation is that firms operating in the local market require a less sophisticated and less capital-intensive technology, so the local dummy is negatively correlated with cost per job, whilst imported technology can be expected to be more sophisticated and capital intensive than local technology, so the imported technology dummy should be positively correlated with cost per job.

Finally three dummies are included to test for a special clothing effect (as clothing is the most dynamic sector and the one dominated by subcontracting), the existence of a scarcity of raw materials (cited as a key problem by firms in the interviews) and the effect of single ownership. If clothing firms are more dynamic, we expect a positive relation between the dummy and both employment growth and profitability. The sign on the cost per job variable is ambiguous. If raw material shortage is a key constraint, we would expect the dummy to be negatively correlated with both employment growth and profits. Finally, the presence of a single owner can work both ways; it may lead to greater efficiency if conflicts between owners are avoided, or it may reflect a weak financial position, which in turn is associated with poor performance. Hence here again the signs are ambiguous.

Taking the three indicators in turn, growth of employment (GE) is found to be most rapid amongst self-financed firms (represented by a dummy variable), and those with either a relatively high rate of profit or growth of total assets. Size of firm has a weak positive relation to employment growth. The positive relationship between employment growth and either asset growth or profitability is of course expected. The relation with self-finance is less obvious, but in their responses to the survey, a large majority of owners replied that their main motive in setting up operations was to provide employment for members of their family. This suggests that amongst firms where owners drew on family funds, employment creation was a primary objective and profitability a secondary one. Within the different groups (results not reported), among clothing, age of firm is found to have a significant negative relation with employment growth, suggesting that it is new entrants to this sector who are benefiting most from subcontracting links with Israeli producers.

In terms of cost per job (CJC), this tends to be higher in large firms (as measured by total assets) and significantly higher amongst local (that is, non-subcontracting) firms. In addition, CJC is higher in firms with higher average wages and in firms that use imported technology (as captured by a dummy variable). These relations are expected. Large firms above a certain size are more likely to employ capital intensive techniques, as are firms that pay higher wages or use imported technology.[8] Age of firm has a negative relation with CJC, implying that older firms use more labour-intensive technology. Alternatively, if the asset figures do not reflect true replacement costs, this relation may be simply due to the use of depreciated equipment, which has not been revalued accurately. Within the groups of firms, the positive relation between use of imported technology and CJC is considerably stronger in statistical terms for clothing than for all firms.

In terms of profitability, a dummy variable for clothing firms is significant with a positive sign confirming the statistical significance of their higher profitability reported earlier. Firms that report raw material problems or have single owners are more likely to have lower than average profits, whilst firms that use bookkeeping are more likely to have above-average profits. There is a weak negative relation between age of firm and PR. Although this relation is not expected, it is justified in the Gaza Strip (GS). There are two main reasons for this negative relation between age and PR. First, when firms get older, machines get older, and their productivity decreases because of the lack of replacement of the machines. Second, the main objective for the owner is high returns in the early years of foundation to minimise the period needed for the return on capital to be realised. This is because of the unstable situation in the GS. The negative sign of the age variable is evidence of uncertainty and instability in the GS. A negative relation between PR and raw material difficulties is expected and the negative relation with single owner-ship is presumably due to difficulties in either obtaining finance or in access to management skills. A strong positive relation between PR and the use of bookkeeping is expected, as book keeping is often taken as a proxy measure of good management practices. Within the groups of firms it is worth noting that age is only weakly significant (at 10 per cent) with a negative sign in clothing, and ceases to be significant at all for food.

A similar pattern of results is obtained by applying logistic analysis (for details, see Migdad, 1999). Here a dichotomous dependent variable is used, taking a value of unity if a firm has a particular characteristic and zero otherwise. We report the results of two such analyses of firms that are either growing or non-growing, or profitable or unprofitable. A growing firm is defined as one where there is an increase in number of workers from the start-up of the firm until the end of 1996; a non-growing firm has zero or negative employment growth over this period. A profitable firm for this analysis is defined as one with a profit ratio (PR) of 10 per cent or more and an unprofitable firm is one with PR below 10 per cent. In this case, 10 per cent is taken as an approximate measure of the opportunity cost of capital.

For the growth of firms taking the two positively significant independent variables, a dummy for clothing firms and a dummy for self-financing, then there is an 85 per cent probability of a firm growing positively if it is in the clothing sector and is self-financed.[9] For the profitability analysis of firms, taking the two positively significant independent variables, a dummy for clothing firms and a dummy for the use of bookkeeping, then there is a 97 per cent probability of a firm being profitable by our definition if it is in the clothing sector and employs good management practices, as proxied by use of bookkeeping.[10] Inclusion of variables with a negative effect on growth and profits reduces the probabilities, but not substantially, so that overall the conclusion is that firms in the clothing sector with certain characteristics have a high probability of success, by either criteria.

5   CONCLUSIONS

Our survey has been the most detailed analysis to date of the industrial sector in Gaza. Our results suggest two distinct sets of conclusions. First, we find considerable support for some of the main stylized facts of international small enterprise development. There is evidence from Gaza for the pattern of 'churning' (Liedholm and Mead, 1999), whereby there is great diversity within the small firm sector with high rates of start-up combined with high rates of closure. In addition, in terms of growth of employment, assets or sales, significant numbers of firms may be contracting whilst at the same time others are growing. The net picture thus masks these divergent trends within the sector. In Gaza we find high rates of closure that average 25 per cent over two years, and very divergent patterns of employment growth within the small industry sector, with two groups of firms shedding workers and the third growing rapidly. Size within the small firm sector does not appear to be a very significant explanatory variable in terms of performance, with few statistically significant differences between micro and small firms.

Several firm characteristics that have proved significant elsewhere are found to be important in Gaza also. Self-financing is important for job creation, suggesting difficulties with the process of financial intermediation, and good management practice, as proxied by use of bookkeeping, is associated with higher profitability. Age of firms has a weak negative relation with profitability, suggesting the absence of any infant industry effects, and broadly in line with results elsewhere.[11] However, entrepreneurial characteristics, relating for example to education levels or family background, are not generally significant. Finally, as expected, firms that perceive themselves to be facing a scarcity of raw materials tend to have below average profitability.

Whilst these results provide few surprises, some distinctive features of small industry development in Gaza are worth noting. First, conventional distinctions between urban and rural small firms and between male- and female-headed firms are not relevant. As a small land area of 360 sq. km, the urban-rural distinction in Gaza has little meaning. Further as a predominantly

Muslim country, female-run businesses are relatively rare.[12] What is clear however, is that the type of small enterprise activity has a strong impact on performance. Clothing firms, particularly those engaged in subcontracting, are far more dynamic than other types of firm. Roughly 40 per cent of firms in the sample are subcontractors, and over 80 per cent of clothing firms are subcontractors. At present this form of activity appears to offer one way out of the one-sided customs union arrangement in the Occupied Territories. Palestinian labour based in Gaza can be combined with Israeli capital in mutually beneficial ventures. Two qualifications can be made however. From the perspective of the economy of the NPE, this is likely to be a considerably inferior arrangement to free access to international markets and free mobility of labour between Gaza, the West Bank and Israel. Second, subcontracting links based on low labour costs are notoriously transitory since they are based on a resource whose value will increase with the success of the strategy. At present the main alternative for Israeli producers is to establish new firms in the border industrial area (Eretz), employing Palestinian workers but outside Gaza, or to establish links with producers in Jordan. Hence, whilst subcontracting may provide an opportunity for firms from Gaza to grow, for the longer term viability of the economy their additional profits will have to be reinvested in either the higher value components of the same commodity chain or a more diversified range of industrial activity.

This raises the issue of what form of industrial policy can be effective in diversifying small industry and increasing internal value added. An improved system of financial intermediation in Gaza with a sound commercial banking system and institutions that can supply long-term finance to dynamic small firms at non-subsidised, but still affordable, interest rates is probably the key to progress.

NOTES

1. Data are from PBS (1995). More recent official data are not available since Israel ceased producing statistics on the area of the New Palestinian Entity after the Oslo Peace Accord and an alternative set has not yet been developed.
2. The figures come from PBS (1995) and are derived from the 1994 census of firms.
3. There is a well-known statement from the late Hitshaq Rabin to the effect that 'Israel will not give any licensing for expanding industry or agriculture that competes with the Israeli economy' (*Jerusalem Post*, 15 Febuary 1985, cited in ASIR 1986).
4. This list is not published and was obtained from the Bureau of Statistics. We do not have the data to establish the share of our sample firms in total industrial employment or value added.
5. Although the absolute values for CJC differ considerably, the earlier study by Okasha and Abo Zarifa (1992) also finds a much lower cost per job in clothing than elsewhere in the industrial sector.
6. Dhar and Lydall (1961) on India is one of the earliest statements of this apparent paradox.

7. The large study of Little *et al.* (1987) found no significant systematic link between size and profitability.
8. Size here is in terms of assets, not employment. We find no evidence that size by number of employees is associated with greater capital intensity. Little *et al.* (1987) also find for India that the definition of size makes a difference and that when they define size by assets not workers, they find the same positive relationship with CJC.
9. To predict the probability in the logistic model in the case of growth rate as a dependent variable, and clothing and self finance as independent variables, we used the following formula:

$$Logit\ (GE) = -2.51 + 1.59(C) + 2.62(S.F)$$
$$Odds\ (GE=1) = e^{logit\,(GE)} = e^{-2.51 + 1.59 + 2.62} = e^{1.7}$$
$$Prob\ (GE=1) = Odds\ (GE=1)/1 + Odds\ (GE=1)$$
$$= e^{logit\,(GE)}/1 + e^{logit\,(GE)}$$
$$= 1/1 + e^{-logit\,(GE)}$$
$$= 1/1 + e^{-[1.7]}$$
$$= 1/1 + e^{-[1.7]} = 1/[1 + .18] = 1/1.18 = 0.85\ ,\ or\ 85\%.$$

10. To predict the probability in the logistic model in the case of profit level as independent variable and type of the firm and bookkeeping as dependent variables, we used the following formula:

$$Logit\ (dPR) = -0.98 + 2.93\ (C) + 1.63\ (BK)$$
$$Prob.\ (dPR=1) = 1/1 + e^{-[-0.98 + 1.63\,(BK) + 2.93(C)]}$$

The result is that the probability of *dPR* =1 is 97%, where *dPR* is dummy for the PR; it equals 1 if the PR is higher than 10% and = 0 otherwise.
11. See for example the results of MacPherson (1996) for some countries in Southern Africa, who finds an inverse relation between age and growth.
12. Islamic law does allow women equally with men to own or manage firms or properties. The reason why women do not do so is related to culture, not to religion.

REFERENCES

Anderson, D. (1982), 'Small industry in developing countries: a discussion of issues', *World Development*, **10**, 11, 913–48.

ASIR (1986), *Industry in the Occupied Territories (West Bank & Gaza Strip) and Scope of its Development*, Arab Scientific Institution for Research and Transfer of Technology, ASIR, Palestine.

Baxendale, S.J. (1989), 'Taxation of income in Israel and the West Bank: Comparative study', *Journal of Palestine Studies*, **18**, 3, 134–41.

Dhar, P. and H. Lydall (1961), *The Role of Small Enterprises in Indian Economic Development*, Asia Publishing House, Bombay.

ICBS (various), *Statistical Abstract of Israel*, Israeli Central Bureau of Statistics, Israel.

Liedholm, C. and D. Mead (1999), *Small Enterprises and Economic Development: The Dynamics of Micro and Small Enterprises*, Routledge, London.

Little I.M.D., D. Mazumdar and J.M. Page (1987), *Small Manufacturing Enterprises: A Comparative Analysis of India and Other Economies*, A World Bank Research Publication, Oxford University Press, New York.

McPherson, M. (1996), 'Growth of micro and small enterprises in Southern Africa', *Journal of Development Economics*, **48**, 2, 253–77.

Mead, D. and C. Liedholm (1998), 'The dynamics of micro and small enterprises in developing countries', *World Development*, **26**, 1, 61–74.

Migdad, Muhammed (1999), *Performance Analysis of Small Scale Industry: Industrial Sector in the Gaza Strip as Part of the New Palestinian Entity*, unpublished Ph.D. thesis, University of Bradford, Bradford.

Ministry of Information (1997), 'Israeli expired foodstuff finds its way to shelves in the Palestinian markets', http://www.pna.org/mininfo/reports/er_index.htm

Okasha, M. and S. Abo Zarifa (1992), *Industrialisation in the Gaza Strip*, Arab Thought Forum, Jerusalem, Palestine.

PBS, Palestinian Central Bureau of Statistics (1995), *The Establishment Census, 1994: Final Results*, August, Ramallah, Palestine.

Roy, S. (1994), 'Separation or integration: closure and the economic future of the Gaza Strip revisited', *Middle East Journal*, **48**, 1, 11–30.

Shaded, M. (1989), 'Israeli policy for development', in Gorge El Abid (ed.), *The West Bank and the Gaza Strip: Development Challenges Under the Occupation*, Arab Unity Research Centre, Palestine.

Wagner, P. and M. Korka (1995), *The Private Sector of Small and Medium-sized Enterprises in Romania, Annual Report 1995*, Romania Centre for Small and Medium Enterprises, Romania.

World Bank (1993), *Developing the Occupied Territories: An Investment in Peace*, World Bank, Washington, DC.

Index